LIVING Off The **POWER** Of Your OIL

40 Invaluable Life Lessons of the Widow's Oil

SANDRA EKPENYONG

JOSEPH DREAM
PUBLISHING CO.

Living off the Power of Your Oil: 40 Invaluable Life Lessons of the Widow's Oil

For spiritual, educational, business, or sales promotional usage, please reach out to the Media Marketing Department at Joseph Dream Publishing.

First Edition, July, 2026

Finance, Life Lessons, business, entrepreneurship, faithpreneur

ISBN-13: 978-1-938613-55-5

www.josephdreampublishing.com
publisher@josephdreampublishing.com

OTHER BOOKS BY SANDRA EKPENYONG

Biblical Dysfunctional Families: The Beginning

Biblical Dysfunctional Families: The Beginning (Workbook)

Woman, God Has Given You Your Voice BACK!

Unlocking the Deborah in You

Unlocking the Deborah in You (18-Week Journal)

Igniting Your Vision (5 Book Series)

The 13 Different Father & Daughter Relationships of the Bible

There will be GIANTS (2026)

The Samson story that was NEVER told (2026)

Biblical Dysfunctional Families (Mini-book series 2026)

The Different Christian Faith Processes (2027)

Jealousy, the Spirit of Destruction (2027)

(All book devotionals are free and downloadable at www.thesandrae.com starting January 2026.)

INTRODUCTION

Living off the Power of Your Oil explores 40 invaluable lessons from the story of the widow's oil, offering insights from a Christian business perspective. In today's ever-evolving business world, Christian entrepreneurs constantly face challenges that test both their business acumen and their faith and integrity. The story of Elisha and the widow's oil, found in 2 Kings 4:1-7, holds timeless wisdom that extends beyond its ancient context, offering powerful insights for modern-day business endeavors.

Oftentimes, Christians focus solely on the miraculous provision of the jar of oil, overlooking the many other valuable life lessons within this story. By doing so, we limit our understanding, reducing the widow's story to just faith, resourcefulness, and seeking divine guidance in times of need, when in fact, it offers much more. The widow's plight, driven by a life-threatening debt, is a struggle that remains all too familiar in today's world, regardless of religion or nationality. Across the globe, mounting debt has driven good people to despair even to the point of taking their own lives. When we consider that she also faced the impending loss of her children, it becomes clear that she was in desperate need of a solution or a miracle.

The widow's story reflects the struggles faced by many Christians today, including entrepreneurs across the globe. Yet, through her obedience, creativity, and reliance on God's provision, she discovers a way out of her dire situation. The 40 lessons drawn from this story are invaluable not only for everyday Christians but also for ministers and aspiring entrepreneurs. This story goes beyond faith—it offers wisdom for those launching a new business as well as those navigating the complexities of an established one. These simple yet profound lessons provide practical guidance rooted in biblical principles that serve as a blueprint for building a business that not only thrives but also honors God.

You've likely heard the saying, "It's not about the destination, but the journey." Every journey carries unique life lessons if you're open to learning. This book teaches the power of communication in developing strategy while leveraging community support in times of need. It explores how strong relationships can transform business ideas into success, the importance of identifying and maximizing the resources God has already placed in your hands, and the ability to recognize divine direction while navigating life's challenges with unwavering faith.

In a world where business decisions are often driven by profit margins and competition, true success is often rooted in foundational life lessons—whatever that may look like for you. We can align our business practices with God's will by seeking His guidance and trusting in His provision, all while maintaining an environment that respects those who do not share our faith. Just as the widow's small jar of oil became the key to her breakthrough, your business—when rooted in faith and guided by these timeless lessons—can become a vessel for God's blessings and a source of meaningful impact in the world.

For those who are in a place of desperation or on the verge of giving up due to financial struggles, I want you to know that I've been there too. My deepest and most sincere prayer is that the 40 lessons in this book will inspire, challenge, and equip you to move from debt to building a thriving business. I also hope these golden nuggets of wisdom serve as a testament to God's faithfulness and provision. And ultimately, may you come to know the God who can turn a simple jar of oil into a million-dollar business.

Peace be unto you,

Sandra Ekpenyong

CONTENTS

CHAPTER 1

THE IMPACT OF CLEAR COMMUNICATION

Crisis Communication

How effective is your communication? Really, what do you consider effective communication? I took an advanced English course while studying Government and Politics and learned that there are different forms of communication and that not all communication is effective. In the story of Elisha and the Widow's Oil, one of the most profound lessons isn't just the miraculous multiplication of oil; it's the simple yet powerful act that sets everything in motion: the widow's cry for help. She communicated!

Her seemingly small gesture was an act of effective communication, and it became the catalyst for her eventual deliverance from a life-threatening situation. For anyone facing overwhelming circumstances, whether it is personal debt, business failure, a medical emergency, or a deep family crisis, the first step to deliverance is unlocking the power of communication!

No solution can be uncovered without this first invaluable step. Throughout the Bible, from Genesis to Revelation, we see the importance of communication starting with God, who is and remains the Great Communicator. When the world was void, He spoke His intention, and the earth was formed in the Old Testament. And this never changed. Even when Jesus walked the earth, He often encouraged people to communicate as a means of finding solutions.

The widow's situation was dire. Her husband, a faithful servant of the Lord and a prophet, had died, leaving her with a heavy debt. Now, creditors stood at her door, threatening to take her two sons as slaves to settle what the couple owed. In her despair, the widow did not remain silent or try to handle the situation alone. Instead, she sought out the prophet Elisha and expressed her need with clarity and urgency. Frankly, many of us would just wallow in self-pity, giving up because we see no way out, but the truth is that communication matters.

While communication is often viewed as a basic life skill, the truth is that many of us struggle to communicate well. This becomes especially clear in moments of conflict or crisis, when effective communication can be the key to resolution. In these moments, the words we choose and how we express them can either open the door to understanding or shut it completely. The widow's decision to speak out was a pivotal moment in her life, opening the door for divine intervention. When facing a difficult situation, especially one as overwhelming as debt, the ability to clearly communicate your needs, fears, and hopes can make all the difference. It allows others to understand your situation and positions you to receive the help you desperately need.

Sadly, in today's fast-paced world, where self-reliance and independence are highly valued, it's easy to overlook the importance of communication. Yet, as the widow's story illustrates, even the most self-sufficient individuals can face situations where they must reach out for help. Understanding how to do this effectively is key to overcoming challenges and moving toward a solution.

Effective communication consists of many different elements, but these can easily fall apart in the middle of a crisis. Calamity has a way of disrupting even the most skilled communicators, often replacing clarity with confusion. Yet the widow's interaction with the prophet Elisha stood out; her message was clear, honest, and compelling enough to stir him to action. What made her words so powerful that they moved him to help?

1. The widow's message to Elisha was clear and direct. She didn't waste time on unnecessary details but stated her problem plainly and with urgency. In times of crisis, clarity is not just helpful; it's crucial. You must keep it simple, eliminate the fluff and get to the heart of the matter. Whether you're reaching out to a mentor, a friend, a family member or even praying before God, He has instructed us to be clear about our wants and needs. Whoever you talk to; ensure that your communication is straightforward, focused on the core issue while speaking from the heart. Walk in complete clarity, while sticking to the main points.

2. Transparency and integrity are crucial in times of crisis, and the widow exemplified this by being honest about her situation. She didn't minimize her needs or try to present herself in a better light. Instead, she embraced humility and spoke honestly about where she stood. Too often, when we find ourselves in difficult circumstances, the temptation to conceal the severity of our struggles out of fear of judgment or shame can be overwhelming. However, if we truly desire the right kind of help, we must resist that urge and choose honesty every single time.

3. Honesty creates space for others to understand your 'real needs' and respond appropriately. When your communication is marked by transparency and vulnerability, it often softens the hearts of those who might otherwise have turned away

from helping you. It took great courage and humility for the widow to approach Elisha and openly admit just how bad her situation was. It was her honesty that unlocked the door to the help she desperately needed.

Take a moment to envision her situation: her late husband, who had likely helped many people, was now gone, leaving her drowning in debt. Picture the whispers around town… the hushed conversations along with the sideway glances. Perhaps even fellow ministers murmured about how he had died, leaving his family burdened and vulnerable. Yet, in the midst of that silence, with no mention of any of his ministerial colleagues stepping forward, there stood his widow—brave enough to cry out to Prophet Elisha for help. The truth is that asking for help often requires more strength than staying silent. It demands that we set aside pride, lay down the mask of self-sufficiency, and admit that we cannot handle everything on our own. Know that this kind of humility is not weakness; it's strength. An inner strength that opens doors for support. A strength that creates space for solutions while securing opportunities. The widow's honest, unassuming plea touched Elisha's heart, compelling him to respond and help save her family.

Everything you do must have a clear purpose. The widow who approached Prophet Elisha was intentional in her communication. She had one focus: to find a solution to the debt that threatened to take her sons away from her. Likewise, when facing a crisis, purposeful communication is key. Know what you are asking for and why. Make sure your words reflect your true goal and keep your message aligned with that purpose.

To help you communicate effectively—whether in everyday life or during times of crisis —here are **5 Key Principles For Purposeful Communication:**

1. ***Identify the Right Person(s) to Communicate With:*** The widow did not take her problem to just anyone—she was strategic. She sought out Elisha, who not only shared a prophetic connection with her late husband, but also carried greater influence and the capacity to help her. Her choice was intentional. She understood the importance of turning to someone who had the wisdom, authority and resources to make a huge difference. In the same way, when you are in need, be deliberate about who you approach. Look for the people who are in the best position to help you—whether they are financial advisors, mentors, trusted friends, or spiritual leaders. Choose those with the knowledge, influence or experience that aligns with the solution you are seeking. Purposeful communication begins with knowing who to speak to and why. **Takeaway:** Be strategic. Choose the right voice.
2. ***Preparing Your Message for the Right Person: Before reaching out for help, take*** time to carefully prepare and practice what you need to say. Be clear about your situation, honest about your needs, and humble in your approach. Writing down key points beforehand can help you stay focused and communicate effectively. Let your tone reflect the seriousness of your situation without losing composure. If speaking in person, remember that body language —your facial expressions, posture and eye contact—can either reinforce or

contradict your words. Ensure that your verbal and nonverbal communication are aligned for maximum clarity and impact. **Takeaway:** Be prepared. Speak with clarity and composure.

3. ***Be Flexible and Open to Guidance:*** Effective communication is a two-way street—it's a dialogue. It's not just about you sharing your needs but also about being open to listening, receiving and responding to others. The widow didn't simply tell Elisha her problem and walk away; she listened ***carefully*** to his instructions and acted on them immediately. Stay humble and receptive. Be willing to follow guidance, even if it challenges your comfort zone or requires you to take actions that you hadn't anticipated. Sometimes, the answers we seek come wrapped in uncomfortable instructions! **Takeaway:** Be teachable. Stay open to direction.

4. ***Follow Through Until the End:*** Communicating your needs is only the first step—what you do next matters just as much. The widow didn't just hear Elisha's advice; she followed it precisely. And, because of her obedience and following through to the end, even though all she had was a small jar of oil, it miraculously multiplied. In the same way, take action on the counsel and solutions you receive. Stay diligent and consistent, as breakthroughs often come not just through what you say but what you do afterwards. **Takeaway:** Be diligent. Apply the instructions fully.

5. ***Learn to Say 'Thank You For Your Help':*** Gratitude seals the exchange. One of the worst things we can do is receive help in a time of crisis and fail to show appreciation—especially if we plan

to return to that source again. Be intentional about expressing thanks. Send a thank-you card, a message, or a thoughtful note of appreciation. A grateful heart not only honors those who helped you but also keeps the door open for future support. **Takeaway:** Be grateful. Never underestimate the power of appreciation.

The widow boldly sought help from Elisha, and that one conversation changed the course of her life. It's a powerful reminder that the right conversation with the right person can transform your situation and become the key to your breakthrough. By appealing to Elisha, the widow embarked on a new path, one that led to her not only to provision but also to entrepreneurship and self-reliance. She didn't receive a handout, but instead discovered a new way forward. In the same way, when we openly express our needs, we may find ourselves unexpectedly launched into a journey of self-discovery, all sparked by authentic conversations about our situations.

The widow had to face the hard truth: she now had to live without her husband who had been the primary provider, had to learn how to provide for herself and her family. Sadly, even today, many wives, whether they are career women or housewives, often find themselves unprepared at the unexpected loss of a spouse. They are left not only grieving but also ignorant of the financial affairs of their household.

The widow's crisis stands as a cautionary tale for us all: knowing the state of your home is not optional, and it is not solely the responsibility of the husband. As a family, we cannot afford to remain blissfully ignorant—because ignorance carries a hefty price.

But here is the beauty of the widow's story: by speaking up and asking for help, she positioned herself to move from lack to abundance. Her breakthrough came not through silence, but through courageous, clear, and purposeful communication. The story of the widow and the oil serves as a timeless lesson: even in our darkest moments, effective communication can unlock divine solutions. She spoke with honesty, humility, and focus—and because of that, she received not just a miracle, but instructions that empowered her to work with her own hands toward her breakthrough.

For the Christian entrepreneur, this lesson is invaluable—never underestimate the power of speaking up and reaching out when you need help. The right connections, the right conversations, and the right relationships can position you for favor, strategy, and provision. Maintaining relationships, networking wisely, and connecting with like-minded people can open doors that talent alone cannot. Communication is more than just a tool—it is a bridge. One that connects you to resources, people, wisdom, and, most importantly, to God—the One who has already assigned help for your life journey.

When we communicate effectively, our lives become like a beautifully woven tapestry, each thread telling a story. It is not just for others to admire as it is on display, but for them to learn from as well.

If we truly want to access the fullness of God's benefits, we must begin with the words we speak. Whether you are starting a new venture or navigating a financial or personal crisis, remember this: your words have the power to open doors, create opportunities, and invite divine intervention into your situation. In the end, only you can harness the true transformative power of communication that God has placed inside of you—and it is for you to use when you need it most.

CHAPTER 2

WHEN HELP DOESN'T COME

Facing Crisis Alone

Have you ever attempted to start a business, build a family, or launch a ministry, and everyone around you promised they would have your back? Their words of support fueled your courage, gave you the confidence to step out, and filled you with hope. But when the moment of true need arrived, they disappeared. Suddenly, their promises turned into silence… their assurances replaced by excuses.

It is called **walking alone**. And it hurts.

Few things sting more than feeling abandoned by the very people you trusted to stand with you. The disappointment cuts even deeper when that betrayal comes from those you counted on the most! The hard truth is this: in some of life's most challenging seasons, you may find yourself standing alone. This was the widow's reality. She faced a giant many know all too well—the giant called "***Indebtedness.***" Her crisis wasn't just emotional; it was financial. The kind of problem that doesn't care whether you're a believer or not. Debt shows no respect for status, gender, race, or education. It does not discriminate. It has the power to reduce kings and commoners alike to the same place of desperation.

Debt can be overwhelming. It crushes hope. And worst of all, it threatens not only your peace of mind but the well-being of those you love the most. It takes **courage** to face debt head-on—whether the debt is the result of your own choices or circumstances outside your control. The widow's creditors were relentless, pounding at her door, making harsh demands, offering no mercy; just like the creditors of today. Their threats were clear: pay up or lose your children.

Indebtedness often brings with it more than just financial strain. It drags in **isolation, shame, and despair** as unwelcome companions. In the quiet desperation of her home, the widow stared down a nightmare no parent ever wants to face: the loss of her sons as payment for debts she couldn't settle.

Her story is not far from the stark reality many face today. For some, the threat is not the loss of children, but the loss of a home, a job, freedom, or the disintegration of family relationships. The pain is real. According to *U.S. News Money,* one in five divorces in America cite debt as a contributing factor.

What makes the widow's story even more heartbreaking is this: her late husband had been a faithful servant of the Lord. A man of God. Yet she was left behind with nothing but unpaid debts, liabilities, and the crushing weight of financial ruin.

The hardest part of debt isn't always about the numbers—it's the loneliness. The isolation is deafening. The crushing weight of carrying a burden so heavy, with no one standing between you and the harsh reality of your circumstances. As the widow's situation pressed down on her, she stood alone. No husband to shield her. No family rushing in to rescue her. Just the cold, unyielding truth of what she was facing. Some of life's most invaluable lessons come wrapped in moments like these—moments that require us to confront our challenges head-on and, sometimes, to do it alone. The truth is, in seasons of great adversity, we all have to arrive at a crossroads where critical decisions must be made.

The widow was no different; she had three choices:

1. ***She could hide***—ignore the problem altogether and hope it would somehow disappear on its own.
2. ***She could wait passively***—doing what many well-meaning believers do which is to pray, but never act, hoping for a miracle to fall from heaven without lifting a finger or working.
3. ***Or she could face the problem directly***—by taking a bold step towards finding a practical solution by seeking help from the prophet Elisha.

I believe the widow chose the third option because she understood the biblical principle: **faith without works is dead**. She put her faith into action by taking the first courageous step towards change and that meant finding a practical solution.

Her decision to face her problem head-on teaches a crucial lesson for anyone battling with the giant of debt—or any other life-altering challenge where you must face your demons squarely. Avoidance only prolongs the pain, while excuses only increase the pressure. Prayer without any action often leads us exactly where we started—stuck, still waiting and with absolutely nothing! The widow acknowledged the severity of her situation and refused to live in denial. Instead, she positioned herself to receive the wisdom, guidance and help she desperately needed to overcome her problem. And in that vulnerable place, in her season of solitude—alone and exposed she began to cultivate something priceless: **resilience**.

This is because in the midst of struggle, we either build character or lose it. Without her husband to lean on and with no loved ones coming to her rescue, she had to make a choice—not just for herself, but for the future of her sons. She had to learn to walk alone. But here's the deeper truth: it is often in those solitary moments that we are forced to dig deep, to discover our inner strength, and to fully trust in God's provision. Alone, yes, but not abandoned. Pressed on every side yet not destroyed. We can face the giant in our lives —but not without faith. And while the weight of debt loomed heavy, and the enemy likely whispered constant reminders of failure and shame... the widow chose courage. She did not remain in seclusion, but she found the strength to face her challenge head-on, recognizing that isolation could work against her rather than for her. She understood something that we often forget in our dark moments; that even when support is lacking, we are never truly alone.

In our own seasons of solitude, we too must remember this truth. No matter how unique your situation may feel or how daunting the road ahead appears, seek help. Reach out. Cry out, if you must. **But don't suffer in silence.** Find someone who will show you mercy, offer guidance, and help you chart a way forward. Walking alone can feel scary, unpredictable, and full of uncertainty, but it also offers something invaluable: the space to self-reflect, to confront who we are, and to discover what we're truly made of. The widow didn't realize the depth of her own capability until she had no choice but to stand on her own without the support of a husband.

The loss of her spouse forced her to lean not on others, but on her own God-given strength as an individual. She was driven to seek out the resources and solutions she needed to survive... and eventually, to thrive. And that is the hidden gift within hardship: when there is no one to lean on, we discover hidden strengths and talents we never knew we had. We uncover abilities buried beneath fear and self-doubt. These hidden strengths turn into valuable assets, not only for overcoming today's challenges but also for equipping us to handle future battles with greater confidence. The process of struggle builds something the comfortable life never could: **resilience.** And that becomes the bridge to true self-reliance. Self-reliance doesn't happen by accident; it must be nurtured. Just as children learn independence through trial and error, stumbling and getting back up, so must we also cultivate the habit of learning how to stand on our own two feet.

For the widow, this was her **'aha'** moment of realization, as the death of her husband forced her to face hard truths: both she and her husband had failed to properly manage their finances, which turned into debt. But now, standing at the crossroads, she had a decision to make. She could either remain trapped by the weight of regret or rise, learn, and lead her family into a new chapter. Blissful ignorance was no longer optional but full dependency on God and a call to action were essential for her survival, that of her sons and her spiritual growth. She also needed to learn independence as she could no longer afford to lean on others for rescue (technically there wasn't anyone). She needed to learn how to navigate complex decisions and challenges with wisdom, courage, and faith.

Here is the reality: without independence, we all risk becoming easy prey or falling to the mercy of others, becoming vulnerable to exploitation, and being trapped in cycles of dependency. But solitude, as painful as it feels, has a way of refining us. It strips away distractions. It sharpens our focus. It teaches us to tune out the noise of the crowd and lean into the still, small voice of God. In the quiet of isolation, we often find the greatest clarity. Solitude creates the mental and spiritual space to weigh options carefully, not settling for the first solution but considering the best one that benefits us.

In that silence, we hear our own thoughts more clearly, causing us in that stillness to align our decisions not with the opinions of others, but with God's purpose, our values, and the life we are called to build. The widow's faith was tested in the crucible of solitude; even as the wife of a prophet, she was not shielded from adversity. But it was in that very place—alone, desperate, and honest—that her faith was not only tested, but strengthened.

Her journey toward breakthrough began the very moment she reached out for help. But the deeper miracle was this: in her loneliness, she learned to trust God's provision above all else. Our faith will be tested, stretched, deepened, and ultimately strengthened. It will be measured by the trials we endure in life. I can imagine that for many years, the widow, like many women of her time, may not have held the authority to make major household decisions. But when she found herself walking alone, she was forced into a new reality: she had to make life-changing and empowering decisions entirely on her own.

That's the truth about walking alone: it teaches us how to grow. As children, our parents made all the decisions for us. But as we grow into adulthood, responsibility slowly shifts onto our shoulders, and we begin to own our choices. Yet, for many who are married, the sudden loss of a spouse can create a moment of crisis, not just emotionally, but mentally as well, because decision-making was shared primarily by one and so the spouse who is left may not have been a developed strength in that area yet. Thus, the widow had no one to consult, no partner to share the mental load. Every decision from that point onwards was hers alone. While that may have felt terrifying at first, it eventually became empowering. Each choice she made became a steppingstone to building her confidence and teaching her how to navigate increasingly complex challenges.

Decision-making is more than just about picking the right solution; it's about growth, ownership, and resilience. As we make decisions, we grow in confidence, wisdom, and discernment. We don't just find solutions; we learn how to work them out! And wherever there is responsibility, personal accountability is close behind. You become responsible not just for the outcome but also for the process; there's no more riding in the backseat because you are at the wheel now. This means no more blame-shifting; you must now own your choices while actively seeking viable solutions that move you forward. Sometimes, it takes loss, the deep pain of losing a loved one, or even the collapse of something valuable, to push us out of our comfort zones. But in that discomfort lies the possibility for change, which is oftentimes for the better.

Solitude, while difficult, can also become sacred—an essential time to disconnect from the noise of the world where we often discover clarity, fresh perspective, and new paths we might never have seen before. And in those quiet, uncertain moments, we learn to lead our lives not by default, but by design.

Solitude often pushes us to take unconventional routes to solve our problems, and that is exactly what happened to the widow in the end. A housewife turned entrepreneur, driven not by ambition, but by crippling debt. How ironic and yet how true that pain and suffering often lead us down paths of creative problem-solving, revealing solutions we might never have discovered otherwise. It is often in seasons of loss that we find the courage to take risks, to step outside of what is familiar and to try something totally brand new. It is here we break away from our old habits and take a chance, and oftentimes, we are pleasantly surprised by what blooms in the soil of our adversity. Now is the time to take a deep breath, focus on yourself, and make the conscious choice to be different. It is time to refuse to blend in with the crowd; dare to march to the beat of your own drum while rising to become the torch bearer that lights the way for others to follow.

One of the greatest misconceptions in today's church is the belief that being a good Christian guarantees a life free from hardship. But the Scriptures, life experiences, and the narratives of faithful men and women throughout history tell a different story. Being a believer does not exempt us from trials but rather equips us to overcome them! Yes, sometimes our challenges are the result of poor choices, but that doesn't mean we are doomed to remain trapped by the consequences of all of them. God's grace makes room for redemption, recovery, and a fresh start.

So, when the path feels lonely...
When you find yourself walking alone...
When the usual support systems fall away—
Ask yourself: *How can I use this season to my advantage?*

This is not the end of your story. It could very well be the beginning of your most creative, courageous, and faith-filled chapter yet. There are several golden nuggets I want to leave you with.

The Courage to Face It Alone: Steps to Turn Crisis into Breakthrough

The first and hardest step in overcoming any crisis is to acknowledge your situation—just like the widow did. No matter how painful it might be, breakthrough begins when you face the reality of your debt, struggle, or circumstance and take ownership of how you arrived here. This is not the time for blame (time is not your **FRIEND** here) nor is it the time to hide behind denial, avoidance, or even the overuse of scriptures on wealth and prosperity without an action plan in place. This is the time for full acknowledgment and accountability! Face it. Own it. And move forward.

Here are six key steps that can guide you through your own journey of walking alone—and walking free:

1. **Acknowledge Your Situation:** Stop running from the truth! Whether the debt, crisis, or hardship was caused by your choices or circumstances outside your control, the first step toward healing and breakthrough is honest acknowledgment and ownership of facts. The widow didn't downplay her reality, instead she named it. Admitted it. And owned it! And by doing so, she opened the door for change in her life. **Key Reminder:** This is not about blame. It's about ownership.
2. **Seek Guidance:** The Bible reminds us, "Where no counsel is, the people fall; but in the multitude of counselors there is safety" (Proverbs 11:14). God often sends help through wise counsel, but we must be humble enough to seek it as well as accept it. Whether through prayer, spiritual mentors, financial advisors, or trusted friends, surround yourself with

those who can offer insight, perspective, and sound advice. **Key Reminder:** You may be walking alone, but you don't have to think alone.

3. **Create a Plan:** Don't just hope—strategize! Write down your next steps and lean on the clarity that comes from solitude, prayer, and seasoned counsel to form a realistic action plan. Outline what needs to be done and break it down into small, achievable steps. If possible, find an accountability partner who will walk the journey with you and help keep you focused and accountable. **Key Reminder:** A goal without a plan is just a wish.

4. **Trust in Your Abilities:** Take inventory of your strengths, your resilience, problem-solving skills, creativity, and most importantly, your faith. Trust that God has already placed within you the tools and abilities needed for this journey. Like the widow, you may not have realized what you were capable of until the moment you had no other choice but to act. **Key Reminder:** God has equipped you for this. Lean into the gifts He's given you.

5. ***Implement Your Plan:*** Execute! Take action even if it's one small step at a time. The widow's journey to Elisha was more than a cry for help; it was a deliberate, faith-filled decision to do something about her situation. Remember, small actions consistently taken create momentum for big change. **Key Reminder:** Faith moves mountains, but action moves you.

6. **Maintain Your Faith:** Above all, hold onto your faith, trusting that the same God who provided for the widow

> is also able to provide for you. Stay open, stay flexible, and trust that while the journey may feel lonely, **you are never truly alone.** Your faith is your anchor when the road feels long, and the nights feel dark and lonely. **Key Reminder:** Faith isn't just belief; it's your source of strength when hope feels hard.

The widow's story teaches us that walking alone in times of crisis, while painful, can become the catalyst for transformative growth, spiritually, mentally, and emotionally. Her journey from isolation to miraculous provision began with one courageous act: facing her problem head-on and taking action. So, whether you're a faithpreneur, a grieving parent, a divorcee, or anyone facing what feels like an impossible situation, let her story remind you of this truth:

Solitude is not punishment, it is preparation. It is the place where faith deepens, strength rises, and breakthroughs are born.

When you embrace your solitary journey with faith, courage, and intentional action, it becomes a powerful testimony. Just as the widow's small jar of oil became a symbol of God's provision, your journey can become a lasting testament to what's possible when you face your giants, even if you must face them alone.

CHAPTER 3

TRANSPARENCY IN TROUBLE

Facing Her Problem Head-On!

How do you handle your problems? Are you someone who confronts them head-on, or do you run and hide, hoping they will somehow magically resolve themselves on their own? A friend once shared something that has stayed with me: "The difference between dishonesty and transparency is communication." In other words, the level of communication you are willing to share reveals just how transparent you truly are about the challenges or joyous things happening in your life. Whenever we minimize, stay silent, or avoid the hard conversations of life, we're not walking in full truth. This often means that we are either in a place of fear or denial.

But here's the good news: there is nothing more liberating than finding the courage to face your problems! This means no more hiding or covering up the truth! It means that you finally understand that there can be no miracle without movement. Freedom begins the moment you decide to confront your challenges boldly and honestly and the widow did exactly that; she refused to shy away from the truth of her situation. She didn't pretend everything was fine but instead, she chose to communicate clearly, directly, and humbly to Elisha. This single courageous step became the turning point that led to her breakthrough.

Many people today hide their issues out of embarrassment, even from their loved ones. However, this was not the case for the widow. In the face of calamity, she made a pivotal decision. And that was to not hide her problem! Despite her desperate situation, the widow chose to speak out, approaching Prophet Elisha with a heavy heart. Though she was in pain, she remained open and honest about her circumstances, laying bare the full extent of her predicament.

One of life's invaluable lessons is the power of transparency and why it's crucial to speak out when facing hardship or debt. Through the widow's story, we explore the importance of seeking help, the strength in vulnerability, and practical steps to address challenges head-on. When the widow's husband died, he left her in a precarious financial position—burdened with debt and facing the potential loss of her sons to slavery. It would have been easy for her to retreat into silence, hiding her struggles out of pride or fear of judgment. However, the widow chose a different path—one marked by transparency and courage. She approached Elisha and openly shared her plight, setting in motion the events that would lead to her miraculous provision. This is called the ***Power of Transparency***.

Transparency, especially in times of crisis, is a powerful tool. It allows others to understand your situation and not only offer their friendship but also open doors to opportunities that could help you. Be completely transparent—do not leave anything out—so that you can invite tailored advice that directly addresses your specific situation. You wouldn't go to a mechanic for advice on baking or ask a baker how to fix a car. In the same way, being open and specific about your challenges ensures that the help you receive is relevant, effective, and truly makes a difference.

Many of us do ourselves a great disservice when we hide our problems or feel ashamed to speak out. The enemy uses our shame and fear to isolate us from potential avenues of support and solutions. Hiding our problems is not just harmful but often creates feelings of isolation and loneliness. Remember this one thing—isolation is the enemy of progress. When you are overwhelmed with debt or a difficult situation, it's easy to feel as though you are the only one struggling with that problem.

This often creates a sense of isolation, which only worsens the problem, making it even harder to find a way out. As a result, stress and anxiety increase, as one feels compelled to hide their struggles. Hiding one's problems often feels like carrying a heavy burden. The weight of secrecy can take a serious toll on both mental and physical health, making it even more difficult to address the issue with clarity and effectiveness.

When we stay silent about our struggles, we miss out on valuable help and support from others. I call these 'missed opportunities,' but many people associate them only with financial assistance. The truth is, support goes beyond financial assistance—it can range from practical advice, like in the case of the widow's oil, to emotional encouragement. You must recognize that there are people willing to help, but only if they know you need it! One of the biggest ways people unintentionally prolong their struggles is through silence, which often leads to debilitating inaction.

Failing to openly address your problems makes it less likely that you'll take the necessary steps to resolve them. Ignoring a problem only allows it to worsen over time. The widow's decision to speak up about her struggles was a decisive turning point in her story. It's a powerful reminder that no matter how dire your situation may seem, there is strength in sharing your struggles with others. This is why it's so important to speak up and share your truth courageously—

it allows us to confront the most difficult areas of our lives. When we open up, we break the cycle of shame that often accompanies financial difficulties or personal challenges. Speaking out empowers us to confront issues head-on, rather than allowing them to fester in the shadows and worsen over time.

There is strength in building a supportive network when we speak up, as it opens doors to opportunities that often remain dormant or untapped. This is when friends, family, mentors, or professionals can offer advice, encouragement, and even share resources that can make a significant difference in your life journey. Do not fall for the misconception that networking is only for the rich and powerful. Many of the most influential people rose from poverty, not because of wealth, but because they were candid about their struggles and found help along the way.

Transparency invites solutions, and by speaking out, you open yourself to new perspectives or strategies you may have previously overlooked. When we are vulnerable and honest, it encourages others who have faced similar challenges to share invaluable insights. This openness often leads to new opportunities and resources that can help you overcome your situation. By sharing your struggles, you empower those who may be shy or less confident to do the same. Your willingness to be vulnerable creates a ripple effect, fostering a culture of honesty, empathy, and support within your community or network. There are several ways to begin looking for viable solutions for those who are struggling under the weight of debt or life difficulties in general, and they are as follows:

1. ***Seek Professional Advice:*** The widow sought out Elisha, a trusted and wise figure whom she and her husband had known for years. Likewise, when dealing with debt or other serious issues, it is crucial to seek professional advice rather than relying solely on the opinions of friends. Look for free financial advisors, counselors, or legal experts who can provide the guidance needed to make informed and sound decisions.
2. ***Build a Support System:*** Sadly, many people realize the importance of building a support system only when they are in crisis—often when it's too late. Start early in cultivating a strong sense of community so you can rely on your tribe—whether it be friends, family, an association, or a faith-based group. It is essential to identify a caring support system that can provide emotional, practical, and, in some cases, financial assistance during times of need. These are the people who can offer encouragement, resources, connections, or even just a listening ear when you need it most. I once lost my job abruptly, and after praying, I began reaching out to people from my past network. Before long, I was working as a consultant and eventually started my own business. None of this would have been possible had I not reached out to those around me.
3. ***Take Inventory of Your Resources:*** Believe it or not, the solution to your problem may be closer than you think. The widow initially believed she had nothing, but Elisha helped her realize that the small amount of oil she possessed could be the key to her salvation. Take inventory of what you do have—the skills, resources, or talents you may have overlooked or

allowed to remain dormant. What assets do you have, and what about those great relationships you have built over the years? Consider how you can best leverage them to address your situation.

4. ***Create a Plan:*** Once you have spoken out and gathered support, it's time to create and implement an action plan. Identify the steps needed to tackle your debt or challenge. This may include budgeting, negotiating with creditors, or seeking additional sources of income. A clear plan can help you regain control and reduce feelings of overwhelm.
5. ***Patience and Perseverance:*** The reality is that you didn't fall into debt overnight, and solving financial or personal problems takes time as well. Be patient and kind to yourself throughout the process. Many people have already been too hard on themselves, but this is when patience and perseverance become essential. These qualities will help you keep moving forward, even if progress is slow.
6. ***Cultivating Love, Faith and Hope:*** A hard but important gift you should give yourself during the most challenging times of your life is to practice self-love. In these moments, we often become our own worst critic, harshly judging ourselves when we are already struggling. Instead, extend yourself some grace and focus on finding a practical solution to your situation. Another important gift that you need is to follow the advice of those who have the experience needed to get out of debt.

Just as the widow had faith in Elisha's guidance, it is essential to cultivate faith and hope in your own journey. Receive this with love, especially if you haven't always heeded wise counsel in the past. Trust that with the right actions and support, you can overcome any challenge. For the 21st-century Christian, there are many viable solutions to financial challenges, which can be vastly different from those faced in the widow's time. However, debt and the principle of transparency remain just as relevant today as they were then. Here are some modern-day financial solutions that you can leverage today:

1. ***Financial Counseling and Debt Management Programs:*** Unlike in the widow's time, today's world offers numerous financial counseling services and debt management programs. These resources can help you develop a plan to manage your debt, negotiate with creditors, and avoid further financial pitfalls. Be sure to carefully vet financial services, as some are predatory and take advantage of the vulnerable. Conduct thorough research and prioritize federal, state, and local resources as your first option.

2. ***Crowdfunding and Community Support:*** Platforms like GoFundMe, Kickstarter, and other crowdfunding sites enable people to share their stories and seek financial support from a wide audience. This modern-day equivalent of borrowing vessels can provide the necessary resources to overcome financial hurdles.

3. ***Online Support Groups and Forums:*** The internet has made it easier than ever to connect with others facing similar challenges. Online forums and support groups offer a space to share your struggles, seek advice, and receive encouragement from those who understand what you're going through.

4. ***Professional Networking:*** In the 21st century, platforms like LinkedIn make it easier to connect with professionals who can offer advice, mentorship, or even job opportunities. Being transparent about your situation can lead to connections that help you discover new ways to generate income or reduce debt.

5. ***Mental Health Resources:*** Dealing with financial stress can take a toll on your mental health. Fortunately, there are many resources available today, such as counseling services, therapy apps, and support hotlines, to help you cope with the emotional aspects of your situation.

6. ***Education and Skill Development:*** Unlike in the widow's time, we now have access to countless educational resources online. If your financial difficulties stem from a lack of skills or education, consider taking online courses or attending workshops to enhance your qualifications and increase your earning potential.

7. ***Transparency in Business Practices:*** For entrepreneurs, being transparent with your team and stakeholders about financial challenges can encourage collaborative problem-solving. Open communication fosters trust and inspires creative solutions that you may not have considered on your own.

In conclusion, the widow's story teaches us a valuable lesson: there is true strength in vulnerability and transparency. While the world may have us believe that these traits indicate weakness, the widow's example shows us that they are, in fact, signs of great strength. It takes courage to speak up, and when the widow spoke honestly about her problem, she discovered the necessary steps to move her toward her miracle!

Today, as you read this chapter, you too can find the courage to take the necessary steps toward your own miracle. Whether you are facing insurmountable debt, personal challenges, or a difficult situation, remember that hiding your problems will only deepen your struggle.

Instead, follow the widow's example: be brave enough to speak out, seek help, and trust that a solution is waiting to be found. In the process, you may discover that the very act of being open about your struggles becomes the key to unlocking the support and solutions you truly need. Just as the widow's oil was multiplied beyond her expectations, your willingness to be transparent can lead to outcomes far greater than you can imagine. It is in moments of honesty and openness that true transformation begins.

CHAPTER 4

WHEN GOOD PEOPLE GET INTO DEBT

The Debt Trap

I want to ask you a question: are you a good person? What do you think makes a person good or decent? My next question is "Can a good Christian end up in debt and does that suddenly make them a terrible person?" What is your debt story? Do you have one? If so, how did you handle it, and are you still trying to dig yourself out? There is an unfair myth that good people do not become victims of debt, but this could not be further from the truth.

The story of the widow and her husband in the biblical account of Elisha and the widow's oil is a powerful example of how even good, faithful people can find themselves in dire financial situations. Despite her husband's devotion to serving spiritually, he left his family in massive debt after his death. This chapter explores how good people can fall into debt due to various life challenges, the importance of financial literacy, and the ways to navigate out of debt using both spiritual and practical tools.

To understand the reality of debt, we must acknowledge life's unpredictability. Life is full of twists and turns; it can be complicated and filled with unexpected events, from illness and job loss to the sudden death of a breadwinner. These challenges can lead even the most responsible individuals into financial turmoil, and no one is exempt from this reality. The widow's husband likely did not anticipate leaving his family in debt, but unforeseen circumstances can thrust even the most prepared individuals into financial distress.

The truth is that many people, including those with good intentions and strong moral compasses, have never been taught how to manage money effectively. Even today, many still lack an understanding of the importance of saving, investing, or planning for their future. While it was a different era for the widow and her husband, it's possible they lacked the knowledge or resources to build a financial safety net. The lack of financial literacy continues to plague many households today, especially those without generational wealth.

In some cultures, there is undue pressure to maintain a certain lifestyle or fulfill societal expectations, which can lead to borrowing beyond one's means. The widow and her husband may have felt compelled to take on debt to meet their family's needs or societal obligations without fully understanding the long-term consequences. I also believe that the couple lacked set boundaries to curb their financial obligations or at least manage their money responsibly.

There are many Christians who believe that faith alone will shield them from financial difficulties, leading to a lack of proactive financial planning. This, along with the 'prosperity gospel' of the 1950s and 1980s, misled many Christians into believing that if they just believed in God, prayed, and paid their tithes, they would one day be rich without much effort. While faith is a powerful tool, God never intended for it to be used as a substitute for practical financial stewardship.

This spiritual misunderstanding, as the widow's story illustrates, shows that even the most devout individuals can find themselves in financial hardship. Many Christians who face such dire straits often turn to their churches for help, only to be declined at times. This has put a lot of strain on the Body of Christ while leaving many Christians financially impacted negatively.

Modern-day Christians must have a better understanding of how to manage money, not just as a practical necessity but also as a spiritual responsibility. The Bible contains numerous teachings on stewardship, emphasizing the importance of managing resources wisely. However, without proper education and tools, even the most well-meaning individuals can make financial mistakes.

Today's world offers a wide array of tools and resources to help individuals and families manage their finances and get out of debt. While the widow had to rely on the miraculous multiplication of oil, modern Christians have access to both spiritual guidance and practical financial solutions.

While I believe the widow and her husband were handicapped in this area, as many Christians also find themselves, we can all learn from the widow's story and leverage the 21st-century tools and opportunities that God has given us.

1. ***Budgeting:*** One of the fundamental aspects of financial literacy is learning how to budget effectively. A budget is a plan that outlines your income and expenses, helping you ensure that you live within your means. The widow and her husband may have avoided some of their financial struggles had they adhered to a strict budget. Throughout the Bible, God teaches about budgeting, and one great example is found in Luke 14:28-30, where we are warned to count the cost of anything we undertake and ensure that we have enough to finish the work we start.

2. ***Saving and Investing:*** Building an emergency fund and investing wisely are crucial steps in protecting against unforeseen financial challenges. In the widow's era, the concept of investing may have been different, but today, there are numerous ways to grow wealth, from savings accounts to stocks, real estate, and life insurance. As much as it is possible, having an emergency fund should cover at least three to six months of living expenses, providing a safety net in case of job loss, illness, or other unforeseen events.

3. ***Debt Management/Consolidation:*** Understanding how to manage and pay off debt is essential. Christians are encouraged to avoid unnecessary debt and to prioritize paying off what they owe. The widow's husband may have taken on debt with good intentions, but without a plan to repay it, his family was left vulnerable. For those struggling with multiple debts, debt consolidation can be a viable solution. This involves combining all your debts into a single loan with a lower interest rate, making it easier to manage and pay off.

4. ***Seeking Financial Advice and Counseling:*** Just as the widow sought guidance from Elisha, Christians today can benefit from seeking financial advice from professionals. Financial advisors, debt counselors, and mentors can provide valuable insights and strategies for managing money effectively. Many organizations offer free or low-cost financial counseling services that can help you create a plan to manage your debt, budget wisely, and build savings. These services provide

practical tools that many people, including the widow and her husband, may not have had.

5. ***Online Financial Education:*** The Internet is a valuable resource for learning about money management. There are countless online courses, videos, and articles that provide education on budgeting, investing, and debt management, helping you become more financially literate.

6. ***Side Gigs and Passive Income:*** In the 21st century, there are many opportunities to earn additional income through side gigs or passive income streams. Whether it's freelancing, starting a small business, or investing in rental properties, these avenues can help you build wealth and repay debt more quickly.

While prayer and faith are essential components of the Christian life, they must be accompanied by action, especially in financial matters. The widow's story reminds us that God provides, but we must also do our part. While our faith is at work, we must take action to experience the fullness of His miracle.

1. ***Faith Without Works is Dead:*** The Bible teaches that faith without works is dead (James 2:26), and this principle applies to finances as well. Praying for financial recovery is important, but it must be accompanied by practical steps such as budgeting, saving, and debt repayment.

2. ***Taking Responsibility:*** It's easy to fall into the trap of believing that God will miraculously solve all our problems without any effort on our part. However, the Bible encourages us to

be good stewards of what we have been given, which includes taking responsibility for our financial situation and making informed, wise decisions.

3. ***Community and Accountability:*** The widow sought help from Elisha, a trusted spiritual leader. Similarly, in today's world, Christians can benefit from being part of a supportive community that offers accountability and encouragement. Whether through a church group, a financial accountability partner, or a mentor, having others involved in your financial journey can make a significant difference.

One of the key lessons from the widow's story is the significance of responsible debt management. For Christians, financial stewardship is an important aspect of faith. Here are some practical steps to help avoid and manage debt wisely:

1. ***Live Within Your Means:*** Avoid the temptation to live beyond your means. Cultivating contentment and embracing simplicity are valuable virtues that can safeguard you from unnecessary debt and financial stress.
2. ***Prioritize Debt Repayment:*** If you are in debt, make it a priority to pay it off as quickly as possible. Develop a clear repayment plan, set achievable goals, and remain committed to them. The sooner you eliminate your debt, the less interest you'll accumulate over time.
3. ***Seek God's Guidance:*** Pray for wisdom and guidance in managing your finances. Seek God's help in making wise

financial decisions and ask for His blessing on your efforts to become debt-free.

4. ***Educate Yourself and Others:*** Take the time to learn about financial management and share your knowledge with others, especially within your Christian community. By educating others on wise money management, you can help them avoid common financial pitfalls.

In conclusion, the widow's story serves as a powerful reminder that even in the most challenging circumstances, there is always hope. Good people may find themselves in debt due to life's hardships, but through faith, financial wisdom, and decisive action, they can regain stability and overcome these obstacles. By embracing financial literacy, taking responsibility for your situation, and seeking both spiritual and practical solutions, you can transform your financial struggles into a testimony of God's provision and grace. Just as the widow's oil multiplied, your efforts to become debt-free can also be blessed and multiplied by God's hand.

CHAPTER 5

LIVING FROM PAYCHECK-TO-PAYCHECK

Retirement without Resources

I don't mean to alarm you, but if you lost your job tomorrow, how long could you sustain yourself financially? Are you among the millions who live paycheck to paycheck? How much do you have saved for emergencies? Do you have life insurance or a retirement plan like a 401(k)? If you're the sole provider for your family, what would happen if an unexpected crisis arose? Do you have a backup plan to protect your loved ones?

The story of the widow and her late husband in 2 Kings 4:1-7 reveals a sobering truth: even those who faithfully serve God can face severe financial hardship if they fail to plan for the future. The widow's husband, though devout and dedicated to his spiritual calling, left his family burdened with overwhelming debt—without savings, investments, or a retirement plan. As a result, his widow was forced to seek divine intervention to prevent her children from being taken by creditors.

This chapter not only examines the financial challenges faced by many 21st-century ministers but also highlights how some Christian families live by an unbalanced code of ethics. Many believe that prayer alone will ensure God provides for all their needs and that their problems will simply disappear. However, this mindset—placing all hope in divine intervention while neglecting the responsibility of hard work—has led to the downfall of many Christian marriages and homes. Financial struggles often become the deciding factor in whether families stay together or fall apart.

This challenge is further compounded by today's working Christian families, who, like the widow's family, live paycheck to paycheck. Many Christians, including ministers, are unprepared for retirement and risk facing serious financial hardship without a 401(k) or government support. Although numerous free financial planning apps are available, money remains an uncomfortable topic for many. However, we all must learn to budget and prepare for the future to ensure financial stability in retirement.

The key takeaway from the widow's story is that by starting financial planning early in life, we can avoid finding ourselves in the same desperate situation. Her experience serves as a crucial lesson for modern-day preachers who rely solely on ministry to support their families. The reality of living paycheck to paycheck is all too familiar—and unfortunately, a harsh truth—for many ministers and Christian families today. Every month, many of us find ourselves in this precarious situation, where each monthly income barely covers our expenses, leaving nothing left for savings or investment.

This lifestyle is fraught with risks, especially as retirement approaches. Statistics show that the average American is just one paycheck away from homelessness—and believers are not exempt from this reality. Living without financial preparation leaves no room for unexpected expenses or emergencies. Without a safety net, a sudden illness, job loss, or financial crisis can quickly spiral into overwhelming debt.

One of the most devastating challenges people face is juggling two crises—financial hardship and the emotional toll that comes with it, often leading to a domino effect. This was the widow's reality, just as it is for many Christian families today. Without savings or solid investments, there is no financial cushion to rely on in times of need or crisis. For many ministers, a lack of financial security can be especially troubling as they approach retirement age without the assurance of a stable income.

As we grow older and enter different phases of life, concerns about downsizing, health issues, fixed income, and retirement become unavoidable realities. It is every Christian's responsibility to take proactive steps toward financial freedom. This is even more crucial for ministers who rely solely on ministry without any additional source of income.

Financial insecurity is a major source of stress, affecting not just individuals but their families as well. The widow's husband likely bore the full responsibility of providing for his family, but his lack of financial planning left his wife and sons in a desperate situation after his passing. This remains true today, especially when a wife is widowed unexpectedly, leaving her financially vulnerable. For many women whose husbands are the primary breadwinners, losing both their spouse and their household income can make life incredibly challenging.

There are several reasons why many ministers find themselves financially unprepared for retirement and they are as follows:

Focus on Ministry Over Money:

"Ministry Over Money," or ***"MOM,"*** describes the mindset of ministers who prioritize their spiritual calling over financial planning. Many believe that if they demonstrate great faith, God will provide for their needs. While faith is essential, it does not eliminate the need for practical financial stewardship—a principle too often overlooked by Christians until it is too late.

Limited Income:

Ministers often earn modest salaries, especially those leading small congregations. In the U.S., the median church attendance ranges from 65 to 250 members. With such limited income, saving for retirement can be challenging—particularly when combined with the financial demands of supporting a family.

Lack of Financial Literacy:

Many ministers and their families lack the financial education needed to make informed decisions about saving, investing, and retirement planning. Without this knowledge, they often fail to recognize the importance of starting early or the long-term benefits of compound interest.

Cultural Expectations:

Many Christian communities expect their ministers to live modestly, prioritizing spiritual work over financial gain. While this humility is admirable, it can become unrealistic if ministers struggle to support their families. This mindset often results in a lack of financial preparation for the future, placing unnecessary strain on family relationships.

In the widow's story, her husband's failure to plan for the future had devastating consequences. As the head of his household, he was responsible for ensuring his family's financial security, even in his absence. This duty remains just as important for modern-day husbands, especially those in ministry, who must take a proactive approach to financial planning for their families' well-being. This is no longer sufficient for 21st-century ministry in today's world with limited financial power and inflation, since many families cannot live off of just one income. Today, many ministers may need to have their wives or even themselves work bi-vocational or take up a secondary job.

1. ***Start Early:*** It is never too soon to begin planning for retirement. The earlier you start, the better. Early planning allows the power of compound interest to work in your favor, making it easier to build a substantial retirement fund over time.

2. ***Budgeting:*** Creating and sticking to a budget is essential for managing finances effectively. A budget helps ensure that you live within your means, allocate funds for savings, and avoid unnecessary debt.

3. ***Investing:*** Most people don't realize that you don't need to work for a major company to have a 401(k). There are many ways to build one, and it is crucial to invest in retirement accounts—such as a 401(k), IRA, or other investment vehicles—to grow wealth over time. For every minister reading this book, prioritizing retirement planning is essential. They should seek out retirement plans offered by their denominations or explore private options to secure their financial future.

4. ***Financial Literacy & Education:*** By educating yourself and your family about money management, investing, and retirement planning, you have a better chance of not being taken by surprise by life's events. Making financial

literacy a family affair helps instill a sense of responsibility early on, fostering a healthy mindset toward money management. It teaches the benefits of both financial literacy and ownership while preparing and securing your family for the future in case of unforeseen life events. While education is key to financial freedom, you do not have to become a financial guru. Simply taking the time to learn about personal finance, investing, and retirement planning can give you the necessary edge you need to build confidence in your retirement. There are many online resources—such as courses, books, apps, and financial tools—that can help you expand your financial knowledge. Many of these are free and user-friendly. Understanding key financial concepts enables you to make informed decisions that benefit your family in the long run and help you to prepare for life's inevitable rainy days.

5. ***Insurance:*** Life insurance is a crucial part of financial planning, offering various options to support your family's future. For instance, an Indexed Universal Life (IUL) policy can provide financial security, while a 529 plan helps fund your children's education. While it is true that life insurance can provide financial protection for your family in the event of your untimely death, it can also help while you are still alive. Having it can help prevent the kind of financial crisis faced by the widow and her children.

While the widow in Elisha's time had limited options, today's ministers and Christian families have access to a wide range of tools and resources to help them prepare for retirement and avoid the struggles of living paycheck to paycheck. One practical step is to take advantage of an employer-sponsored retirement plan offered by your denomination. Take advantage of your church's 401(k) or a similar retirement plan, contributing as much as you can afford. If that option isn't available, consider opening an Individual Retirement Account (IRA). Both Traditional and Roth IRAs provide tax benefits that can help you grow your retirement savings more effectively.

Another solution is seeking advice from a financial advisor who can help you create a personalized retirement plan to manage your investments. Financial advisors can ensure that you are on track to meet your financial goals and prepare adequately for the future. Passive income, or "side gigs" as many call them, is essential for anyone looking to build multiple streams of revenue. Side businesses such as rental properties, freelance work, or even taking on a second job can significantly boost financial stability. These income streams can provide extra funds for saving and investing, reducing the pressure on your primary income.

Debt management is a crucial aspect of achieving financial freedom. Prioritizing debt repayment allows you to carry less financial burden into retirement. As you approach retirement age, avoid taking on new debt and focus on paying off existing obligations. Balancing debt management, budgeting and financial literacy adds up to an effective retirement plan because you have a sure roadmap to retirement.

Failing to clearly understand your income, expenses, and financial goals can easily lead to the trap of living paycheck to paycheck and neglecting retirement savings. Start by creating a realistic budget, which is only possible by tracking your income and expenses. Identify areas where you can cut back and allocate those funds towards savings and investments.

It deeply saddens me to hear how the unexpected death of a parent who is often the primary provider can drastically alter the course of a family's future due to a lack of preparation. Wives, in particular, should be aware of essential details such as their mortgage lender, utility providers, and other key financial obligations. In the 21st century, we can no longer remain ignorant when it comes to understanding our individual roles in our family's financial planning and expenditures. Husbands who hide their assets do themselves a great disservice. The best friend who knows all your financial secrets may end up taking your money and never supporting your children after you're gone.

Too many Christian families, especially ministers, have suffered due to a lack of financial preparation and literacy. It is essential to have a living will and life insurance, and if you own a safety deposit box, someone you trust should be aware of it. Starting today, take proactive steps to ensure your entire family is prepared for the future. Work together toward financial security by planning wisely.

In conclusion, the widow's story reflects the reality of many people around the world who are unprepared for a secure future—even in a great country like the United States. Her story, like countless others, serves as a powerful reminder of the importance of financial planning. The truth is that living paycheck to paycheck is a burden that can have serious consequences, particularly as one's retirement approaches.

By proactively budgeting, saving, and investing, your family can avoid past mistakes and build a secure future. Cultivating healthy financial habits today can protect your loved ones from future struggles and challenges. For the modern-day preacher, the widow's story—and the lessons it holds—has been around for generations. Yet, many continue to fall into the very traps this story warns us about.

As a minister and spouse, it is essential to balance spiritual responsibilities with practical financial stewardship. Preaching the Gospel or serving in the church does not exempt you from your financial duties to your family. Faith alone cannot replace wise financial planning—prayer must be paired with action. Retirement planning is not just a worldly concern; it is a reflection of your commitment to providing for your family and securing their well-being. God will not come down from heaven to handle your finances, as it is your responsibility to ensure that your loved ones are cared for both financially and spiritually.

Today, I want to plead with you as the reader to circumspectly learn from the widow's story and take the necessary steps to ensure that you can live off the power of your oil. Commit to building a legacy that will endure for generations by embracing both the spiritual and financial responsibilities of your calling—as a minister, a Christian, and a provider. There is no joy in a lifetime of labor if your future is put at risk simply because you failed to prepare adequately for retirement. Diligence without direction shows a lack of adequate preparation. Many people are devoted and hard workers but have no firsthand knowledge of how to manage their money for the future. Let us all embrace the lesson of the widow and her jar of oil!

CHAPTER 6

LEVERAGING HER WIDOW'S NETWORK

The Power of Connection

If you were to go through your phone right now and identify three people in your network who could support you in a time of need, who would they be? Excluding your pastor and family members, which friends could you call during a crisis, knowing they would step up to help because they are truly part of your network? If you're unsure who those people might be—those who will show up for you when it matters most—it may be time to reevaluate some of your friendships.

I have often felt that the widow's story in the Bible is overlooked and underestimated due to personal biases. Some may wonder, what could the wife of a great prophet possibly teach us? Or what lessons can a widow offer to those with thriving careers and families? The answer is "many" if we allow God to open our hearts to them! In 2 Kings 4:1-7, we see a widow in desperate need, facing the threat of losing her children to creditors. What saved her in the end? It was not just her faith but her connection to the great prophet Elisha himself.

The widow and her husband had built a relationship with Elisha, a man renowned for his spiritual insight, prophetic word, and countless miracles. This connection would later become her lifeline in a time of trouble. The question remains: *Who is your lifeline if you find yourself in a difficult situation?* This is a serious question every Christian must ask. After her husband's passing, the widow leveraged his relationship with Elisha to secure the help she desperately needed.

In today's world, connections often serve as the bridges that lead us out of difficult situations. For 21st-century Christians, nurturing and maintaining relationships—whether in the workplace, church, or personal circles—is essential. Yet, I often encounter Christians who have severed important relationships simply because they believed those connections were no longer necessary or had run their course. Too often, this decision proves to be to their own detriment.

Relationships can open doors, provide support in times of need, and even create opportunities for growth and advancement. This chapter delves into the importance of building strong networks, drawing key lessons from the widow's story and the power of relationships. The widow's connection to Elisha wasn't coincidental; it stemmed from her husband's dedication. As a faithful servant of God, he had worked alongside Elisha or was known well enough to earn the prophet's regard.

While the Bible doesn't detail their relationship fully, we can see that the widow's husband had built a connection with Elisha based on respect and trust. This relationship became her lifeline when crisis struck. Though they may never have preached together or shared a platform, this connection proved to be her saving grace in her darkest hour

The lesson here is simple: relationships matter. The widow may not have had great financial wealth, but she had a connection to someone who could change her circumstances. This same principle applies today. Whether you are an entrepreneur, a corporate professional, or someone facing personal challenges, your network can be one of your most powerful resources.

Christians are often encouraged to build relationships based on love, support, and mutual care within the church. However, nurturing relationships is not just a spiritual mandate—it is also a practical necessity. By building meaningful connections, you create a support system that can sustain you in times of trouble, much like Elisha helped the widow. I must also state that it is not enough to build relationships within the church only but also outside as well. I often feel that many 21st-century Christians limit themselves to church relationships while excluding secular ones simply because those individuals are unsaved. Yet, these same Christians pray for the wealth of the unjust. How limiting, myopic, and even contradictory this mindset can be! We must do better. One way to grow is by recognizing the importance of vital relationships.

Here are three key reasons why we should nurture our relationships—whether Christian or not.

1. ***Emotional and Spiritual Support:*** In difficult times, a strong network of relationships can provide both emotional and spiritual support. Friends, family, and fellow believers can offer prayer, encouragement, and practical assistance when needed. For the widow, Elisha was more than just a prophet—he was a source of spiritual guidance and a solution to her immediate crisis.

2. ***Opportunities for Growth:*** Building and nurturing relationships can also create opportunities for personal and professional growth. In the workplace, a strong network can offer mentorship, career guidance, and connections that open doors for advancement. In the church, meaningful relationships can foster spiritual growth and a deeper understanding of your faith.

3. ***A Safety Net in Times of Crisis:*** As seen in the widow's story, a strong network can serve as a safety net when life takes an unexpected turn. Whether facing financial hardship, loss, or a personal crisis, the relationships you have cultivated can provide support in ways you may never have anticipated.

There are connections, and then there are true connections—and there is a difference. Have you ever faced a challenge, reached out to a connection, and realized they were unwilling or unable to help? Now, let me be clear: no one is obligated to help us, and we are not entitled to anyone's support. However, we all hope that when the time comes, we will have people in our corner who are willing to step up when we need them most. Well, here we are going to discuss the benefits that having the right connections can afford us as individuals. Having the right connections is crucial, especially in times of trouble. Here are some of the key benefits of maintaining a strong network:

1. ***Access to Resources and Expertise:*** When you have the right connections, you gain access to resources that might otherwise be out of reach. For the widow, her connection to Elisha provided divine wisdom and a miraculous solution to her crisis. In today's world, building relationships across various fields can open doors to solutions for financial, professional, and personal challenges.
2. ***Opening Doors for New Opportunities:*** A strong network can open doors to new opportunities in business, ministry, and personal life. The right connections can recommend you for jobs, introduce you to potential clients, or help you

launch a new venture. Your network can serve as a gateway to opportunities you may never have discovered on your own.

3. ***Support during Difficult Times:*** When tragedy strikes, a strong support network can make all the difference. The widow relied on her late husband's connection to Elisha, which ultimately saved her family. Similarly, in today's world, a well-built network can provide emotional, spiritual, and financial support when life becomes overwhelming.

4. ***Mentorship and Guidance:*** One of the greatest benefits of having strong connections is the opportunity for mentorship. Just as Elisha guided the widow through her financial crisis, mentors in your network can provide valuable advice, share wisdom from their experiences, and help you navigate life's challenges.

Building meaningful relationships requires time, effort, and intentionality. It's not enough to simply know people—you must actively invest in those connections for them to flourish. Here are some practical steps to build and maintain a strong network:

1. ***Be Genuine:*** People can sense when you're not being authentic. Whether in the workplace or church, approach relationships with sincerity. Show genuine interest in others and be willing to offer help whenever possible.

2. ***Stay Connected:*** Don't wait until you need something to reach out—it can be frustrating for others. Instead, regularly check in with your network. Whether through phone calls, messages,

or face-to-face meetings, staying connected strengthens relationships over time.

3. *Give and Take 'Reciprocity':* Relationships should be mutually beneficial. Be willing to support others in your network without expecting anything in return. Genuine generosity builds trust and strengthens the bonds between you and your connections.
4. *Leverage Social Media:* In the 21st century, social media is a powerful tool for maintaining relationships. Platforms like LinkedIn, Facebook, and Instagram allow you to stay connected with people worldwide and keep your network active.
5. *Attend Networking Events:* Whether in your profession or church, attending events where you can meet new people is a great way to expand your network. Conferences, seminars, and social gatherings offer valuable opportunities to build meaningful connections.

In my women's leadership book titled *"Unlocking the Deborah in You, the Traits of a Great Female Leader,"* I often emphasize the importance of building your network, as it is directly linked to your net worth! As often as this is said, I still believe that the average Christian has yet to fully grasp this concept the way the modern world has. A strong network can open doors to opportunities that may have a lasting impact on your financial future. Here's how networking can help you build both your personal and professional net worth:

1. ***Job Referrals and Career Growth:*** Many people secure jobs through referrals from their network. Strong connections increase your chances of hearing about job openings, business opportunities, and potential clients. This can lead to career growth and higher income.
2. ***Partnerships and Collaborations:*** In business, having a network can lead to partnerships and collaborations that can grow your company and increase revenue. A strong network opens the door to new ideas, resources, and markets.
3. ***Financial Advice and Mentorship:*** Your network can also include financial advisors, mentors, and experienced professionals in wealth management. These connections can offer invaluable advice on growing your investments, managing your finances, and securing your financial future.

Whenever I hear a person state that they do not have many friends or connections, I often feel a sense of apprehension for them. I am afraid that in their most desperate moment, they might not have anyone to run to because they did not invest in building relationships. There is a Nigerian adage that says, "Rain will fall on everyone's roof." This means that challenges and hardships are not exclusive to one person; they will come to everyone at some point, regardless of status or position, signifying a shared human experience. And it is in this shared experience that you will need your connections the most. Failing to build and maintain healthy relationships can leave you vulnerable, especially in difficult times. Without a strong network, you may find yourself isolated, with no one to turn to for support or guidance. Here are some potential pitfalls of not having strong connections:

1. ***Limited Opportunities:*** Without a strong network, you may miss out on job opportunities, partnerships, and collaborations that could advance your professional and financial growth.
2. ***No Support in Times of Crisis:*** Without strong relationships, you may struggle to find help when you need it most. Like the widow, you could face financial hardship or personal difficulties without the safety net a network provides.
3. ***Isolation:*** Lacking a strong network can lead to feelings of isolation and loneliness. As social beings, we thrive on meaningful relationships, which are essential for emotional well-being.

Even after experiencing a loss, like the widow, it's important to keep the lines of communication open with your network. Here's how to stay connected during challenging times:

1. ***Reach Out:*** Don't hesitate to ask for help when you need it. Like the widow who sought out Elisha, reaching out to your network in times of need can provide valuable support and solutions.
2. ***Stay Transparent:*** Be honest about your situation. Whether facing a financial crisis or a personal loss, transparency allows others to understand how they can support you.
3. ***Offer Support:*** Even in times of grief, be willing to support those in your network. Reciprocity strengthens relationships

and fosters a support system that will be there for you when you need it.

The widow's ability to rely on her late husband's connection to Elisha suggests that her husband was well-regarded and had built strong relationships during his life. His work likely positioned him as a man of integrity, which opened the door for his widow to receive help when he was no longer there. This teaches us that the relationships we build during our lifetime can have lasting benefits for our families. As Christians, it's important to ensure that the people we connect with know not only us but our families. Building strong relationships with family friends, church members, and colleagues helps ensure that if we are ever in need, our loved ones can rely on those connections for support.

In conclusion, the widow's story reminds us of the power of relationships and why they are vital. By nurturing our connections, we create a safety net that can support us and our families in times of need. To secure the future of the 21st-century Christian, one must build relationships with both their own future and that of their family in mind. You must be intentional about building and maintaining the networks that you have around you if you want to be successful.

CHAPTER 7

A LEGACY OF TIMELESS CHARACTER

Diligence and Distinction

If I were to ask a few of your closest friends, how would they describe your character? Are you warm and friendly, or more serious and refined? Do you have a playful side, or do some friends see you as straight-laced and reserved? Are you courageous and compassionate? Are you kind and resilient? How would you define character? According to the Merriam-Webster Dictionary, character is "one of the attributes or features that makes up and distinguishes an individual."

In the story of the widow and her jar of oil, one key detail that is often overlooked is how she leveraged her husband's reputation as a diligent worker and a man of sound character in her time of need. Without acknowledging the integrity of her late husband, the prophet, the widow's story would be incomplete. People often quote Scripture about how gifts or charisma can bring us before kings, but character and integrity are just as crucial in shaping our legacy.

A gift does wonders;
it will bring you before men of importance!
Proverbs 18:16 (TLB)

Yet, I often remind people that while your gift may open doors to leaders and decision-makers who can shape your future, only your character will keep you in their presence and grant you lasting access. We are living in perilous times where talent often seems to matter more than character or reputation—but this should not be so. The widow's story presents an intriguing paradox: how can a person possess strong character and still be in debt? It's a question that could spark a lively debate at any dinner table.

As I mentioned in earlier chapters, good people can fall into debt due to unforeseen circumstances. The widow's late husband was one such example. Despite his family's financial struggles, the deceased prophet must have been a man of integrity and respect. His legacy was so strong that even after his death, his character continued to carry weight, offering his wife a foundation to seek help in her time of need.

The question we must all ask ourselves is this: How do others truly perceive our character? If an unexpected life event were to occur, would our reputation be strong enough for our family to receive help if needed? It's essential to reflect on our character and consider whether we have built a legacy that our loved ones can rely on. The widow's husband had a relationship with the prophet Elisha that proved invaluable—it allowed his widow to seek help in her time of desperate need. The Amplified Bible offers a powerful perspective on the value of a good name compared to gold and silver.

A good name [earned by honorable behavior,
godly wisdom, moral courage, and personal integrity]
is more desirable than great riches;
and favor is better than silver and gold.
Proverbs 22:1 (AMP)

Boom!!! The Scripture says it all—it tells us exactly how we can secure a good name through good character! This chapter dives deep into the importance of being not only a diligent and ethical worker but also the significance of maintaining a strong reputation, both in life and after we are gone. For 21st-century Christians, these lessons are crucial—not just spiritually, but physically as well. It serves as a sharp reminder that our character, work ethic, reputation, and the relationships we cultivate during our lifetime don't just shape our own destiny. They have a lasting impact on the lives of our loved ones long after we're gone.

Imagine the widow's conundrum—being in debt and yet still respected! Her situation presents a fascinating paradox worth exploring. How could a man of good standing, known personally by the great prophet Elisha, die and leave his family in such financial distress? I can just hear the church gossip now! In fact, some would even go as far as to suggest that if this broke prophet was Elisha's friend, then perhaps Elisha's character should also be called into question. And let's be real—if we're going to be totally honest, a few of us might find ourselves chiming in on the conversation too, even though we don't have the full story.

The truth is, this conundrum offers several valuable lessons about life, character, and work ethic—lessons that all of us as believers can learn from, beginning with the widow's late husband and his profession as a prophet. Since he was neither a major nor a minor prophet, we can consider him a nameless prophet. It's safe to assume that his work may not have been financially lucrative, yet he remained diligent and dedicated in his service to God. This reminds me of my father, who once worked for the World Bank but later chose to dedicate himself to teaching as a college professor.

I can tell you without a doubt that teachers are among the most unappreciated and underpaid workers in the world. Many don't do it for the money, but for the love of their students, people like my father. The late prophet may not have accumulated wealth, but he built something far more valuable: a reputation of integrity and faithfulness. His life and work had earned the respect of Elisha, one of the most powerful and revered prophets in Israel. And it was this very reputation that the widow leaned on in her time of need.

She may not have had financial resources, but she possessed something just as powerful—relational capital, built by her husband's years of diligent work.

What is relational capital? In a nutshell, it is the value derived from strong, positive relationships founded on trust, respect, goodwill, and mutual understanding. The widow's story demonstrates that being in debt does not automatically erase one's good reputation. Even in financial hardship, her husband remained a man of high standing, and his legacy ultimately helped her find a solution to her problem. Now, ask yourself: What does your relational capital look like? How have you nurtured it over time?

Do you see relational capital as an asset, or do you only value your relationships when you are in need? What is the quality of your relationships with others? When was the last time you took stock of your relational capital? In today's world, reputation and work ethic are just as vital as they were in ancient Israel—perhaps even more so, given our increasingly interdependent world. As 21st-century Christians, we are called to display excellence in everything we do, recognizing that our work and character speak for us even when we are not present.

The Bible places significant emphasis on the value of hard work and integrity.

"Do you see a man diligent in his business? He will stand before kings; he will not stand before obscure men."
Proverbs 22:29 (AMPC)

This verse underscores the idea that diligent work and a good reputation can open doors, leading to favor in high places. The widow's husband may not have stood before kings, but he stood in the good graces of Elisha—and that alone was enough to save his family from financial ruin and slavery! In Colossians 3:23-24, Paul encourages the church to work with sincerity, as unto the Lord, so they may receive an inheritance from Him. This passage reminds us that our labor is not just for earthly recognition but is ultimately for God.

By maintaining this perspective, we are motivated to excel in all we do, knowing that our labor is not in vain. However, we should also recognize that when we work with a spirit of excellence, there is an even greater reward if we ever find ourselves in a difficult or unexpected situation.

Whatever may be your task, work at it heartily (from the soul), as [something done] for the Lord and not for men, knowing [with all certainty] that it is from the Lord [and not from men] that you will receive the inheritance which is your [real] reward. [The One Whom] you are actually serving [is] the Lord Christ (the Messiah).
Colossians 3:23-24 (AMPC)

Now, let us flip the perspective inferred in the Scriptures and imagine if the widow's husband had been of poor character and a lazy worker. What would that have meant for his widow in her greatest time of crisis? If he had been unreliable, dishonest, or lazy, it is unlikely he would have had a relationship with Elisha. Instead, he would have squandered any opportunity to build meaningful connections, leaving his family without a support network when tragedy struck. As a minister, I have heard countless stories of men who passed away after either refusing to mentor others or living dishonestly. More often than not, their widows and children suffered immensely due to their lack of character.

Lazy hands make for poverty,
but diligent hands bring wealth.
Proverbs 10:4 (NIV)

Laziness, a poor work ethic, and a lack of integrity are all traits that can lead to financial, relational, and spiritual poverty. Had the widow's husband been such a man, his family's plight could have been far worse. They might have been left with no one to turn to, with creditors closing in and no hope of divine intervention through the prophet Elisha. In that case, we would be reading a very different story—one of a failed prophet whose household God did not intervene to save.

This is a valuable lesson for today's Christians. You must understand that the work you do, the relationships you build, and the character you display are investments—not only in your future but in that of your family as well. Hard work, diligence, and integrity create a legacy that can be relied upon in times of need, even long after you are gone. The value of good character cannot be underrated because a good reputation is everything. From Genesis to Revelation, we are constantly reminded that a good name or reputation is paramount—more valuable than gold and silver.

The long-lasting impact of a good reputation is seen in our everyday interactions with people, especially those who know your family's name or reputation. A person's wealth may diminish or be lost, but their reputation and the relationships they build through a life of integrity often remain for generations. The widow's husband may not have left behind great riches, but his good name provided her with an opportunity to receive the help she needed from Elisha.

A good name speaks of trustworthiness, reliability, and faithfulness—traits that reflect the character of God. For Christians, maintaining a good reputation isn't about seeking personal glory but about reflecting God's character to those around us. This is why it is so important to be a person of integrity in all aspects of life, from the workplace to personal relationships. In the widow's story, we see the power of a good name. Though her husband was no longer there to provide for his family, his reputation opened the door for divine provision!

The same principle applies today: when we live lives of integrity, we leave behind a lasting legacy that can bless others long after we are gone. The widow's story clearly teaches us that diligent work and integrity create opportunities for help and support when we need them most. Had her husband been a different kind of man, she might never have gained access to Elisha's assistance—or could have even been denied it. However, because of his character and years of faithful service, he built a relationship with the prophet that, in turn, became her lifeline when she needed it most.

There is an adage that says, *"No news is good news."* While we never heard of the mighty things the late prophet accomplished, we certainly did not hear any bad news either! Though he owed creditors, there is no indication that he borrowed recklessly or lived beyond his means. This tells me that he did his very best to work hard, remain independent, and live a simple yet honorable life. In the book of 1 Thessalonians, we are once again reminded of the importance of hard work, ethics, and independence. Living a respectable life ultimately leads to success, both in the present and the future.

And to make it your ambition to lead a quiet life: You should mind your own business and work with your hands, just as we told you, so that your daily life may win the respect of outsiders and so that you will not be dependent on anybody.
1 Thessalonians 4:11-12 (NIV)

As 21st-century Christians, we must approach our work with dedication and purpose, understanding that it is also the legacy we leave behind. Working diligently creates opportunities for God's favor to flow in our lives. By doing so, we open doors for divine help when we need it most. The widow's story holds a crucial lesson for modern-day Christians, especially those in ministry—it can no longer be ignored. Her ability to leverage her husband's reputation serves as a powerful reminder that our professional and personal relationships matter, even beyond death.

In today's world, many people prioritize accumulating wealth and success, often at the expense of character and integrity. Even Christians are following this trend, forgetting that we are called to a higher standard. Our work should not be solely about financial gain but also about building a legacy that reflects the values of the Kingdom of God. Here are a few key takeaways that 21st-century Christians can glean from the widow's story:

1. ***Build a Reputation of Integrity:*** First and foremost, your reputation is everything, and therefore you should guard it as one of your most valuable assets. Whether in the workplace, in ministry, or in your personal relationships, your highest priority should be to strive for integrity. Remember this: a bad name closes doors, while a good name not only opens them but keeps them open for your loved ones long after you are gone.
2. ***Work Diligently:*** Whatever you do, do it with a spirit of excellence—always bring your very best to the table. Whether you hold a high-powered corporate position or a seemingly insignificant role, your work ethic reflects your character. Diligence in your work can lead to greater opportunities, unexpected support, and even surprises from places or people you least expect.
3. ***Cultivate Meaningful & Healthy Relationships:*** The widow's husband's relationship with Elisha teaches us all about the power of building meaningful relationships and that without them, we cease to exist even as a society. We all need relationships that can provide emotional, spiritual, and practical support in times of need. However, they cannot exist without investing the time and commitment into building them.
4. ***Leave a Lasting Legacy:*** You are not just defined by your work but by your character at work—whether in a secular job or in

> ministry. Remember, your character will speak for you long after you are gone. Be intentional and authentic in building your legacy. When integrity, hard work, and faithfulness serve as your cornerstone, there will always be someone who remembers your family when it matters most.

One of my favorite stories in the Bible is that of Jonathan and David. In today's terms, we might call their bond a 'bromance,' and it was especially evident after Jonathan's premature death. Jonathan did everything by the book—he walked with integrity even when his father, the king, acted dishonestly. He cultivated healthy relationships, and in the end, his legacy endured long after he was gone.

When David ascended the throne as king of Israel, he not only wept over the death of his best friend, Jonathan, but also ensured that Jonathan's crippled son, Mephibosheth, received special care for the rest of his life, treating him like family. This is the true impact of hard work and good character—it continues to speak even after one is gone!

In conclusion, the power of a good reputation has far-reaching effects long after we are gone. Whether it is through divine help, as seen in the case of Elisha and the widow, or through tangible assistance, as in the case of Mephibosheth, Jonathan's lame son, a strong legacy endures. Jonathan's kindness to David, even in the face of rejection, set the stage for future generations of his family to be blessed!

In a world that often prioritizes wealth and success over character, the story of the widow and her jar of oil reminds us that integrity, diligence, and a good name are far more valuable than riches. As

Christians, we must never forget this truth. Instead, let us strive to leave the world better than we found it—reflecting God's character in all we do. By doing so, we create a legacy that serves as a source of blessing and provision for those we truly love.

CHAPTER 8

THE BENEFITS OF BI-VOCATIONALISM

Navigating The Bi-vocational Life

How long have you been attending your church? Is your pastor among the thousands who serve in bi-vocational ministry, balancing the demands of both ministry and secular work? How do you feel about a pastor who juggles these responsibilities? If you are a pastor, what are your thoughts on bi-vocational ministry? What's your story? How did you begin your journey in ministry, and why do you believe this topic is relevant in today's world?

The story of the widow and her jar of oil reveals that the root cause of her family's financial crisis stemmed from the choices made by her late husband. As a prophet, he devoted his life to spiritual work, fully relying on his calling for financial provision. However, his decision not to secure a secondary source of income left his family vulnerable after his passing. I believe that many modern-day ministers, as well as those from the past, have faced similar hardships due to their resistance or reluctance toward bi-vocational ministry.

Somehow, Satan and the relentless pursuit of building mega-churches have fostered a mindset that having a secular job alongside ministry is a sign of weak faith. This dangerous ideology has led to the breakdown of many Christian homes, creating role reversals between husbands and wives. It places unrealistic expectations on men who, despite not providing for their households, are still expected to lead them with authority and respect. The truth is, unless both spouses mutually agree on this arrangement, without one imposing their will on the other, it can lead to deep resentment and instability within the family. Negating your responsibilities while demanding that both your wife and children fall in line is totally unrealistic and hypocritical. I have often stated, *"The shoulders of a woman were never built to handle the responsibilities of a man."* And when it does happen, every man should expect that woman to move according to the responsibilities that she has been made to shoulder!

The widow's desperation and indebtedness highlight a critical issue: could her family's financial crisis have been avoided if her husband had embraced bi-vocational ministry—working both in a secular job and in his calling as a prophet? I believe the outcome might have been drastically different had he chosen this path. This chapter explores the importance of modern-day ministers considering bi-vocational roles, particularly when serving small congregations or facing financial instability. It is crucial that this discussion is approached without judgment or condemnation toward those who choose to take on secular work alongside their ministry.

It would be ideal if bi-vocational ministers received more support from mega-churches, kingdom celebrity preachers, and, most importantly, from congregants who often fail to recognize that ministry can be an unforgiving and thankless task. However, the Bible also reminds us to count the cost of what we commit to—including ministry. Should we expect others to carry our responsibilities to the point that it becomes a burden for them as well? And if ministry alone becomes too overwhelming or financially unsustainable, when should we make the decision to balance both ministry and secular work? These are hard but necessary questions that modern-day ministers must prayerfully consider. The widow's story gives us the opportunity to correct certain outdated ideologies of bi-vocational ministry while exploring the benefits and challenges of balancing secular work and ministry.

One of the most valuable aspects of studying bi-vocational work is the ability to draw from biblical examples of individuals who successfully balanced their work while serving God. Additionally, it is crucial to explore the dynamics within families where both spouses must navigate the balance between ministry and secular work in a way that benefits both partners. When only one spouse makes the decision, it can lead to resentment, strain, or even divorce. Throughout Scripture, God provides us with numerous examples of successful ministers—many of whom were well-known and respected—who still chose to work in order to avoid placing undue financial pressure on the people of God.

I am one minister who strongly believes in bi-vocational ministry, as I have always worked while serving in ministry. In the case of the widow's husband, his decision to focus solely on ministry may have stemmed from his deep devotion to God. While his faithfulness to his prophetic calling is admirable, the consequences for his family were devastating. Without a financial plan in place, he left them vulnerable, burdened by debt that not only threatened to enslave his children but also risked tearing his family apart altogether. This reality brings into focus the practical need for ministers, especially those serving small or struggling communities, to consider a bi-vocational approach.

Bi-vocational ministry refers to ministers who balance both a secular job and their spiritual calling. This approach enables them to provide for their families while remaining dedicated to their ministry work. Had the widow's husband chosen this path, he might have been able to reduce or even eliminate his debt, ensuring that his family would not be left in financial distress after his passing. In today's world, many preachers face similar challenges, particularly those leading small congregations where financial support is limited. Such churches are unable to provide a stable income to the pastor, thus relying solely on donations/tithes. This often leads to financial stress for the minister and the church.

The reality is that the average median-sized church, according to the Hartford Institute for Religion Research, has a weekly worship attendance of around 65-75 people. While many associate the term "mega-church" with congregations in the thousands, the truth is that a church with 150-200 attendees can be considered a large congregation in many contexts. Factors such as location, denomination, culture, socio-economic conditions, and community engagement all play a significant role in determining a church's size and growth. In recent years with the church's consolidation with 'hub/satellite' churches, the truth of church growth is often misrepresented. The impact of COVID-19 and online service has also shifted how attendance is reported.

With all these factors at play, I believe we are entering a time where even mega-church leaders will be compelled into bi-vocational ministry—not by choice, but by necessity. The era of pastors owning private jets is coming to an end. More and more, choosing a secular job alongside ministry to supplement one's income will become the norm. Any responsible minister who truly wants to provide for their family while reducing financial pressure on their congregation will have to consider this shift.

The Bible presents numerous examples of men and women who served both in ministry and secular roles. Through their stories, we gain valuable insights into the art of balancing these responsibilities effectively. Here are five extraordinary individuals from the Bible who exemplified bi-vocationalism:

The Apostle Paul (Scribe + Tentmaker)

Paul is perhaps the most well-known example of a bi-vocational minister of his time. On one hand, he was a scribe, and on the other, a tentmaker by trade. He frequently relied on tentmaking to support himself financially during his missionary journeys.

> *After these things Paul departed from Athens and went to Corinth. And he found a certain Jew named Aquila, born in Pontus, who had recently come from Italy with his wife Priscilla (because Claudius had commanded all the Jews to depart from Rome); and he came to them. So, because he was of the same trade, he stayed with them and worked; for by occupation, they were tentmakers. And he reasoned in the synagogue every Sabbath and persuaded both Jews and Greeks.*
>
> *Acts 18:1-4*

Despite his deep commitment to ministry, Paul understood the importance of providing for his own needs. This approach enabled him to preach without becoming a financial burden to others. His work not only sustained him but also granted him the freedom to continue his ministry without depending on the generosity of others, allowing him to follow wherever the Spirit led. I have heard some ministers ignorantly state that Paul did not have enough faith, which is why he was a tentmaker! Wow, a man whom the Bible records performing at least seven miracles. I just chuckled and asked each of them to show me their Eutychus.

The Apostle Peter (A Key Disciple + Fisherman)

Peter was casting his net in the Sea of Galilee when Jesus called him into ministry. He was a fisherman by trade when Jesus told him to follow him. He used his identifying trade to call him a "fisher of men."

> *Walking along the beach of Lake Galilee, Jesus saw two brothers: Simon (later called Peter) and Andrew. They were fishing, throwing their nets into the lake. It was their regular work. Jesus said to them, "Come with me. I'll make a new kind of fisherman out of you. I'll show you how to catch men and women instead of perch and bass." They didn't ask questions but simply dropped their nets and followed.*
>
> *Matthew 4:18-20 (MSG)*

While Peter did not actively practice his fishing skills while following Jesus, he immediately returned to his trade after Jesus' death, demonstrating his commitment to providing for his family and ministry. Notably, when Jesus appeared to Peter for the second time after His resurrection, it was by the seaside—just after Peter had made a significant catch of fish.

Many ministers have used this scripture to justify their decision to pursue full-time ministry. However, the key distinction here is that Jesus appeared to Peter at a moment of lost hope, not as an endorsement of abandoning secular work. His appearance to the disciples was meant to encourage them to continue their mission, as they would become the pioneers of spreading the Gospel worldwide. It is important to emphasize that Peter would have balanced both his practical and spiritual needs if it had been required of him!

Dorcas "Tabitha" (Seamstress + Charity)

I must begin by noting that Dorcas is introduced to us as a disciple living in Joppa—one who also happens to be a woman. She is described as someone who was constantly doing good and helping the poor through her sewing skills. Dorcas masterfully balanced ministry and secular work, using her talents to serve the disadvantaged in her community.

> *In Joppa there was a disciple named Tabitha (in Greek her name is Dorcas); she was always doing good and helping the poor. About that time, she became sick and died, and her body was washed and placed in an upstairs room. Lydda was near Joppa; so, when the disciples heard that Peter was in Lydda, they sent two men to him and urged him, "Please come at once!" Peter went with them, and when he arrived, he was taken upstairs to the room. All the widows stood around him, crying and showing him the robes and other clothing that Dorcas had made while she was still with them.*
>
> *Acts 9:36-39 (NIV)*

Dorcas used her skills to serve her community, channeling her income into charity by making clothes for the poor, allowing her to be a blessing to others. No one had done as much for the widows and orphans in her community as she had, which is why Peter was summoned to raise her from the dead in the same chapter.

Joseph (Prime Minster of Egypt + Dreamer Interpreter + Preserver of God's People)

One of the main reasons I love Joseph's story in the Bible is that it highlights his ability to transition from a spiritual gift to a marketable and relevant secular skill. We are introduced to Joseph's primary God-given gift—dream interpretation—when he interprets Pharaoh's dream in Genesis 41:16. While his gift secured his release from prison, it was his wisdom and strategic advice on preparing for the seven-year famine that elevated him to the position of second in command.

> *Then Pharaoh said to Joseph, "Inasmuch as God has shown you all this, there is no one as discerning and wise as you. You shall be over my house, and all my people shall be ruled according to your word; only in regard to the throne will I be greater than you." And Pharaoh said to Joseph, "See, I have set you over all the land of Egypt."*
> *Genesis 41:39-41*

I'm sure you've heard the saying many times: When you solve someone's problem, that's where you'll find your promotion. Joseph not only used his gift but also provided a solution—and he was promoted because of it. In this case, his actions not only secured his own advancement but also led to the survival of the entire tribe of Israel. He skillfully balanced his spiritual gift with his secular responsibilities, preparing the land for famine while simultaneously increasing Pharaoh's wealth.

Lydia (Merchant + Church Supporter)

We are briefly introduced to this remarkable businesswoman and kingdom supporter, whose specialty was selling purple cloth. She generously hosted ministers of God, including Peter, in her home. As a kingdom financier, she played a crucial role in establishing the early church in Philippi. Her story serves as a powerful reminder that we all have the ability to balance the spiritual and the practical to fulfill our ministerial responsibilities if we allow God to use us.

These five examples demonstrate that working while ministering is not only possible but also highly impactful. In many cases, it makes us more relatable to the very people we are called to serve. Paul's ministry thrived, Peter became a pillar of the early church, and Dorcas was deeply loved by her community because of her charitable work.

I believe there are several benefits to being a bi-vocational minister. For me, the top three are financial stability, a greater reach into the secular world, and the ability to remain open-minded and flexible in order to connect with the people we are called to serve. Let's explore these three in depth.

1. ***Financial Stability:*** One of the most immediate benefits of being bi-vocational is financial stability. Ministers with secular jobs can reduce their reliance on church tithes and offerings, allowing them to focus on their ministry without the constant stress of financial insecurity. This stability is a blessing not only for the minister's family but also for the congregation, which may already be facing financial challenges.

2. ***Reaching the Secular World:*** Working in a secular environment also provides an opportunity to minister to people outside the church. Ministers with secular jobs often interact with individuals who may never set foot in a church. Their presence in the workplace enables them to demonstrate Christ-like character, share their faith through everyday conversations, and build relationships that could lead to evangelistic opportunities. I cannot tell you how many opportunities I have had due to being a bi-vocational minister in the job that has ended up being a tremendous blessing in the long run.
3. ***Maintaining a Balanced Perspective:*** Being bi-vocational also helps ministers maintain a balanced perspective. Working in the secular world keeps them grounded in the everyday realities their congregation faces. Because they experience similar financial, familial, and professional challenges, they can better relate to their parishioners. This deeper understanding allows ministers to connect with their congregations in a more meaningful way.

Of course, bi-vocational ministry comes with its challenges. Balancing two vocations that are vastly different in nature can be both taxing and demanding. One requires the exercise of faith, while the other may not, making it difficult for some ministers to navigate between spiritual and practical responsibilities. To succeed, ministers must be intentional about how they allocate their time and energy while also ensuring they minister in the workplace without offending their colleagues. I often tell people that it is a fine balance so do not overstep your boundaries. You must also respect everyone's choice and religion at the workplace. It's important that both our work and ministry responsibilities are handled with the spirit of excellence.

1. *Time Management:* One of the greatest challenges for bi-vocational ministers is time management. Secular jobs often require significant time and attention, which can sometimes pull ministers away from their spiritual responsibilities. To navigate this, ministers must cultivate strong organizational skills and establish clear boundaries between work and ministry. Prioritizing tasks, setting aside dedicated time for prayer and spiritual study, and delegating responsibilities within the church can help prevent burnout.
2. *The Emotional Toll:* Juggling two roles can also take an emotional toll on ministers. Managing the demands of family, a secular job, and ministry can lead to stress, fatigue, and feelings of inadequacy. To maintain their well-being, ministers must be mindful of their emotional health and seek support when needed—whether from mentors, spiritual advisors, or family members.

The role of the family in bi-vocational ministry is crucial. I have often been called to mediate when one spouse independently decides to enter full-time ministry without considering their partner. This lack of communication can strain the relationship, allowing bitterness to seep into different areas if not addressed promptly. Sadly, some spouses attempt to pressure their partners into accepting their decision as "the will of God"—without any discussion or mutual agreement.

The widow's story raises a very important point about the role of family in financial and ministry decisions. If the prophet had been a bi-vocational worker, perhaps the wife could have contributed in several ways to ease the financial burden on the family as well. While the Bible does not provide much detail about the widow's role before her husband's death, it underscores the importance of preparation and responsibility. Families must engage in open and honest discussions about financial obligations and ministry commitments. There are practical tools available to help start this conversation today, beginning with joint financial planning.

1. ***Joint Financial Planning:*** What is joint financial planning? If you are married and have never practiced it, you may already be experiencing some strain in your marriage! In today's world, especially for families involved in ministry, honest discussions about finances are essential. Couples must agree on their respective roles in supporting the household. If one spouse is fully committed to ministry, the other may take on a secular job to ensure financial stability. They must also agree if this is practical or just wishful thinking. If so, together, create a plan that allows you both to serve God while adequately providing for your family's needs.
2. ***Timing Conversations around Ministry and Work:*** Every minister should also know when it is time to transition to a bi-vocational role. If financial strain becomes too great, or if the demands of the congregation grow too heavy, ministers should feel free to pursue a secular job, even temporarily, without feeling as though they are stepping away from their calling or made to feel guilty about it. I also want to say that having your children suffer because you

> are in the ministry is not a flex to have in the 21st century. The idea that your entire family must endure hardship—and that God will bless them for it—is a misconception that needs to be re-examined. Should we get everything we want in life? No. Should children learn that life requires some level of sacrifice? Absolutely. But when we can no longer provide them with the basics, it becomes necessary to embrace a bi-vocational approach. It is time for many of us to reassess our perspectives on ministry and make the necessary adjustments in regard to finance, ministry, and family.

In conclusion, the lessons from the widow's story emphasize the importance of financial planning and the consequences of lacking a second source of income when necessary. By choosing to be solely a prophet, the widow's husband placed his family in an unnecessarily precarious position. Had he taken on a second job, he might have prevented the debt that nearly led to his children's enslavement. While today's world no longer sees creditors coming to enslave children over unpaid debts, financial hardship can still trap us in other ways if we fail to plan properly.

Sadly, many 21st-century ministers face the same dilemma, especially those leading smaller congregations that do not always provide sufficient financial security. By choosing to become bi-vocational, modern ministers can avoid the pitfalls of financial instability and ensure their families are not left vulnerable in times of crisis. The widow's story serves as a powerful reminder that financial planning, diligence, and practical work are just as essential as spiritual ministry.

For modern-day ministers, especially those serving small congregations, being bi-vocational can provide financial stability and prevent spiritual burnout while opening doors for them to minister in the secular world. While ministers must carefully weigh the pros and cons of holding a secular job, the decision can ultimately safeguard their families and strengthen their ministries. Additionally, families should openly discuss the role of work and ministry in their lives, ensuring that both spouses are involved in decisions about finances and career paths. The lessons from the widow's story are applicable in today's world of ministry, showing that even devoted ministers must plan.

CHAPTER 9

A SPECIFIC NEED FOR A SPECIFIC CRISIS

The Power of a Clear Ask

Have you ever had someone come to you for help but start by going all over the place—jumping from Chicago to France, then to South Africa? Often, I prefer things to be clear and straight to the point, so I simply ask, "What do you want?" It's never my intention to be rude, but if the explanation drags on too long, it's time to get to the point.

Over time, I have learned to practice what I want to ask before approaching someone. You've probably heard about the three-minute elevator speech; it's crucial to rehearse it to sound confident, certain, and persuasive when making a request. In the story of the widow with the jar of oil, she had mastered the power of a clear ask when she approached Prophet Elisha. Despite her dire situation, she articulated her needs masterfully—a feat in itself.

Let me paint a vivid picture for you. She was trapped in a desperate situation: her husband was dead, debt was suffocating her, and creditors were on the verge of taking her sons as payment. With no financial resources to escape this crisis, the weight of her circumstances was overwhelming. And these were just the pressing issues we know about. What about the smaller struggles? Was she homeless or on the brink of losing her home? Had her only means of transport already been taken? When was the last time she and her sons had a proper meal?

Had her lights been turned off (okay they probably did not have electricity back then, but you get my message!)? Could they have been in famine or what was the political climate at that time? Was this when Elisha was still friendly with Ahab or on the run from Jezebel? Now, let's step back for a moment; how easy would it be to deliver a three-minute elevator speech when facing crises of this magnitude? Yet, the widow was remarkable. Instead of becoming paralyzed by distress or speaking in vague terms, she articulated her problem with clarity. She knew exactly what she needed and presented her situation to Elisha with precision, tailoring her request to her urgent reality.

It is crucial for Christians today to clearly define and articulate their needs, especially in times of trouble. The widow's example serves as a powerful template for effective communication. No one was coming to rescue her—no ex-boyfriends, no in-laws, no government support systems. The creditors were closing in, and without a solution, her family would be torn apart. She could have been vague, simply asking for help without clearly explaining what was at stake, but instead, she laid out the specifics to Elisha and held back nothing!

She told him everything about her financial trouble, the impending enslavement of her sons, and her need for a solution. This allowed Elisha to understand the nature of her crisis and offer the best and most appropriate solution; a miraculous provision through the multiplication of her small jar of oil. This is an essential lesson for modern-day Christians. Too often, we let pride keep us from admitting when we need help and, in some cases, that hesitation is understandable. There are several reasons for this. Firstly, when facing a crisis, especially a financial or personal one, it's easy to fall into the trap of speaking in generalities. We might say, "I need help" or "I'm struggling," without clearly defining what we actually need. Secondly, we fear that expressing our struggles might come across as complaining, whining, or a simple lack of faith.

Thirdly, no group can be more judgmental than the church (Can the church say Amen!). Oh, my goodness—there will always be those saints who assume your struggles stem from a generational curse, a major unaddressed sin or financial mismanagement. And while that may be true in some cases, more often than not, it isn't. The real issue? A staggering lack of empathy. Statistics show that the average American is just one paycheck away from homelessness. If that's the reality, then we all have a much bigger problem on our hands!

The truth is, in many cases, the solution to our problems hinges on how well we communicate our needs to those who can help us. The widow understood this—she needed a financial solution, and her sons' freedom was at stake. By being clear, honest, and direct with Elisha, she opened the door for the exact miracle she required. We must take a page from her book and embrace the power of clear, honest communication. More importantly, we should practice it long before we find ourselves in a crisis.

Christians in the 21st century must learn to be specific, especially given the multitude of challenges we face today—personal, financial, professional, and spiritual—often all at once. Like the widow, we frequently need help, whether from God, our community, or professionals. Yet, one of the most common mistakes we make is failing to articulate our needs with clarity. When we are ambiguous in our requests, we risk receiving solutions that don't fully address our problem, or worse, we may receive no help at all because those around us don't understand the depth of our need or crisis.

For example, if someone is struggling with debt but only says they are "having financial trouble," they may receive generic advice that fails to address the root of their problem. However, if they clearly state that they have a specific amount of debt, are facing the threat of homelessness, outline their current income, and express their need for a debt relief plan, they are far more likely to receive advice and assistance tailored to their situation.

The 3-Minute Elevator Pitch: Ready, Set and Go!

So, here's a question for you: How well do you articulate your needs? Have you ever considered that you might need to practice? One way we, as Christians, can develop this skill is by crafting a three-minute elevator pitch. This business world concept is designed to be a short, concise summary of what you need, what you're asking for, and the expected outcome. In today's fast-paced world, whether seeking help from a mentor, a financial advisor, or even in prayer, we must learn to communicate our needs quickly and effectively.

Here's how to structure a 3-minute elevator pitch:

1. ***State the Problem:*** Be clear about what your specific challenge is. For the widow, it was her debt and the impending enslavement of her sons.
2. ***State What You Have:*** The widow stated that she had nothing but a jar of oil. This detail is crucial because it helps the person you're seeking help from understand what resources you already have.
3. ***State What You Need:*** Be specific about what you are asking for. The widow's unspoken request was for a financial solution, and because of her clarity, Elisha was able to provide instructions tailored to her needs.

4. ***State the Expected Outcome:*** Articulate what you hope to achieve. For the widow, it was the preservation of her sons' freedom.

By practicing this, we as Christians can gain confidence in our ability to communicate our needs, especially in difficult situations. The more we practice, the more natural it will become, allowing us to clearly and confidently express ourselves even in moments of desperation. The key lesson here is that the three-minute pitch isn't just a business tool; it is also a life tool, one essential in times of crisis.

God has never favored ambiguity. He has always made it clear that when we approach Him, we must do so with honesty and transparency and not in vagueness. Ambiguity carries great risk, and the Bible provides a compelling example of this danger. The story of the young and inexperienced king who visited Elisha on his deathbed in 2 Kings 13:14-19 serves as a powerful reminder of what happens when we fail to articulate our needs properly.

The young king was instructed to shoot arrows as a symbolic act of securing victory over his enemies. However, he only shot a few arrows and failed to ask for complete victory or seek clarification on its extent. As a result, Elisha rebuked him for his half-hearted effort and warned him that his victory would be incomplete.

Then Elisha said, "Take the arrows," and the king took them. Elisha then instructed him, "Strike the ground," so the king struck it three times and stopped. The man of God was angry and said, "You should have struck five or six times; then you would have defeated Syria completely and

destroyed it! But now, you will strike Syria
only three times."
2 Kings 13:18-19

Here, we see two contrasting stories: the widow, who clearly articulated her crisis and, in the end, received more than she had asked for or expected, and the young king, who failed to express his desire for complete victory. His lack of specificity and conviction resulted in a partial and unsatisfactory outcome. This serves as a warning to modern-day Christians: if we are unclear or half-hearted in our requests, we may miss out on the full solution that God has for us, even through those who can provide help around us.

It takes confidence to articulate your needs, especially in desperate situations, which most times can be totally intimidating. It is the reason why many people shy away from clearly stating what they need because of fear, embarrassment, rejection and ego, but for most, it is about a lack of confidence. By exploring the widow's story, we learn that there is no shame in asking for help and that clarity can lead to breakthrough solutions. Here are four confidence-building strategies to help you articulate your needs effectively:

1. ***Practice Speaking About Your Problems:*** Before approaching someone for help, take time to practice speaking about your problem clearly. Try rehearsing with a trusted friend, a family member, or even in front of a mirror. The more you practice, the more confident you'll become in expressing your needs, refining your elevator pitch in the process.

2. ***Write It Down (WID):*** As a writer, I often enjoy putting my thoughts into words, whether on paper or my tablet. Writing things down brings clarity and helps keep my thoughts focused rather than scattered. Similarly, writing down your problem along with your request can help you process your emotions and refine your thoughts. When you see your request in writing, it becomes much easier to articulate it in conversation.

3. ***Pray for Boldness:*** The Bible encourages us to approach God's throne of grace with confidence (Hebrews 4:16). If you are struggling with fear or hesitation, ask God for the courage to articulate your needs clearly.

4. ***Understand Your Worth:*** One reason people hesitate to ask for help is that they don't feel worthy of receiving it. I have a small plaque in my office that reads, "**Know your worth—then add tax.**" While the widow found herself in a desperate situation, she never lost sight of who she was or the fact that her sons were worth saving. She may not have been able to save her husband, but she was determined to fight for her sons. You must understand that you are valuable and deserving of help, especially when you have helped others.

21st-century Christians have more tools than ever to help them build confidence in articulating their needs. From public speaking courses and communication workshops to mentorship programs and self-help books like the one you are reading right now, you have access to all sorts of resources designed to teach clear and confident communication. Whether in a business setting, a personal crisis, or even in ministry, mastering this skill can make a world of difference.

Additionally, technology is a powerful tool for clear communication. Email, messaging apps, and video conferencing platforms give you the opportunity to organize your thoughts before making a request. You can even rehearse difficult conversations or record yourself explaining your needs to build confidence.

Let's be very clear: if the widow had been vague or failed to express her desperation, her discussion with Prophet Elisha and the outcome would have been drastically different. Likewise, if you don't communicate your needs clearly, others may struggle to understand how best to help you or may offer solutions that don't fully address your problem.

Clear communication isn't just about stating facts; it's about creating a connection that is often empathetic and relatable. When you articulate your needs, you invite others into your story, allowing them to become part of the solution. Whether you're asking for financial help, emotional support, or spiritual guidance, the clearer you are, the more likely you are to receive the help you truly need.

In conclusion, the widow's ability to clearly articulate her needs reminds us that effective communication is crucial. This is especially true in today's world, where communication is often rushed, unclear, and emoji-filled 😊☹. The widow remains our prime example of the power of a well-defined request. Whether in prayer, relationships, or professional settings, we must learn to communicate our needs with clarity, confidence, and conviction.

By practicing clear communication, developing tools like the 3-minute elevator pitch, and building confidence through prayer and practice, 21st-century Christians can ensure that their needs are understood and addressed. When we articulate our needs clearly, authentically, and transparently, we open the door wide for God and others to meet us at our point of need. Let us continue to practice the art of effective communication.

CHAPTER 10

SHIFTING LEGACIES TO EMBRACE A NEW IDENTITY

Building a New Identity

If I were to ask you what your family's legacy is, what would you tell me? What would that story look like? What does that mean to you? Have you ever thought about the legacy you're building? What do you want to be remembered for? Are you striving to create something entirely new, or do you hope to build upon your family's history? Legacy holds deep significance, shaping how we are remembered and the impact we leave behind. As Christians, it is essential to reflect on the kind of legacy we want to leave—not just for our families but for future generations. What values, actions, and faith-driven choices will define your legacy?

One of the most striking aspects of the widow's story and her jar of oil is how she had to depend on her late husband's reputation and connections to receive help from the prophet Elisha. She was left with nothing—no assets, no income, and no options of her own. The only thing she could rely on was her husband's legacy, his past service as a prophet, his work, and his reputation. She had no personal achievements to reference, no accomplishments of her own to present.

Her total dependence on her husband's accomplishments was a precarious position, raising an important question: What happens when a woman has nothing of her own to claim or show for? Yet, thousands of modern-day women—many of them Christian and married—find themselves in a similar bind, whether due to widowhood or divorce. Times have changed, and if we are to remain relevant and secure, we must adapt and grow with them.

This chapter delves into the dangers of not having your own resources or accomplishments to lean on, especially for Christian women today. In a world where financial independence and personal accomplishments are essential, the widow's story offers a timeless lesson: the importance of building your own résumé and relationships beyond your spouse or family. Every individual, especially women, must cultivate their own skills, reputation, and financial security. In doing so, they ensure they have something to rely on, no matter their circumstances.

The widow's situation was dire—her late husband had left her with a mountain of debt, and she was on the brink of losing her sons to slavery. If not for her husband's connection to Elisha and the prophet's willingness to help, she might have been left utterly stranded. This underscores a critical point: her survival depended entirely on her husband's reputation. But what if he had not been a man of good standing? What if he had no relationship with the prophet Elisha? Or worse, what if Elisha had chosen not to help her at all? What options would she have had then?

This is a sobering reminder that relying solely on a spouse—or anyone else—for reputation, skills, or financial stability leaves one completely vulnerable. I have met widows from all walks of life, from businessmen's wives to ministers' spouses, whose husbands were pillars in their communities. Yet, when these men passed away, no one came to their widows' aid. In some cases, people even sought to exploit them and their children. What a dangerous world we live in. The widow's lack of personal accomplishments or assets left her without any leverage of her own, trapped in a situation where she had little control over her future. Her story serves as a cautionary tale for both women and men in the 21st century, particularly for those who rely heavily on their spouse or family for financial security and social standing.

The only way to combat this situation is for every individual, especially women, to build their own "resume" not just in terms of employment, but in terms of skills, relationships, and personal achievements. A résumé is more than just a document—it is a reflection of your legacy and your ability to stand on your own two feet. In the 21st century, Christians—both men and women—must be equipped with more than just spiritual knowledge. They should develop practical skills, build strong relationships, and work toward financial independence. Had the widow possessed a business, a skill, or a network of her own, she might not have found herself in such a desperate situation.

For stay-at-home parents whose primary role is caring for their family, this lesson is especially relevant—they, too, need to build something of their own. It's easy to believe that if you are supported by a spouse or family, there's no need to develop your own skills or relationships. But the widow's story is a stark reminder of how quickly circumstances can change. When her husband died, she was left with nothing to fall back on.

Every stay-at-home parent (female or male) should have something of their own, whether it is a small business, a side hustle or a skill that can be leveraged when it becomes essential to take care of their family. It should not only provide financial security in case something happens to the primary breadwinner but also offer a sense of identity and purpose beyond the family. For stay-at-home mothers in particular, Proverbs 31 highlights the example of the virtuous woman. While devoted to her household, she was also engaged in commerce and trade.

The Proverbs 31 woman possesses many qualities that make her not only a great mother and wife but also a savvy businesswoman. When we break down various parts of Scripture, we see that she demonstrates all the traits necessary for successful entrepreneurship—from business acquisition to managing her household.

> *She seeks wool and flax and willingly works with her hands. She is like the merchant ships; she brings her food from afar. She also rises while it is yet night, and provides food for her household, and a portion for her maidservants. She considers a field and buys it; from her profits she plants a vineyard. She girds herself with strength and strengthens her arms. She perceives that her merchandise is good, and her lamp does not go out by night. She makes linen garments and sells them and supplies sashes for the merchants.*
>
> *Proverbs 31.13-18, 24*

This particular woman "considers a field and buys it" and "trades profitably." She is a triple threat if you ask me, as this woman has several entrepreneurial traits. They are as follows:

1. She seeks out quality materials (wool and flax), showcasing her entrepreneurial ability to source the best while keeping costs low.

2. Her resource management is evident in her pursuit of merchant ships and their offerings, as she actively seeks alternative options for her business and family.
3. While maintaining a healthy work-life balance is important, she oversees household operations, showcasing her ability to delegate, organize, and manage effectively.
4. She demonstrates a keen understanding of investments while actively engaging in trade and commerce.
5. She is creative and is also a supplier. She provides economic security for her household in case of future needs.
6. She is wise as she is also influential due to the success of her business ventures. She balances her workload and is recognized for her achievements within her community.

The Proverbs 31 woman is likened to the 21st-century Christian woman—industrious, entrepreneurial, resourceful, and self-sufficient. Today's women can embrace all these qualities while fulfilling their roles within the family. This lesson also applies to modern households where men have taken on the role of stay-at-home fathers. They, too, can draw inspiration from the Proverbs 31 woman and forge their own path in home-based entrepreneurship or business.

There are significant pitfalls to having no personal point of reference, whether in the form of past business experience or a developed skill set. What if the widow's husband had not been a man of good standing? She would have had nothing to fall back on. This highlights a crucial point: relying entirely on someone else's reputation or resources leaves you vulnerable when they are no longer available. Yet, many households continue to depend solely on a spouse's income, skills, and connections without developing any of their own.

The pitfalls of this kind of dependence are numerous:

1. ***Financial Instability:*** If the family's breadwinner passes away or loses their job, the household can quickly fall into financial ruin because there are no secondary sources of income. As a minister, I cannot count the number of times I have heard people share stories of sudden hardship following the death of a parent—often coupled with the devastating reality of homelessness caused by the financial instability that loss brought to their family.

2. ***Loss of Identity:*** If your entire identity is tied to someone else's accomplishments and connections, you may feel lost or insignificant when they are no longer present. This is evident even in cases of divorce, where one spouse often loses the friendships and connections they once shared with their partner, leaving them struggling to rediscover who they truly are. This can be a significant challenge, and some individuals never fully recover if it is not properly addressed or if they do not seek counseling.

3. ***Lack of Agency/Autonomy:*** Without your own set of skills, knowledge, or resources, you may struggle to make crucial decisions or take action during a crisis, leaving you and your family vulnerable. Lacking the necessary tools or expertise can hinder your ability to navigate challenging situations effectively. Marriage should not mean giving up your autonomy—it should enhance it. Invest in building your skill

set, pursue certifications at least once a year, and find ways to stay engaged in your field, even through volunteer work. Each of these steps contributes to your independence and personal growth.

I don't want you to read this chapter and feel that all is lost—because that is not the case. The good news is that it is never too late to start fresh and begin building your own legacy, and it doesn't require a tragedy to do so. There are countless benefits to developing your own resume, skill set, and relationships. Here are a few key advantages:

1. ***Financial Independence:*** Having your own business, job, or skill set ensures that you are not solely dependent on someone else for financial security. Whether it's a full-time job or a side hustle, having your own source of income gives you agency and freedom.

2. ***Emotional Security:*** When you have your own accomplishments and relationships, you develop a sense of self-worth and identity that is independent of anyone else. This emotional security is invaluable, especially in times of crisis.

3. ***Better Relationships:*** When both spouses contribute to the household in different ways, it strengthens the relationship. You become partners rather than one person being entirely dependent on the other.

4. ***Legacy Building:*** Your accomplishments, whether personal, professional, or spiritual, become part of your legacy. They

represent the impact you've had on the world and provide something for your children and community to look up to.

There are several biblical examples of independent and successful women who built their own legacies and made a significant impact. Consider Lydia, a dealer in purple cloth. This successful businesswoman used her resources to support the early church. She had her own connections, and through her business, she made major contributions to the spread of the gospel.

Another example is Deborah, who held dual roles as both judge and prophetess in Israel. She was a highly influential woman, demonstrating wisdom, resilience, and leadership while acting independently of any male figure. Her guidance was crucial in leading Israel through a time of war and turmoil, ultimately helping to restore peace and stability. There are also other women in the Bible who built their own legacies independent of husbands, children, or communities. Their stories show that women can indeed create their own legacies—unapologetically.

I want to encourage you at this very moment—yes, right now—whether you are a man or a woman reading this book, to take the time to build your own resume. Do this for your family, but most importantly, for yourself, even if your primary focus is on your family or ministry:

1. ***Develop a Skillset:*** Whether it's learning a trade, acquiring a new language, or mastering a craft. Having a skill that you can monetize is invaluable and it serves as a safety net in case of financial difficulties.

2. ***Start a Small Business:*** I love the Internet! Thanks to it, starting a small business has never been easier. Whether it's selling handmade goods, offering freelance services, or working as a virtual assistant, there are countless ways to earn an income from home. Various platforms allow you to get started and build your own little empire right from your living room!
3. ***Invest in Relationships:*** It's time to take out your phone, black book, Rolodex or whatever you use and start building relationships beyond your immediate family. Cultivate friendships, professional connections, and mentors who can support you in times of need. Join an association, attend your alumni functions, take a pottery class, or even join a running club. You never know where these connections might lead or how they could help you in the future!
4. ***Pursuing Education:*** The greatest investment you should make is in yourself. Invest in your education. This makes you a marketable subject matter expert. Whether it's going back to school, taking online courses, certifications or attending workshops, education is a powerful tool for building independence and building your network.
5. ***Stay Financially Involved:*** Even if you are not the primary breadwinner, stay involved in your family's finances. Know where the money is going, how it's being saved, and what the long-term financial plans are. There should be a monthly financial meeting—not just with your spouse, but also with your children, especially the older or most responsible ones. They need to understand the family's financial situation so

> that, in case anything happens, they are prepared. After all, it's always better to be safe than sorry.

The story of the widow and her jar of oil serves as a sobering reminder that while faith calls us to rely on God and our network, it is equally crucial to cultivate our own unique set of skills, relationships, and resources. As Scripture states, *"Faith without works is dead."* This truth applies to anyone who remains unprepared for life's unexpected twists and turns—because they will surely come.

21st-century Christians, especially stay-at-home parents, must not rely solely on their spouse's accomplishments or income as their only source of security. Invest in a small business, a hobby, or a professional career to build your own resume for both financial and emotional stability. By doing so, you can stand strong in times of crisis, contribute meaningfully to your family and community, and leave behind a lasting legacy.

CHAPTER 11

LIFE WITHOUT A SAFETY NET

No Plan B

When was the last time your company had a fire drill? Do you remember being told to leave your handbag or briefcase at your desk? With over twenty years of experience in corporate America, I have participated in numerous workplace fire drills. In these drills, we are expected not only to evacuate the building but also to gather at the designated meeting site identified by the company. Most companies have a contingency plan in case of a fire, from getting their staff out of the building to backing up their information onto the cloud. What contingency plan do you have in place for your family in case there is an earthquake, the stock market crashes or one of you loses your job?

How prepared are you and what plan do you have in place? If you don't have one, now might be the time to start putting one together. Are your passports current? Do you have an account outside of the United States in case you become stranded? Who are your designated guardians for your children in the event of an unforeseen situation? The truth is, the widow was unprepared for the worst, and it became her wake-up call. Yet, many of us also put off preparing for the unexpected, assuming we have plenty of time to write a will, open a safety deposit box, update our life insurance, or show our children where we've stored our stocks and bonds. But time waits for no one.

In the biblical story of the widow and her jar of oil, one underlying lesson that many overlook is the absence of a backup plan. Somehow, modern Christians have come to believe that having a contingency plan signifies a lack of faith—but nothing could be further from the truth! God was the first planner. He meticulously designed everything, from the formation of the earth to the creation of mankind. Throughout the Bible, preparation is emphasized—sometimes explicitly and other times indirectly.

The young man David was prepared to fight Goliath because God had used his past experiences—fighting bears and lions—to equip him for the battle that would change the trajectory of his life and lead him to the throne of Israel. Without preparation and a backup plan, David could have died at the hands of King Saul. His ability to foresee danger and devise a contingency plan allowed him to escape Saul's attempt to kill him at dinner.

Jonathan said: I swear by the Lord God of Israel, that two days from now I'll know what my father is planning. Of course, I'll let you know if he's friendly toward you. But if he wants to harm you, I promise to tell you and help you escape. And I ask the Lord to punish me severely if I don't keep my promise.
I Samuel 20:12-13 (CEV)

Jonathan and David had a backup plan regarding King Saul's intent to kill David. Their plan required Jonathan not only to inform David but also to help him escape. Later in the same passage, both young men made a vow to protect each other's families in case of unforeseen circumstances. This exemplifies true preparation for the unexpected and highlights why modern Christians must also equip themselves for life's uncertainties.

Nothing prepared the widow for the death of her husband. Imagine being unable to mourn properly because you have no income, assets, or strategy for providing for your family. With overwhelming debt, the threat of creditors, and no clear provisions for her children, her late husband's status as a prophet was not enough to rescue them from their struggles. While will or estate planning is a modern concept, the consequences of being unprepared remain just as relevant in today's Christian society.

Sadly, this issue is not a thing of the past. Many 21st-century Christians remain trapped in the same vicious cycle of unpreparedness. They avoid setting up a last will and testament, mistakenly believing that preparation is either unnecessary or a sign of weak faith. However, the reality is that failure to plan creates chaos and emotional strain and leaves loved ones vulnerable to exploitation in times of grief. Having a backup plan and preparing adequately for unforeseen circumstances reflects the true care and love one has for their family.

This debunks the myth that having a plan indicates a lack of faith. On the contrary, planning is a demonstration of wisdom, love, and foresight—grounded in both biblical and practical principles. The truth is that preparation and having a backup plan are rooted in the biblical concept of counting the cost—whether it's starting a business, beginning a family, or making any significant decision. The Bible provides several examples, such as the following:

> *For which of you, intending to build a tower, does not sit down first and count the cost, whether he has enough to finish it lest, after he has laid the foundation, and is not able to finish, all who see it begin to mock him, saying, 'This man began to build and was not able to finish'? Or what king, going to make war against another king, does not sit down first and consider whether he is able with ten*

thousand to meet him who comes against him with twenty thousand?
Luke 14:28-31

While this Scripture has to do with counting the cost of following Jesus Christ, it is very applicable to our everyday lives. We have to count the cost from when we wake up in the morning to when we go to bed at night (should I sleep early or late and pay the price for it?). Here, we see that there is a financial cost to building a tower, which is vastly different from the cost of life when preparing for war. Everything comes at a cost—even when you are adequately prepared. However, the consequences are significantly worse when you are unprepared and lack a contingency plan.

The widow must have felt overwhelmed by the cascade of events unfolding all at once. Imagine her state of mind—grappling with the loss of her husband while facing financial instability. On top of that, the looming threat of creditors seeking to enslave her sons only added to her distress. Emotionally drained and struggling to think clearly, she found herself in a desperate situation. The absence of a backup plan only exacerbated her grief, leaving her scrambling for help. She was without a safety net, a set of instructions, and even without an inheritance. She must have been scared, vulnerable and desperate!

Unfortunately, this remains a harsh reality for many families when a loved one passes away without any preparation. Tragically, Christian families—including ministers—often seem the most unprepared for this inevitable stage of life. The emotional toll of losing someone dear is already overwhelming, but the added burden of unresolved financial and legal matters can push a family to the brink. Without a plan or a set of instructions, loved ones are left vulnerable to exploitation, and often make poor life decisions in the fog of immense grief.

This is why many courts have a clause around signing documents under duress so that one does not get taken advantage of. Having only the hope that a solution to the situation will come is no way to live one's life. The best solution is to create a plan while you are in the right frame of mind and spirit to do so. The importance of having a backup plan cannot be overstated—whether it's a will, a financial safety net, or an emergency strategy, having a contingency plan provides stability in times of uncertainty. The widow's story illustrates the chaos that follows when no plan is in place. However, modern Christians have access to tools and resources to prevent such situations, yet many still fall short of preparing adequately.

Planning ahead is not a sign of fear, doubt, or a lack of faith. It is a demonstration of wisdom, strength, and love for the people you leave behind. Having a contingency plan offers numerous benefits, especially when young children are involved. Here are some essential reasons to consider having a backup plan in place:

1. ***Peace of Mind for Your Family:*** With a clear plan in place, your loved ones won't be left in a state of confusion and uncertainty. They will understand your wishes and how best to carry them out, easing some of the emotional strain that comes with losing a loved one.

2. ***Protection from Exploitation:*** In the midst of grief, people are vulnerable and are often taken advantage of by creditors, opportunistic family members, and unethical legal entities.

Having a will and other legal safeguards in place can protect your family from such exploitation.

3. ***Continued Financial Stability:*** A backup plan, whether it's a life insurance policy, a savings account, or an investment portfolio, ensures that your family has financial support after you're gone. This prevents them from falling into debt or poverty, as the widow did.
4. ***Clarity in Decision-Making:*** In times of crisis, people often make impulsive or emotionally driven decisions that they later regret. A well-laid-out plan provides clarity and guidance, helping your loved ones make sound decisions when emotions are running high.
5. ***A Lasting Legacy:*** By planning, you are leaving a legacy for your children and grandchildren. A well-thought-out estate plan or will allows you to pass down not just material wealth, but also your values, principles, and wishes for how your family continues after you.

Proper planning and preparedness go hand in hand, and the Bible offers numerous examples that serve as a model for modern-day Christians. There are two powerful biblical examples, along with a well-known secular one, that highlight the necessity of having a contingency plan:

1. ***Joseph's Foresight in Egypt:*** In Genesis 41, Joseph's interpretation of Pharaoh's dream—foretelling seven years of abundance followed by seven years of famine—enabled him to develop a contingency plan that not only saved Egypt but

also his people and the surrounding nations that traded with Egypt during that time. By storing grain during the years of plenty, Joseph ensured survival during the years of scarcity. His story powerfully illustrates the importance of planning, preparedness, and having a contingency plan to protect against unforeseen disasters.

2. ***Noah's Ark:*** In Genesis 6, Noah was God's contingency plan for replenishing the earth, so he was instructed by God to build an ark in preparation for the flood. While the flood seemed unlikely at the time, Noah's faith-driven obedience to prepare the ark saved his family and preserved all of humanity. The ark represented God's physical backup plan for man's preservation down to the materials and the boat designs. Why is that? The ark had to be built not only to withstand the coming storm but also to ride out the flood that would cover the entire earth. In the same way, Christians today must create plans that enable them and their families to endure both life's storms and the challenges that follow.

3. ***The Guard in 9/11:*** One of the most striking modern examples of the power of preparation is the story of Rick Rescorla, the security chief at Morgan Stanley during the 9/11 attacks. A military veteran, Rescorla had long anticipated the possibility of a terrorist attack on the World Trade Center. For years, he rigorously trained employees in evacuation drills, ensuring they were prepared for an emergency. When the planes struck the towers, Rescorla calmly led nearly 3,000 employees down

> the stairwells, even singing songs to keep them calm. His foresight and preparation saved thousands of lives.

Just like Joseph and Noah, Rescorla's actions illustrate the immense value of having a backup plan and preparing for even the most unimaginable scenarios. The evacuation drills he implemented—once considered tedious or unnecessary—became the difference between life and death on that fateful day. Yet, a common misconception among some Christians is that creating a plan or preparing for worst-case scenarios signals a lack of faith or doubt in God's provision.

However, faith and preparation are not mutually exclusive—rather, they complement each other. Having a backup plan is a demonstration of wisdom, reflecting the responsible use of God's resources to protect your family and secure your future. Proverbs 16:9 reminds us that while we make plans, it is God who ultimately establishes our steps, reinforcing the importance of preparation aligned with His purpose.

A man's mind plans his way [as he journeys through life],
But the Lord directs his steps and establishes them.
Proverbs 16:9 (AMP)

In life, having a plan is essential—whether for personal growth, career advancement, or financial stability. You've likely heard people, including employers, ask, 'What is your five-year plan?' Without a clear direction, others may not take you seriously. Proverbs 16:9 acknowledges that while God ultimately directs our steps, it remains our responsibility to plan wisely and make informed decisions based on the knowledge and resources He has provided.

Planning is an act of stewardship—taking responsibility for the resources and duties God has entrusted to you. When you create a will, establish a financial safety net, or prepare for emergencies, you demonstrate wisdom and accountability in fulfilling this role. Even Jesus, upon His resurrection and return to the Father, ensured that His disciples would not be left without guidance. He promised them a Helper—the Holy Spirit—who would provide comfort and direction in His absence. This serves as a powerful example that having a contingency plan is not just practical but deeply biblical.

And I will ask the Father, and He will give you another
Helper (Comforter, Advocate, Intercessor—Counselor,
Strengthener, Standby), to be with you forever
—the Spirit of Truth
John 14:16-17

For modern-day Christians, there are numerous tools and resources available to help you create a backup plan. Here are some practical steps you can take to ensure that your family is protected in the event of an unforeseen tragedy:

1. ***Create a Will:*** A will ensures that your assets are distributed according to your wishes and that your family's needs are taken care of. It's a simple yet essential document, and with many online resources available, some even free, creating one has never been easier or more affordable.

2. ***Life Insurance:*** Life insurance offers financial security for your family in the event of your passing. It can help cover funeral

expenses, settle outstanding debts, and provide ongoing income to support your loved ones.

3. ***Emergency Savings:*** An emergency fund is essential for handling unexpected financial challenges, such as medical emergencies or job loss. Experts recommend setting aside enough to cover at least three to six months of living expenses, ensuring financial stability during tough times.
4. ***Power of Attorney and Health Directives:*** These documents ensure that your medical and financial decisions are handled according to your wishes if you become incapacitated.
5. ***Estate Planning:*** For those with more complex assets, such as property or businesses, an estate plan can help ensure that everything is passed down according to your wishes, minimizing legal complications for your family.

The widow's story teaches a powerful lesson: failing to prepare for life's challenges can leave us vulnerable and unable to protect those we love. Proper preparation shields our families from chaos, confusion, and exploitation by unscrupulous individuals who often take advantage of grief. Planning is not driven by fear but by wisdom—an enduring act of love that ensures we continue to provide for our loved ones even after we are gone.

Modern-day Christians can learn from the widow's mistake—her lack of a contingency plan led to a disaster that could have been prevented. We must not repeat the errors of those who lived centuries before us but instead take proactive steps to secure a better future for our loved ones.

CHAPTER 12

BREAKING FREE FROM A BORROWER'S MINDSET

Owning Your Future (The Widow's Guide)

Let me ask you a question—what kind of mindset do you have when it comes to finances? Are you someone who constantly borrows, to the point where people start avoiding your calls? Or are you someone who takes charge of their finances—perhaps an entrepreneur or even a faithpreneur, diligently working to build wealth and financial stability? Do you find it easy to depend solely on others or do you strive for independence? The fact of the matter is that we are our mindset, shaped by our experiences and our upbringing. The story of the widow and the jar of oil in 2 Kings 4 is a powerful one, not just because of the miracle performed by Elisha, but also because of the underlying lessons it teaches us about the dangers of dependency.

The widow's story highlights a crucial issue that remains relevant today: the dangers of total dependence on another person for financial and emotional well-being. Her reliance on her late husband for survival left her and her children vulnerable to severe hardship. She had absolutely nothing—no income, no savings, and no plan for her future—placing her in a precarious situation that many modern-day Christians can relate to, especially in today's unpredictable economic climate. Without a second source of income or established relationships beyond her immediate circle, she faced the heartbreaking possibility of losing her children to creditors.

This tragic scenario mirrors the challenges of modern life, where individuals and families can find themselves in crisis when they fail to cultivate independence and diversify their sources of support. Relying entirely on others—whether a spouse or even an unbalanced understanding of faith—can leave you vulnerable to hardship. It is, therefore, imperative that we explore why independence, particularly financial freedom, is essential for 21st-century Christians. More importantly, we must learn how to cultivate a mindset of independence in both ourselves and our children so that we can thrive in a world where inflation, economic shifts, and global interdependency impact every aspect of our lives.

Ancient Israel's social structure often left women financially dependent on their husbands, and the prophet's widow was no exception. Like many women of her time, she relied entirely on her husband's income to sustain their family. When he died, she was left with nothing, forcing her into survival mode. This abrupt shift from dependence to desperation highlights the precariousness of her situation. It didn't just expose her to emotional turmoil and potential exploitation; in today's world, where mental health struggles are increasingly recognized, such a crisis could easily lead to severe distress or even a nervous breakdown.

This is a cautionary tale for modern Christians—a reminder that while marriage and partnership are designed for mutual support, complete financial dependence on another person can be risky. In today's unpredictable world, marked by inflation, job instability, rising living costs, and the growing influence of artificial intelligence, particularly GenAI, financial security has become an even greater concern. For those without a contingency plan, the fear of financial disaster is more real than ever.

Relying on a single source of income—or someone else's—can be risky, or even disastrous. As global interdependency grows, Christians must take proactive steps toward financial independence, both for their own security and for the well-being of their families. This means equipping our children and spouses with the necessary skills and mindset to be self-sufficient, especially as relying on just one income stream has become increasingly unsustainable. Everyone has a critical role to play, including children. You should teach them how to manage money, encourage entrepreneurial thinking, and foster practical life skills that are essential for their own survival. Flexibility and adaptability are essential to financial freedom. With that said, independence doesn't necessarily mean rejecting help or refusing to work together as a family; it's about having the tools to contribute, make wise decisions, and navigate financial challenges effectively.

One of the greatest challenges facing modern-day Christians is the spirit of passivity, which fosters dependency on their faith. Many mistakenly interpret faith as passively waiting on God to provide, rather than actively combining faith with action. As James 2:17 declares, faith without works is dead.

In the same way, faith by itself, if it is not accompanied by action, is dead.
James 2:17 (NIV)

Passive Christianity would have left the widow sitting at home, merely praying for deliverance—an approach that has led to the downfall of many well-meaning Christians. Instead, Elisha required her to take action after providing a strategy. He didn't simply perform a miracle; he called on her to demonstrate faith through action. Her willingness to gather jars, pour out her oil, and sell it to repay her debts was faith in motion—her faith at work!

Sadly, many Christians today fall into the trap of waiting for divine intervention without making any effort themselves. *They pray but refuse to prepare; they have faith but refuse to act.* God expects us to do our part—putting in the work and being good stewards of the resources we have, no matter how small. The widow's story teaches the crucial balance between relying on God and taking personal responsibility. Dependence on Him should not lead to complacency or passivity but should instead fuel our efforts with hope and purpose.

Independence isn't just about having a second source of income—it's about cultivating a mindset that is resourceful, adaptable, and proactive. Throughout the Bible, many women were financially independent or made significant contributions to their households. One shining example is Ruth. Though she initially relied on her mother-in-law, Naomi, after her husband's death, she quickly took ownership of her circumstances.

Ruth could have easily returned to her family, as Orpah did, and depended on them for sustenance. Instead, she chose to follow Naomi and work in the fields, providing for their household independently. Her willingness to take initiative, work hard, and rely on her own efforts—while maintaining faith in God—ultimately sustained her and positioned her to marry Boaz, securing her future (Ruth 2:1-12).

Ruth's story illustrates the power of independence and resourcefulness. She didn't wait for someone to rescue her; instead, she took the initiative to secure her own survival—and, ultimately, her future. Several key attributes demonstrate that Ruth possessed an independent mindset:

1. ***Ruth the Loyalist:*** Ruth chose to stay with Naomi despite having no obligation to do so, demonstrating both her independence and loyalty to the older widow. Returning home would have been the safer, more predictable choice, but true independence often requires making difficult, sacrificial decisions rather than simply following the expected path.

2. ***Ruth the Believer:*** She boldly declared her position and faith, standing firmly by her conviction. Ruth chose to adopt Naomi's faith even when it seemed that Naomi's God was not working in her favor.

3. ***Ruth the Explorer:*** She chose to follow her to a strange country that she knew nothing of—this was faith in action. Stepping into the unknown based on a word and a promise!

4. ***Ruth the Leader:*** She took the initiative by volunteering to glean in the fields to take care of Naomi and herself. She was self-reliant instead of waiting for someone to solve their problem; no one was coming to their rescue!

5. ***Ruth the Hard Worker:*** Ruth was committed, persistent, and hardworking—never complaining as she toiled from morning until evening. True independence is marked by diligence and resilience, especially in life's most difficult seasons.

6. ***Ruth the Strategist:*** She was a strategic thinker and planner. When Naomi advised her on how to approach Boaz, she listened carefully and applied wisdom, tact, and respect. True independence requires not only the ability to strategize but also the wisdom to advocate for yourself.

7. ***Ruth the Risk Taker:*** Ruth refused to return to Moab and her old way of life. Instead, she was determined to build a new future despite the uncertainty ahead. True independence requires stepping out of your comfort zone and embracing new beginnings.

8. ***Ruth, A Woman of Good Reputation:*** Ruth was not just a woman of integrity but one of good reputation. She didn't manipulate her way into favorable circumstances but earned respect through her actions.

9. ***Ruth, Truster in God's Providence:*** While life was hard, Ruth trusted in God's plan for her life and continued to work until the maturity of His plan came to pass.

10. ***Ruth the Responsible:*** While Ruth might have followed Naomi, she did not rely on her to 'fix' her life but stepped up and took action to create a better future for both of them. Independent people seize ownership of their future rather than blame or expect others to do it for them.

11. ***Ruth the Blessing:*** Ruth's independence and diligence brought redemption to Naomi's life, while her marriage to Boaz secured her a legacy, including the lineage of Christ. Independent people empower others and build a legacy for the people around them.

Ruth's story highlights the importance of having a proactive attitude and being willing to work for your own well-being. Modern-day Christians, including stay-at-home parents and homemakers, can learn from her example. While staying at home to care for the family is a noble and important role, homemakers can still cultivate independence by having their own side hustle or work.

The dangers of over-dependence on others can lead to an unproductive life—one that expects God, as our ultimate provider, to wave a magic wand and do everything for us. No! He also expects us to work, plan, and use the gifts He has given us to secure our livelihood and future. Nothing demonstrates this expectation more clearly than when the children of Israel entered the Promised Land.

Then the manna ceased on the day after they had eaten the produce of the land; and the children of Israel no longer had manna, but they ate the food of the land of Canaan that year.
Joshua 5:12 (NKJV)

There is a dangerously false narrative that when God takes us to our Promised Land, we will no longer have to work and that everything will be given to us on a silver platter. This could not be further from the truth! If God has made you a promise, expect to put in hard work and effort to see it fulfilled—including in marriage. The children of Israel had to work to gain every part of the land God promised them, and those who refused to do so either never inherited their land or lived unproductively in it.

While God provided manna from heaven, He also commanded them to gather it daily. They had to put in the effort to collect the food and were instructed to save some for the Sabbath. This is a reminder that while God provides, He expects us to be active participants in His provision.

Let us also consider the example of the ant in Proverbs 6:6-8, which teaches us to be industrious and prepare for the future. The ant does not depend on another creature to provide for its needs; instead, it works diligently to gather food during the summer so that it has enough to survive the winter. This is a powerful metaphor for the importance of independence and preparation. If we are too dependent on others, we may find ourselves unprepared when difficult times come.

Consider the ant, you lazy bum. Watch its ways and become wise. Although it has no overseer, officer, or ruler, in summertime it stores its food supply. At harvest time it gathers its food.
Proverbs 6:6-8 (GW)

While I am in no way suggesting that the widow was lazy, both she and her husband should have been thinking about a rainy day, especially since they were already so far in debt. What was their plan for paying off their creditors? What was their strategy? While they were not lazy, they were unprepared when the time finally came.

For stay-at-home parents, independence can take many forms, even if they are not earning an income outside the home. It is essential for homemakers to have skills, knowledge, and relationships that extend beyond the household. This could be as simple as developing a hobby, starting a small business from home, or building a network of friends and mentors who can provide support and guidance in times of need.

One practical example of how homemakers can cultivate independence is by developing a "side hustle" or small business. Many stay-at-home parents today are turning their hobbies—such as baking, crafting, business consulting, or writing—into profitable ventures. This not only provides additional income but also gives them a sense of purpose and accomplishment outside of their roles at home. It's their way of contributing to the household while maintaining a level of financial independence.

One of the most critical lessons from the widow's story is the balance between faith and work. While the widow cried out to Elisha for help, it's important to note that she still had to take action. Elisha did not simply give her money or a handout; instead, he instructed her to gather jars and pour the oil she already had. This required following instructions, effort, initiative, and faith.

While faith is essential, it must be accompanied by action. God expects us to use all our resources—whether it's our skills, talents, or relationships—to improve our situation. Faith is not passive; it is active and requires work. Depending solely on others or waiting for a miracle without putting in any effort is neither a sustainable nor a biblical approach. Independence provides a sense of security, self-worth, and freedom.

The flipside of complete independence is that it can lead to pride and isolation—traits that we should not have as Christians. As believers, we are called to be part of a community, to bear one another's burdens, and to help those in need (Galatians 6:2). The goal is to find a balance between being independent enough to take care of ourselves and our families while also being willing to rely on others and help those in need.

Parents have a crucial role to play in teaching their children the value of independence. In the widow's story, her children were at risk of being taken by creditors because there was no financial plan in place. This is a sobering reminder of the importance of preparing the next generation to be independent and self-sufficient through practical skills like budgeting, saving, and investing. It also means encouraging them to develop their talents and pursue education or careers that will allow them to stand on their own two feet. Children should be taught the value of hard work and the importance of not relying solely on others for their livelihood.

Modeling is one of the most effective ways to teach our children independence. Parents who demonstrate strong work ethics, financial responsibility, and resourcefulness pass on those traits to their children. Additionally, parents should encourage their children to build relationships and networks outside the family so they have a support system in times of need. It has been suggested that parents with poor financial habits raise children who demonstrate the same characteristics. We must do better for our children.

Most of us, by now, have heard about diversifying our portfolios or having multiple streams of income. This is important in modern times, as even the Bible encourages us to be wise stewards of our resources and to be prepared for the unexpected. Ecclesiastes 11:2 warns us about the importance of diversifying—not just financially, but also in our relationships, skills, and personal development. Everyone will experience a rainy day, according to a Nigerian adage "Rain will fall on everyone's roof at some point." Meaning that calamity is bound to happen, it is just a matter of when it will be your time. The Bible gives us the same warning.

Put your investments in several places, many places even because you never know what kind of bad luck you are going to have in this world.
Ecclesiastes 11:2 (GNT)

To be successful in today's world, Christians must shift their mindset about independence. Relying solely on others—or even on God—without taking action is a recipe for failure. We must learn to balance faith with work, dependency with independence, and prayer with practical action. Too often, fear lurks in the shadows, keeping people trapped in dependency. The fear of failure, the fear of stepping out of one's comfort zone, and the fear of the unknown can paralyze individuals and prevent them from pursuing independence of any kind. However, as Christians, we are called to live in faith, not fear (2 Timothy 1:7).

The widow likely felt fear and uncertainty as she faced the prospect of losing her children and being left with nothing. Yet, it was only when she acted in faith—obeying Elisha's instructions and using her small jar of oil—that she was able to break free from her dire situation. We must trust that God has already equipped us with the tools we need to succeed, but we must also be willing to step out in faith and take action. Her story encourages us to push past fear, embrace practical steps toward independence, and trust that God will bless our efforts.

In conclusion, the widow's story is a powerful reminder of the dangers of complete dependency, whether on a spouse or unbalanced reliance on God without taking personal responsibility for our actions, as it can lead to disaster! The widow's initial lack of a backup plan left her in a vulnerable position, but her willingness to act on Elisha's instructions ultimately led to her deliverance. True love means teaching our children and spouses the value of independence and self-sufficiency—whether by developing multiple streams of income or cultivating relationships beyond the family. In an unpredictable world, we must all take personal responsibility for our own well-being.

By balancing faith with work and fostering independence within our homes and communities, we can build lives that are both spiritually strong and practically prepared for whatever challenges arise. The widow's story is more than a tale of miraculous provision—it is a lesson in personal responsibility, resourcefulness, and the power of taking action.

CHAPTER 13

FROM SCARCITY TO INGENUITY

Strategy Over Scarcity

Let's be clear, no one likes scarcity or tragedy but let me ask you a question. Can you name a time in your life when scarcity brought about ingenuity, and sparked an idea of some sort which at least during your famine season sustained you until you came out of it? An idea or skillset that once lay dormant can suddenly find purpose and become a source of income. Sometimes, life places us in difficult situations, and we discover a way to emerge—whether through our own ingenuity or the support of those around us.

In 2 Kings 4, the widow's tragic situation turned into a business opportunity when she sought the help of Elisha. What seemed like an insurmountable obstacle—her husband's death and the impending loss of her children to creditors—was transformed into a blessing through divine wisdom and strategy. Elisha's response was not to simply hand over financial resources but to open the widow's eyes to what she already possessed, a small jar of oil. Through this simple yet profound act, her life was changed forever. Her story teaches an invaluable lesson: it's not always about what we lack, but how we use the little that we have.

Life will have its tragic moments—its highs and lows—and it's at those critical times that we need to pull ourselves together and think strategically about our resources. The widow's oil was a small resource, but with the right mindset and strategy, it became the foundation for her business and a tool for deliverance from debt. Too often, we as Christians get caught up in what we lack, overlooking the power of the small resources we do have in our arsenal. We must learn to transform what appears to be scarcity into opportunity, using biblical wisdom, principles, and real-world examples as a guide for the modern-day believer.

The widow's story highlights a key principle: scarcity can be a fertile ground for both ingenuity (innovation) and opportunity. The widow failed to realize that an opportunity for innovation lay within her possession! While her small jar of oil might have seemed insignificant in value, it offered more than she had imagined. Elisha didn't instruct her to seek additional resources or accumulate more debt; instead, he guided her to use what she already had strategically.

This lesson is especially important in today's world, where Christians often look outward for resources or wait for *"big breaks"* before believing they can succeed. But God has often used the smallest of resources to perform the greatest of miracles. Consider the story of the five loaves and two fish in Matthew 14:13-21. Jesus took what seemed like an insufficient amount of food and used it to feed thousands. The same principle applies to us: it's not about the quantity of our resources but how we strategically utilize them.

The widow's small jar of oil, when used strategically, became her business opportunity. She was instructed by Elisha to borrow empty vessels, pour her oil into them, and sell the filled jars. The key to her success was not merely the oil itself, but the strategy behind its use. What we often perceive as scarcity can actually be the starting point for God's provision. Our role is to approach it with ingenuity, obedience, and faith.

One of the biggest barriers to success is the scarcity mindset; the belief that we don't have enough, that we're not enough, or that we need more to achieve our goals. This becomes even more challenging when we are already in a tough spot or facing a tragedy. It's easier to have faith when you have money in the bank and a roof over your head. The widow could have easily fallen into this mindset—after all, she had only a small amount of oil, and her situation seemed hopeless. However, with Elisha's guidance, she shifted her focus from what she lacked to what she possessed.

As modern-day Christians, we must also learn to shift our focus from what we lack. We should ask ourselves: What do I have that I can use? How can I be resourceful with the little that I have? Many of us are sitting on untapped potential, waiting for the "right" conditions—yet success often begins with a single step of faith and a shift in perspective.

A scarcity mindset can paralyze us in many areas of life—not just in finances, but also in relationships and careers. We may feel that we need all the answers or resources before taking action, but the widow's story reminds us that small beginnings should never be underestimated. As Zechariah 4:10 reminds us, "Do not despise these small beginnings, for the Lord rejoices to see the work begin."

The power of strategic thinking played a major part in the widow's success; it was not just the oil alone, but in the strategy that Elisha gave her. Elisha didn't give her any money or tangible goods; he gave her a *plan*. The strategy was simple: collect as many vessels as possible, fill them with oil, and sell them to pay off her debt. The simplicity of the plan underscores that success often lies in straightforward, practical strategies rather than complex, unattainable solutions. In my book *"Igniting Your Vision, Part 1: Keeping It Simple,"* I emphasize that every great businessman or woman often starts with just one product.

Identify a product and become a subject matter expert in it, and when you are making crazy profit then you can think of diversifying your product. The simplicity of the product and execution is important for success. This is an essential lesson for modern Christians as we often look for miraculous solutions to our problems or wait for someone to give us a handout. Sometimes, the solution lies in a strategy that uses what we already have. The widow put in the work—collecting jars, pouring the oil, and selling it. Elisha didn't perform the miracle for her; he gave her the tools to do it herself. Her obedience and willingness to follow the strategy were crucial to her success.

The question for us today is: What strategies are we following? Are we waiting for a miracle, or taking actionable steps toward success? Like the widow, we must be willing to implement the strategies God gives us, even if they seem simple or unconventional. In the secular world, there are countless examples of individuals and companies that have turned small resources into massive success. One notable example is **FedEx**. Its founder, Frederick Smith, had an idea for a company that would deliver products overnight. His teacher failed him, yet he pursued it anyway.

He started his company with a small amount of capital and an idea. At some point, his company was on the brink of collapse and he was unable to pay his workers. Smith was resourceful; he took the last bit of money the company had and gambled it in Las Vegas to pay for jet fuel. His bold strategy worked, and FedEx became a multi-billion-dollar corporation. Smith's ability to see opportunity in scarcity and take calculated risks was key to its success.

Another example is **Apple**, which started in a garage with two people, Steve Jobs and Steve Wozniak, and a small budget. What they lacked in resources, they made up for in ingenuity and strategic thinking. Apple's success wasn't instantaneous, but it stemmed from turning small beginnings into groundbreaking innovations. These examples, like the widow's story, show that success isn't about starting with abundant resources but using what you have wisely, efficiently, and strategically.

The Bible is filled with examples of people who took small resources and turned them into something great. In addition to the widow and the five loaves and two fishes, consider the story of **David and Goliath**. David, a young shepherd, had only a sling and five smooth stones, but he used these small resources to defeat a giant and change the course of Israel's history and eventually the King (1 Samuel 17).

> *Saul put his battle tunic on David, placed a bronze helmet on his head, and dressed him in armor. David fastened Saul's sword over his clothes and tried to walk, but he had never trained in them. "I can't walk in these," David told Saul. "I've never practiced with them." So he took them off. Instead, he took his staff, chose five smooth stones from the riverbed, and put them in his shepherd's bag. With a sling in hand, he approached the Philistine.*
> *1 Samuel 17:38-40 (GW)*

David's success wasn't about the size of his weapon but his faith and strategy. He didn't try to use Saul's oversized armor. Instead, he relied on what he knew—his sling—and trusted God for the victory. Another prime example is the **parable of the talents** in Matthew 25:14-30. In this story, a master gives three servants different amounts of money, or "talents," to manage while he is away. Two invest and multiply their talents, while the third buries his out of fear. The servants who took risks and used their resources were rewarded, but the ones who did nothing lost everything.

This parable highlights the importance of using the resources God gives us, no matter how small. We should use them wisely and diligently. Many people have untapped gifts and talents they've never considered turning into a business opportunity. Just like the widow, who didn't realize the potential of her oil until Elisha pointed it out, we often overlook the gifts that are right in front of us. Whether it's a creative skill, a knack for organization, or a passion for teaching, all of these gifts can be the foundation for a successful business or career.

Here are a few questions you need to ask yourself to get started and the first step is to identify what you have.

1. What am I really good at?
2. What do people come to me for?
3. What resources do I already have that I can use?

Once you identify your gifts, the next step is to develop a strategy to turn them into a business. This might start with offering services to friends and family, creating a side hustle, or freelancing. The key is to start with what you have and build from there. Don't overthink it. As the widow's story teaches, success isn't about having everything in place before you start—it's about taking the first steps in faith. Use the resources you have and trust God to multiply your efforts.

The widow's story is not just about strategy but about balancing faith with action. She could have waited for a miracle, but instead, she took action. Her faith was shown through her obedience to Elisha's instructions, and her willingness to use what she had was the key to her success.

As Christians, we are called to walk by faith, but faith is not passive. We must take steps of faith, even when resources seem small or inadequate. God often works through our actions to bring His provision. In today's world, this may mean taking a risk, starting a business, or investing in your skills and talents. It might mean working diligently with the little you have, trusting that God will bless your efforts and bring about an increase.

In conclusion, consider your strategy. The widow's story reminds us that success isn't about what we have but how we use it. She turned tragedy into triumph by using her smallest resource—a jar of oil—and following the simple strategy given by Elisha. This very same principle applies to us today. As modern-day Christians, we must shift our focus from what we lack to what we already possess. We must develop strategies for using our gifts and resources wisely, trusting that God will multiply our efforts when we act in faith.

Whether it's starting a business, pursuing a new career path, or simply using your talents to serve others, the key is to take the first step and trust that God will provide the increase. So again, what's your strategy? How will you turn your small resources into something greater? Just as the widow's oil became the foundation for her business, what gifts and talents do you possess that could become the foundation for your success? It all starts with a shift in mindset, a step of faith, following instructions and a willingness to work with what you have.

CHAPTER 14

DANGERS OF GENERATIONAL INDEBTEDNESS

Debt Ends with Me

What if I told you that debt isn't just a personal issue—it can have generational consequences, enslaving not only individuals but entire families? What debt is your family still paying off from a previous generation or a spouse? How is that debt affecting your family today? What have you denied yourself because of that debt? What have you denied your children because you are paying off someone else's debt? How has that made you feel about debt altogether?

Okay, I want you to take a deep breath, as this might be an uncomfortable chapter for you to read but it is a necessary one for you to overcome. I will have to walk you through the mess to get you to your miracle. So let us do this together without fear. The truth is, overwhelming debt enslaves—just as it did in biblical times, it does today. The widow's story in 2 Kings 4 exemplifies the dangers of generational debt, as her children faced the prospect of slavery to pay their deceased father's creditors.

If generational wealth can positively impact a family, imagine the dangers of generational indebtedness. Modern-day debt can entrap families, making it crucial for Christians to break the cycle that affects generations. Beyond its financial burden, debt also carries legal implications, highlighting the need for practical solutions to achieve financial freedom.

Let us be clear, debt is not a new phenomenon. In fact, it is as old as Genesis when Adam and Eve ate the fruit in the Garden. It caused us to be indebted to sin. However, we really get to hear about God addressing debts in Deuteronomy 15: 1-2 when He talks about the cancellation of debt after seven years. It is the same premise that is used to cancel some of our credit card debt after seven years if you live in America.

At the end of every seven years, you must cancel debts. This is how it is to be done: Every creditor shall cancel any loan they have made to a fellow Israelite. They shall not require payment from anyone among their own people, because the Lord's time for canceling debts has been proclaimed."
Deuteronomy 15:1-2 (NIV)

God instituted the "Year of Jubilee" to prevent generational financial indebtedness from devastating families. He recognized the destructive power of debt and sought to provide an economic reset and restoration for all people. In ancient times, debt was not just a personal burden but a family one. When a person incurred debt and could not repay it, creditors often seized their family members, forcing them into servitude to settle the debt.

This is what the widow in 2 Kings 4 faced after her husband's death; she is left with not only mourning his loss but also financial ruin. The creditors demanded payment, and when she could not provide it, they sought to take her sons as slaves. It was not uncommon in that era to use family members as collateral—a powerful metaphor for how debt continues to enslave families today. The widow's children were on the brink of generational bondage due to decisions made by their father, a religious man by all accounts. This illustrates how debt can impact future generations, both financially and emotionally, indiscriminately on title, career or faith.

Today, physical enslavement as a result of debt is illegal and amoral, yet financial bondage still traps families for generations. The effects of debt ripple through generations, creating cycles of poverty, limiting opportunities, and passing down financial instability. This ongoing burden leads to endless family trauma. Here are several ways modern-day indebtedness can entrap families:

1. ***Student Loans:*** In the Western world, particularly in the United States, student loan debt has become a major financial burden that impacts families for years. Many parents take out loans to support their children's education, leaving both the parents and children in financial hardship. The burden of student loans can limit career choices and delay major life milestones such as buying a home or starting a family. Former President Obama once shared that he finished paying off his student loans only after becoming President of the United States—highlighting the crippling cost of student debt.

2. ***Credit Card Debt:*** Credit card debt is one of the most insidious forms of modern-day financial entrapment. Families often rely on credit cards to cover basic needs or emergencies, but as balances grow and interest compounds, repayment becomes nearly impossible. This leads to financial stress that can impact family relationships and mental health.

3. ***Medical Debt:*** In countries without universal healthcare, medical debt can devastate families. Unexpected health crises often result in insurmountable bills, leaving families trapped in debt they had no choice but to take on. Medical debt, like other forms of debt, can result in the loss of assets like homes

or savings. In developing countries, upfront payment is often required for medical services, leading to the premature death of many who could have been saved if doctors accepted payment plans or financial assistance programs.

4. ***Mortgages and Foreclosures:*** Many families take on mortgages with the hope of building wealth through homeownership. However, unforeseen circumstances such as job loss or economic downturns can make it difficult to keep up with mortgage payments, leading to foreclosure and the loss of their home. This not only destroys financial stability but also disrupts the family unit.
5. ***Generational Poverty:*** Families trapped in poverty often take on debt as a means of survival. This can become a generational cycle, as children inherit financial habits from their parents. Without intervention, they are more likely to fall into the same pattern—accumulating debt and passing it down to their own children.

In modern times, indebtedness carries serious consequences for families, including garnished wages, seized assets, and diminished credit scores—factors that can negatively impact future borrowing opportunities. Similarly, the widow in 2 Kings 4 faced the legal threat of losing her sons to creditors due to her husband's unpaid debts. Though the circumstances have changed, today's world still has legal mechanisms that can trap families in financial bondage.

One of such legal mechanisms used today, especially in Western countries, is **bankruptcy**. This is often seen as a last resort for individuals or families who can no longer manage their debt. While bankruptcy can provide temporary relief by eliminating some debt, it also carries long-term consequences, such as damaging credit scores and making it difficult to secure loans or mortgages in the future. For those in certain professions, bankruptcy may not even be an option—for example, a CPA cannot file for bankruptcy and expect to maintain their license. So, while it may offer short-term relief, it is not always the best choice for everyone.

Another legal tool that is used is **estate seizure.** When someone with overwhelming debt passes away, creditors often have the legal right to claim portions of the deceased's estate. This can include homes, savings accounts, and other assets, potentially leaving surviving family members with little or nothing—especially if there was no will or financial plan in place. The same applies to individuals with civil judgments against them. In such cases, estate sales are often held, where assets are sold to the public until the debt is paid in full.

The inheritance of debt is a legal process in which financial obligations are passed down to children or other family members. This typically occurs when they have cosigned a loan, or in a worst-case scenario, when the estate is unable to cover outstanding debts.

The widow avoided losing her children to creditors because God, through the prophet Elisha, provided an earthly solution that enabled her to pay off her debts and save her family. This story teaches us that escaping generational debt is possible—but it requires intentionality, discipline, and, most importantly, a plan.

There are practical steps modern-day Christians can take to avoid generational indebtedness, many of which I have outlined in other chapters. A key strategy is financial education combined with a solid plan to break the cycle of debt. Avoiding unnecessary debt means steering clear of high-interest loans, excessive credit card use, and unaffordable luxury items. If you haven't already, consider estate planning and creating a proper will to ensure your family isn't left in financial chaos after your passing. A will allows you to distribute assets, designate guardians for your children, and ensure that your estate is managed according to your wishes.

Another crucial step is teaching children financial responsibility early, including the importance of saving money and the dangers of over-reliance on credit cards and loans. By instilling good financial habits in children, parents can help prevent them from falling into the debt trap. This also includes practicing realistic budgeting and living within one's means. In many cases, this means avoiding expensive vacations, luxury cars, or high-end gadgets that can lead to unnecessary financial strain and heavy indebtedness.

Teaching the importance of an emergency savings fund is crucial for avoiding debt during unforeseen circumstances. Aim to save at least three to six months' worth of living expenses in an easily accessible account. Finally, rather than accumulating debt, families should focus on building wealth through assets such as real estate, investments, or entrepreneurship. These assets can be passed down to future generations, creating a legacy of financial stability and prosperity instead of debt.

As Christians, while we trust in God's provision, we are also called to be wise stewards of the resources He has given us. Just as the widow put in the work by collecting jars and pouring oil, we too must be proactive in managing our finances and preventing debt. Avoiding generational debt is not just about earning more money—it's about adopting a mindset of stewardship and fiscal responsibility. Christians must reject the notion that faith alone will solve financial problems without taking practical steps. Instead, we should trust God to bless the work of our hands as we make wise financial decisions.

Families who are free from the bondage of debt experience many blessings, both financial and spiritual. Living without the constant pressure of debt allows families to give generously, invest in their children's future, and enjoy peace of mind. Proverbs 13:22 speaks directly to this principle, reminding us of the importance of leaving a legacy for future generations.

Good people leave an inheritance to their grandchildren,
but the wealth of sinners is stored away
for a righteous person.
Proverbs 13:22 (GW)

By taking the time to avoid the debt trap and managing finances wisely, parents can leave behind a legacy of financial freedom rather than a burden of debt. This requires intentional effort to break the cycle of generational indebtedness through discipline, faith, and wisdom. Parents should proactively manage their finances while also investing in the next generation by teaching them the importance of financial stewardship. This way, they can avoid the pitfalls of debt and experience the blessings of financial freedom for generations to come.

In conclusion, the widow's story of the oil highlights the extreme dangers of debt and its potential to enslave future generations—an issue that continues to affect modern families. For contemporary Christian families facing similar financial challenges, it is imperative to change the way they see and approach money. By taking proactive financial steps, families can break free from the cycle of generational indebtedness and build a foundation of financial freedom for future generations.

It is only when families are debt-free that they can experience the blessings of financial freedom and live full lives while leaving behind a generous and lasting legacy for their children and grandchildren. As Christians, we are called to be wise stewards of the resources God has given us. We honor Him and protect our families from the dangers of debt by managing our finances responsibly. By making wise financial decisions today, we can secure a brighter future for generations to come.

CHAPTER 15

THE POWER OF PROBLEM-SOLVING

A Widow's Hidden Provision

What if I told you that sometimes when we're in the thick of things, our problem-solving skills just go kaput? They fly right out the window! We become so overwhelmed that we can't even think clearly enough to develop a plan—let alone an executable one! I remember a friend calling me once, completely distraught and in tears. As they explained their situation, I reminded them that they had a major connection they could leverage—but in the moment of crisis, they had completely overlooked it. Her response was, "Oh I forgot about him." Twenty minutes later, she was on the phone thanking me for reminding her of her friend.

The story of the widow and her encounter with the prophet Elisha should be one that resonates deeply with all of us when it comes to the nature of problems and problem-solving. At some point in our lives, we've all faced situations so overwhelming that we struggled to think strategically, unable to find a way out. Such was the case for the widow who approached Elisha, burdened by a crippling debt that threatened to take her sons into slavery.

What's interesting is that the widow approached Elisha without a well-thought-out plan to resolve her predicament. Instead, she simply presented her problem, trusting his wisdom to provide a solution. This chapter explores the importance of not pre-judging those who come to us with a problem but no plan. I often hear questions like, "What is your three-, five-, or ten-year life plan?" But how can someone map out their future if they were never given the tools to do so? Now, imagine that same person suddenly facing an unexpected, life-altering event—how could they possibly be prepared?

The significance of seeking help from the right sources is just as important as learning to cultivate problem-solving skills that apply both inside and outside the church. While it may be true that the widow's approach was "problem first, plan later," the fact remains that when she approached Elisha, she had no clear course of action in mind. She simply knew she was in trouble and needed help. Her lack of a plan did not stop her from seeking assistance, and Elisha did not turn her away just because she lacked a detailed strategy.

Instead, he listened to her problem and asked a critical question: "What do you have in your house?" Then, he gave her clear instructions that ultimately led to her salvation from debt. People who seek help without a plan often do so because they are overwhelmed by life's difficulties, lacking the mental or emotional space to devise a solution. Rather than expecting everyone to have a detailed action plan before seeking assistance, we should be open to listening and using our skills and resources to help them formulate solutions.

Our communities play a major role in problem-solving and the cultivation of beneficial relationships. Elisha did not give the widow money or material resources; instead, he provided her with a strategy. His wisdom was the key to her financial breakthrough! This highlights that there are people within our circles who often hold the solutions to our very problems. However, we must be willing to recognize and leverage those relationships.

As believers, it is important to build relationships with people who have problem-solving abilities—not simply because of their financial status. Our connections should never be about exploiting others for their talents, wisdom, or wealth, but about cultivating humility to recognize when someone in our circle has an answer we lack. The Bible encourages us to seek wise counsel and acknowledge that solutions may come from those with insights, experiences, or ideas we have not yet considered.

Where there is no [wise, intelligent] guidance,
the people fall [and go off course like a ship without
a helm], But in the abundance of [wise and godly]
counselors there is victory.
Proverbs 11:14 (AMP)

In the New Testament, the apostle Paul was a vital source of guidance for early Christian communities that struggled with spiritual and practical challenges. His letters were filled with advice, solutions, and strategies that helped these churches navigate issues such as sin, conflict, and theological confusion. Because they trusted in Paul's wisdom and actively sought his counsel, they were able to grow and thrive.

The widow's story teaches us that seeking help isn't just about presenting a problem to someone—it's also about being willing to act on the advice given. When Elisha instructed the widow to collect jars and pour out her oil, she obeyed without hesitation. This step was critical to the process; she didn't just receive the strategy—she implemented it. This is a trait that contemporary Christians should cultivate: the habit of researching and actively seeking solutions to their problems.

Today's world is filled with resources—from Google to generative AI—so there's no shortage of ways to find answers. However, doing so requires both intentionality and commitment to the process. Just as the widow had to gather jars, we too must gather information, explore options, and seek counsel when facing challenges. Many Christians are often encouraged to "just pray about it and leave it alone." While prayer is absolutely necessary, it should never be where the effort stops. Faith and action go hand in hand. After praying, it is our responsibility to search for solutions, seek advice, and be proactive in solving our problems.

In the parable of the talents (Matthew 25:14-30), the servant who hid his talent out of fear was reprimanded, while those who actively used and multiplied their resources were rewarded. His master told him that even investing the money in a bank for the smallest return would have been better than doing nothing with it.

> *"Then the one who received two thousand dollars came and said, 'Sir, I knew that you are a hard person to please. You harvest where you haven't planted and gather where you haven't scattered any seeds. I was afraid, so I went off and hid your money in the ground. Look! Here is what belongs to you.' "His master responded, 'You evil and lazy servant! If you knew that I harvest where I haven't planted and gather where I haven't scattered, then you should have invested my money with the bankers. When I returned, I would have received my money back with interest.*
>
> *Matthew 25:24-27 (GW)*

This scripture is rich with lessons, one of which is that passivity and inaction are not options for Christians. We cannot ask God for abundant resources only to bury them, return them unused, and expect to be celebrated. Secondly, we must not waste the time of others in the process. We are called to use the resources—both material and intellectual—that God has given us to solve problems and improve our lives.

If we are going to seek counsel to help solve our problems, we must be open to flexibility. The widow likely expected financial help from Elisha or a direct solution to her debt crisis. Instead, she received what seemed like an unrelated set of instructions—to gather empty jars and pour oil into them. In modern terms, Elisha was asking her to trust a process that didn't make immediate sense to her at the time.

Sometimes, God's solutions—including those given through wise counsel—do not always align with our expectations. Modern-day Christians should be willing to explore unconventional methods and ideas if they truly want their problems solved. This includes being open to solutions that extend beyond the church setting, as answers can come from unexpected sources. These may include a mentor at work, a non-Christian friend, or even a stranger.

Never dismiss a potential solution simply because it doesn't fit your preconceived notions of how help should arrive. In Chapter 3 of my book, "*Unlocking the Deborah in You: The Traits of a Great Female Leader,*" I discuss how some of the greatest leaders often come in unassuming or even undesirable packages. This pattern is evident throughout the Bible and continues in modern times. A prime example is Naaman, a Syrian general who nearly missed his healing because he expected a grand gesture from the prophet Elisha (2 Kings 5).

When Elisha instructed Naaman to wash in the Jordan River, he initially rejected the idea because it seemed too simple and beneath him. However, his servants convinced him to follow the prophet's advice, and when he did, he was completely healed of his leprosy. Rahab, the prostitute turned spy; David, the shepherd boy turned giant slayer; Mary, the mother of Jesus—the list goes on. Stories like these illustrate the importance of being flexible in receiving help and open to different solutions.

I dislike problems as much as the next person. However, as painful and frustrating as they may be, problems are often great opportunities for personal growth and transformation. The widow's problem became the catalyst for her journey from debtor to business owner, enabling her to pay off her debt and live off her surplus. The challenge she faced pushed her to rely on her resourcefulness and act on the prophet's advice. Problems compel us to develop new skills, expand our understanding, build resilience, and evolve spiritually.

Problems not only stretch us but also shape us into better individuals when we face them head-on. They become opportunities to deepen our faith, sharpen our problem-solving abilities, and enhance our adaptability. Problems challenge our assumptions, prompt us to ask critical questions, and push us to think creatively beyond our comfort zones.

Joseph, in the Old Testament, faced a myriad of problems—from being sold into slavery to being wrongfully imprisoned. Yet, each challenge allowed him to develop specific skills, and the wisdom he gained strategically positioned him as second-in-command in Egypt.

His trials refined him, teaching patience, leadership, and the ability to manage complex situations.

In fact, with each problem Joseph solved, he moved closer to his destiny. This means that when we refuse to confront our problems head-on, we hinder our growth and remain stagnant, unable to mature into what God has prepared for us. Joseph was introduced to us as a dreamer, but when he interpreted Pharaoh's dream, he provided a solution for the coming famine. He advised the king to build storehouses to prepare for the impending food shortage.

> *"Now therefore, let Pharaoh select a discerning and wise man, and set him over the land of Egypt. Let Pharaoh do this, and let him appoint officers over the land, to collect one-fifth of the produce of the land of Egypt in the seven plentiful years. And let them gather all the food of those good years that are coming and store up grain under the authority of Pharaoh and let them keep food in the cities. Then that food shall be as a reserve for the land for the seven years of famine which shall be in the land of Egypt, that the land may not perish during the famine."*
> *Genesis 41:33-36*

Joseph provided a solution to an upcoming problem and was promoted because of it. However, it was his trials that refined him in preparation for leadership. In the same way, when we face our problems, they refine us—if we approach them with the right mindset and a willingness to learn.

The Bible is filled with examples of people who sought help with their problems—some followed the advice they received, while others did not. Those who heeded wise counsel often experienced deliverance, whereas those who ignored it faced negative consequences. When Moses became overwhelmed by the responsibility of leading and judging the people (Exodus 18), his father-in-law, Jethro, observed the problem and provided wise counsel.

Jethro advised Moses to delegate some of his leadership responsibilities to capable men who could handle minor issues, allowing him to focus on more important matters. Moses accepted this advice, which alleviated his burden and enabled him to lead more effectively. The solution here was delegation. Moses had capable men around him, but he failed to recognize their potential until Jethro brought it to his attention!

In contrast, King Rehoboam ignored the wise counsel of the elders, who advised him to be a kind and considerate leader to the people of Israel. Instead, he followed the poor advice of his young peers, which led to rebellion and the ultimate division of the kingdom (1 Kings 12). Rehoboam's failure to heed sound advice resulted in long-term consequences for both his reign and the nation of Israel. Seeking the right counsel—and being humble enough to accept advice, even when it does not align with our initial expectations—is something all Christians should learn to do.

One of the greatest benefits of seeking help with our problems is recognizing that we don't have to carry the burden alone. God places people in our lives—mentors, friends, family, and even professionals—who can offer solutions, guidance, and support.

Recognizing the resources around us can alleviate much of the stress associated with our problems. Additionally, sharing our challenges with the right people fosters connection and allows us to gain valuable insight. Listening to the right people and implementing their advice not only helps solve our immediate problems but also builds essential life skills such as critical thinking, problem-solving, and resilience. Over time, these skills equip us to handle future challenges more effectively and wisely.

Today's Christians can leverage technology, including AI-based tools like ChatGPT and Claude.ai, which offer an endless supply of information and ideas for tackling various challenges. These tools can provide creative solutions, research options, and expert advice that may not be readily available in our immediate circles. For instance, if you have no idea how to start a will, there are free online platforms that can guide you through the process without the high cost of hiring an attorney. Similarly, budgeting tools and financial counseling services are accessible online to help manage finances effectively. By utilizing modern tools, we can become more proactive in addressing our problems and finding solutions.

One vital lesson Christians can draw from the story of the widow and Elisha is the need for empathy and patience when people come to us seeking help. When the widow approached Elisha, he did not pre-judge or criticize her. Instead, he listened to her concerns and responded with compassion, providing her with a solution that changed her circumstances. This act of empathy and patience should serve as a model for today's Christians. There will be times when people come to us with a problem—not necessarily seeking a solution, but rather a compassionate ear and a heart of grace to hear them.

Empathy allows us to connect with others in their time of need. The Bible teaches us to "bear one another's burdens" (Galatians 6:2) and to show compassion toward those who are struggling. Empathy does not mean having all the answers; rather, it calls us to offer support and understanding to those who come to us in distress. It can be frustrating when someone has not yet figured out their next steps, but it is best to show grace to those who may be in a fragile state of mind as they work toward solving their own problems.

Many people do not know where to start and are often too ashamed to admit it. This is where we can extend empathy and understanding to them. It is not the time to ask for their five-year plan or question why they didn't save for a rainy day. Instead, by putting ourselves in their shoes and acknowledging their struggles, we can better understand their position and respond with kindness and patience.

In many ways, the widow's approach to Elisha reflects how many people handle crises. She knew she was in trouble but lacked the tools or knowledge to resolve her debt. Elisha, acting out of compassion and wisdom, did not rebuke her for lacking a plan but instead helped her find a way forward. Christians should strive to be like Elisha, responding to others with empathy rather than judgment.

Patience is a critical virtue when helping others with their problems. The process of problem-solving takes time, and those seeking help are often in a state of confusion or desperation. Rushing them or expecting instant results adds to their stress rather than alleviating it. Instead, we are called to practice patience, guiding those in need through their challenges at a pace that respects their emotional, mental, and spiritual journey.

The Bible frequently emphasizes patience as a fruit of the Spirit (Galatians 5:22). This virtue not only enables us to support others during difficult times but also gives them the space to process their issues and seek God's guidance in finding a solution. When people come to us without a plan, developing one may take time. It requires patience to walk alongside them, helping them think through their options and decisions.

Elisha demonstrated patience by not rushing the widow or insisting that she already had a solution. Instead, he carefully asked about the resources she possessed and then gave her instructions on how to use them to solve her problem. It's important to note that she wasn't a businesswoman when she met Elisha, but a housewife who now had to learn how to think outside the box in her decision-making. Christians today can learn from this example by taking the time to listen, offering thoughtful advice, and guiding others in a gentle and patient manner.

Patience cannot exist without tolerance, yet many Christians struggle with being tolerant of one another—this should not be the case. We must be willing to extend tolerance to those who come to us without a fully formed plan, recognizing that each person's situation and capacity to handle stress are different. Tolerance means accepting people as they are, even when they are not in an ideal state to solve their own problems. It involves extending grace to those who are struggling and refraining from judgment or impatience.

I love the biblical story of tolerance, empathy, and patience in the parable of the Good Samaritan (Luke 10:25-37). In this parable, a Samaritan stops to help a man who has been beaten and left for dead. The injured man is in no condition to ask for help, let alone devise a plan for his own rescue. Notably, the Samaritan does not question why the man was in that part of town or how he ended up in such a dire situation. Instead, moved by compassion, he cares for him without hesitation. He does not demand an explanation or inquire about how the man plans to recover—he simply helps him in his time of need. This story powerfully illustrates the importance of offering help without conditions or expectations and extending tolerance to those who cannot help themselves.

Empathy, tolerance, and patience are not just virtues for helping others—they are essential problem-solving tools as well! When someone approaches us with a problem but no plan, it's easy to focus on what they lack—whether it's resources, ideas, or foresight. However, empathy allows us to shift our perspective and see their potential for growth, patience helps us guide them through the process of finding solutions, and tolerance serves as a reminder that we, too, could find ourselves in a similar situation.

By exercising empathy, tolerance, and patience, we can help others feel seen, heard, and valued—motivating them to take steps toward solving their problems. We can gently encourage them to think critically, explore different options, and tap into resources they may not have realized were available. The key is to remain patient and empathetic, reassuring them that even without a plan, they are not alone and that solutions are within reach.

In conclusion, the story of the widow and Elisha serves as a powerful reminder for Christians to exercise empathy, patience, and tolerance while removing any form of pre-judgment when approached by those in need. This is especially important when they come to us with problems but no plans. As followers of Christ, we are called to bear one another's burdens and provide support without judgment. Empathy allows us to connect with those who are struggling, while patience gives us the endurance to walk alongside them as they work toward solutions.

By being open and understanding, we can help those in need discover their own resources, explore problem-solving strategies, and ultimately find success in overcoming their challenges. Moreover, we must encourage a mindset of resourcefulness, research, and active problem-solving—not only within church settings but also in our daily interactions and relationships. In the end, the widow's story is not just about the miracle of the jar of oil and debt cancellation, but also about how we treat each other when things are not working out the way we would like them to. May we all find our kind, tolerant, empathetic and patient side. Amen.

CHAPTER 16

HELPING HAND VS. HANDOUT

The Faith 'Investment'

Have you ever needed help and what did you get in return? Did you get a helping hand, perhaps a small amount of startup money for a company or a downpayment on a car that you had to repay? Or did you get a handout, which you didn't have to pay back, and how did that make you feel? With the helping hand, were you able to stand on your own after a few months—what about the handout? Did you have to think of where you would have to go next to get help again?

The story of the widow and Elisha highlights the importance of seeking solutions rather than relying on handouts in times of distress. When the widow approached the prophet Elisha, she did not simply ask for charity—she sought a way forward. Faced with a serious debt that threatened to consume her family, she needed more than temporary relief; she needed guidance. Elisha, recognizing her sincerity and determination, understood that what she required was not just assistance but a divine and practical solution. Instead of offering a handout, he provided wisdom that would empower her to overcome her situation.

Elisha's guidance came with clear instructions on how the widow could use the little she had to solve her problem and avoid future indebtedness. This story underscores the vital distinction between seeking a solution and seeking a handout—and the importance of recognizing the difference. Both those who offer assistance and those in need must understand this distinction. True help empowers, providing a path toward self-sufficiency rather than ongoing dependence.

As modern-day Christians, it is imperative that our mindset evolves beyond merely expecting to live off God's miracles. While faith is essential, we must also embrace practical and actionable ideas that lead to self-sufficiency, opportunities, and growth. It's unlikely that the widow expected Elisha to simply hand her a wad of cash—especially since he probably didn't have the amount she needed in the first place. Instead, she turned to him in the hope that he would provide a solution. While she sought relief from her debt, what she truly needed was financial direction to overcome her situation.

She understood that her problem required more than a temporary fix—it needed a lasting solution that would transform her circumstances and set her on the path to financial freedom. The widow likely realized that she and her husband had been merely covering up their financial struggles instead of addressing the root cause. Now, those unresolved issues had placed her family in danger of enslavement. So, let me ask you: in what areas of your life have you been applying a temporary bandage, changing it over and over when what you truly need is a permanent, lasting solution? This was the crossroad where the widow found herself—faced with the choice between another quick fix or a transformative, long-term answer.

Elisha's response to the widow is instructive. He didn't offer her charity or an easy way out—besides, he wasn't known for giving out money. Instead, he asked, "What do you have in your house?" When she replied that she had only a small jar of oil, he gave her a divine strategy to escape poverty. His solution was practical, requiring effort, faith, and action on her part. She was giving a helping hand by way of a strategic idea; she was being empowered to use what she had to solve her problem!

In many situations, people in need may approach others seeking assistance versus a solution. The key distinction between those genuinely seeking a solution and those merely looking for a handout is commitment. A solution requires effort, initiative, and a willingness to work toward resolving a problem—with humility. A handout, on the other hand, is a temporary fix that demands no long-term commitment from the recipient—just words, with no action to back them up.

For those offering help, it is crucial to recognize the difference between a solution and a handout. Solutions empower people to take control of their situations, equipping them with the skills and resources needed for self-sufficiency. Handouts, while sometimes necessary in emergencies, can foster dependency and hinder the resilience and creativity needed to overcome life's ongoing challenges.

Elisha's approach to the widow is a prime example of offering a solution rather than a handout. He didn't simply give her money to pay off her debt; instead, he provided a plan that required her to take action and use the resources she already had. This is the model Christians should follow when helping others—empowering people to solve their problems rather than just alleviating immediate needs until the next crisis.

Unfortunately, many modern-day Christians approach God with a handout mentality, expecting Him to solve their problems without any effort, commitment, or initiative on their part. Many pastors share the blame for promoting a prosperity message without emphasizing responsibility or work ethics. They pray for financial blessings, success, and opportunities, but often neglect the practical steps needed to make those blessings a reality. This mindset is akin to waiting for manna from heaven—expecting God to provide for all their needs without engaging in the work He has called them to do. Even when He did provide them manna, they complained about not having enough because handouts eventually build a sense of entitlement if we are not careful.

Throughout the Bible, God provided divine ideas and strategies to His people—ideas that required responsible action and commitment. He didn't simply give handouts; He offered opportunities to work, create, and build something that led to lasting success, benefiting not just individuals but entire communities. Handouts are unsustainable in the long run, which is why when the children of Israel entered the Promised Land, manna ceased from heaven.

Take Joseph in Egypt, for example. God gave him divine insight to interpret Pharaoh's dream and a strategy to save Egypt from famine by building storehouses. Joseph didn't just sit back and pray that God would prevent the famine. *(Some religious Christians today might have simply "bound the devil" while insisting that no famine was coming!)* Nor did he wait for God to make provision; instead, he proactively worked for seven years to store up grain during the years of plenty to prepare for the years of famine. His faith was not passive; it was active, and it required planning, effort, discipline, commitment and foresight.

Similarly, when the widow was given a divine idea, she took immediate action by getting her sons to gather up the vessels while she poured the oil to sell. Her solution came through her willingness to follow God's instructions and work toward resolving her problem. On the other hand, the Bible also gives examples of those who sought handouts or easy solutions. In John 6:26, after feeding the 5,000, Jesus told the crowd that they followed Him not for His teachings but for free food—a handout. Jesus recognized their motives and rebuked them, saying, "You seek me, not because you saw the signs, but because you ate of the loaves and were filled." These individuals were seeking a hand-out rather than the spiritual nourishment and wisdom that Jesus offered.

Building relationships and expressing gratitude when seeking help worked in the widow's favor. Her ability to approach Elisha for assistance likely stemmed from the bond her husband had established with the prophet over time. As one of the sons of the prophets, her husband likely had a close-knit relationship with Elisha, which created an opportunity for his widow to seek help in her time of greatest need.

What does your relationship look like with your spouse, their friends, or even their family? Is it strong enough that, if you were in trouble, your wife, husband, or child could reach out for help, just as the widow did? If cultivating relationships has not been a habit for you, now may be the time to start—not merely for the possibility of future help, but because relationships are inherently valuable. As Christians, we should recognize the importance of building strong connections with others, both within and outside the church.

When we cultivate genuine relationships built on mutual respect and trust, we establish a reliable support system for times of need. Furthermore, expressing gratitude for the help we receive not only strengthens these relationships but also ensures that we are not perceived as individuals who merely take advantage of others' kindness. As believers, we are warned not to take advantage of others. In 2 Thessalonians 3:10, Paul reminds us that "if anyone is not willing to work, let him not eat," emphasizing the importance of contributing rather than relying on others to do the work for us. This serves as a stern reminder that while seeking help is necessary at times, we must also put in the effort to solve our own problems.

In conclusion, the story of the widow and Elisha teaches us that God understands we will face difficult times. While there may be moments when we receive help, His expectation is that we actively seek solutions when confronted with challenges. We must learn to approach God with a willingness to take action and follow His guidance, rather than merely extending our hands and expecting continuous miracles to solve our problems. The key lesson here is that the resources we need to overcome our difficulties are often within reach—we just need to recognize and use them.

All Christians must evolve from a hand-out mentality and embrace an evolutionary mindset of seeking divine but practical solutions. Whether through prayer, research, or seeking advice from trusted individuals, we must be proactive in addressing our problems and finding ways to create opportunities from our challenges. Our "faith investment" begins with the understanding that while we may need help, what we truly need is a solution. At the same time, we must cultivate empathy and patience toward those who seek our help, recognizing that not everyone will have a clear plan. However, that does not make them unworthy of assistance.

Finally, we must remember the importance of building relationships, expressing gratitude, and contributing to the solutions we seek. When we approach life's challenges with this mindset, we not only solve our immediate problems but also set ourselves up for long-term success and growth. In doing so, we fulfill God's expectations for us as His followers, while also extending our eventual success to our community.

CHAPTER 17

DIY WEALTH: DOMESTIC INCOME

From Jar to Jackpot

I will be totally honest; I'm not a DIY person at all when it comes to fixing things around my home. However, when I bought my second house, I had a group of friends determined to teach me how to handle DIY projects. From friends to family members, everyone was eager to show me the importance of taking on these tasks myself. While I've learned a lot, I still call on a few friends when I'm not quite ready to climb a ladder or hang something around the house!

What if I told you that you can take the very concept of DIY and ensure that you build your own domestic income that can lead to wealth? Many of the things we can do ourselves often present an opportunity for domestic income, if we can see the value in what we are doing. More often than not, others see our passion and love for something more clearly than we do ourselves. They recognize that the very thing we're passionate about could change our destiny, just as it did for the widow in 1 Kings 4:1-7. When she encountered the prophet, she told him she had nothing at all. In modern terms, he might have asked her, "What do you enjoy DIY-ing around your house?"

Today, that widow might be someone who loves collecting stamps or a man who enjoys collecting autographed baseballs. Like the widow in the Bible, we often overlook the key to our own breakthrough. Through the miraculous act of gathering and selling her oil, the widow discovered that what she thought was insignificant had the power to change her life forever. Similarly, there are countless DIY opportunities in our lives that have the potential to inspire modern-day Christians to find solutions to their problems right within their reach.

Many times, we overlook the resources, skills, and ideas that God has already placed within our grasp. Feeling inadequate, like the widow, we believe we have nothing left. But in reality, what we need is already in our house, in our minds, or in our hands.

The first lesson of DIY is identifying the hidden resources around you. While these resources are often in plain sight, they can be the most difficult to recognize because we've deemed them insignificant, thus downplaying their importance. When Elisha asked the widow what she had, her initial reaction was to focus on her lack: "I have nothing." Yet, even in her desperate situation, she had something—a jar of oil. This small resource was what God used to bring her out of debt.

At some point, we've all focused on our lack, inadequacies, and shortcomings, telling those around us that we have nothing. Many Christians find themselves in similar situations—burdened by debt, unemployment, or a sense of hopelessness—believing they have nothing to offer. However, what they need to realize is that within their homes, there may be hidden resources that God wants to use. It could be a skill, a hobby, or even an idea they've overlooked.

I will give a real-life example as I have a young man who does home car detailing in my neighborhood. One morning, I ran into him on my way to work, and he mentioned that he could clean my car at home. When he came over, he shared how he got into the car-washing business during COVID. You see, he was a federal government employee, but he had always loved washing his car. One day, his brother said to him, "Why don't you turn car washing into a business?" He scoffed at his brother but decided to take his little jar of oil—let's call it soap and water—and began washing cars after work.

Three years later, he retired comfortably from his six-figure government job and is now in business for himself. It started with his DIY and he has now grown his business from IT professional to a mobile car washing owner. That side hustle that you are disdaining might be the one that God wants to multiply to get you into early retirement! The second challenging step is to shift your mindset from one of lack to one of abundance. The widow's initial mindset was rooted in lack, as she herself said, "I have nothing." She failed to see the potential in the jar of oil, which is a common struggle for many Christians.

A mindset that focuses on what we don't have, rather than what we do, or the willingness to partner with others whom we perceive as having the same idea or concept, limits our potential. To experience God's provision, we must shift our focus from lamenting our lack to asking God to open our eyes to the resources He has already placed within our reach. This is the only way we can break free from the paralysis of debt, despair, and fear that leaves us stuck.

One powerful tool in aiding our mindset shift is prayer, especially when faced with financial or personal crises. If we can take a moment to pray instead of succumbing to fear, we will overcome. One of my favorite scriptures speaks about the renewing of our minds, and this is how we can experience a mindset shift, as stated in Romans 12:2.

Don't become like the people of this world. Instead, change the way you think. Then you will always be able to determine what God really wants—what is good, pleasing, and perfect.
Romans 12:2 (GW)

To be honest, it's normal to feel afraid, especially when you're unsure of what will happen next—whether you'll have a place to sleep or where your next meal will come from. But God has told us not to be like the people of this world. The only way to do that is by changing the way we think. When we do, we'll also be able to change our approach to life and embrace the best things God has reserved for us.

Ask God today, "What do I have in my house?" Through fervent prayer, God can reveal hidden talents, ideas, or resources that you may not have considered before. When I asked various businesswomen what inspired them to start their own businesses, most of them shared one thing in common with the widow. They were tired of someone determining the outcome of their life; for some, it came from an unfair boss, a recession, a divorce or just wanting to take control of their own destiny. One of the most practical lessons from the widow's story is the concept of starting a business or income stream from what you already possess, and everyone possesses something. For the widow, it was oil.

For modern-day Christians, it could be anything from skills, crafts, ideas, or even one's property in which they can be a landlord or sign up for Airbnb! The key is to ask God for insight into how to use what you have to create wealth. A stay-at-home mother might realize that her passion for organizing can become a business, helping others declutter their homes. A man who enjoys woodworking could turn his craft into a business by selling handmade furniture. In today's world, the rise of the gig economy and online platforms has made it easier than ever to transform hobbies and skills into thriving businesses.

A major sign for starting your own business is when you do not feel that you have reached the pinnacle of success in life yet. This was the case with Jacob and Laban in Genesis 30:25-43. After twenty years of working for his uncle, Jacob had little to show for his labor. His wages had been reduced six times over that period. I can understand how the lure of more money might make someone set aside their dreams—but for less money? That should never be the case. So, God gave Jacob a divine idea: to breed sheep in a specific way that increased his wealth exponentially.

Then he put three days' journey between himself and Jacob, and Jacob fed the rest of Laban's flocks. Now Jacob took for himself rods of green poplar and of the almond and chestnut trees, peeled white strips in them, and exposed the white which was in the rods. And the rods which he had peeled, he set before the flocks in the gutters, in the watering troughs where the flocks came to drink, so that they should conceive when they came to drink. So the flocks conceived before the rods, and the flocks brought forth streaked, speckled, and spotted. Thus the man became exceedingly prosperous, and had large flocks, female and male servants, and camels and donkeys.
Genesis 30:36-39, 43

Jacob was extremely wise. First, he put a three-day journey between himself and his uncle before using the resources available to separate the flock. Just as the widow shut the door when she gathered the vessels, you, too, may need to put some distance between yourself and certain people in your circle. Second, Jacob combined his knowledge of animal husbandry with God's guidance, turning it into a strategy that brought him financial success. If you do not like where you are career-wise or financially, it might be time to DIY your financial life.

Know that Jacob's success wasn't just the result of God's strategy—it was also because he had a better understanding of animal husbandry than his uncle Laban. Likewise, there are things you understand better than those around you, and that knowledge could be your ticket out of poverty and limitations. Think outside the box. Think beyond the scope of your debt, because debt has a way of paralyzing us, making us feel trapped and powerless. The widow was in a similar position with the threat of her creditors coming to take her children and no way to pay her debts; she was in a hard place. However, instead of allowing her situation to defeat her, she sought help from the prophet of God.

One of the most important lessons Christians can learn is not to let debt define their future. While it may feel overwhelming, debt is not the end. Instead, like the widow, ask God for direction. Rather than focusing on what you don't have, shift your focus to what you can create. You are made in the image of the Creator of the universe—God Himself—so ask Him to give you divine and creative ideas that will lead you out of financial bondage.

He did it for Jacob—until that time, nothing like that had been achieved in history. We have the power to create. As Plato stated, "Our needs will be the real creator," a concept now commonly known as *"Necessity is the mother of invention."* So, what is your necessity? Identify it, then begin to create solutions to address that need! Throughout the Bible, we find testimonies of individuals who found themselves in difficult situations but received divine ideas that led to their financial breakthrough. One example is Nehemiah the cupbearer who was in exile but had a desire to rebuild the ruins of Jerusalem.

He had no self-interest at all but asked God for favor and the king's permission to rebuild the city. His vision, faith, and leadership transformed a dire situation into a successful mission. He had a strategy—to build with one hand while holding a weapon in the other. A classic example of DIY—constructing an entire city in just fifty-two days with no prior building or architectural experience! Some of our best work emerges when our backs are pressed against the wall of life, forcing us to respond out of necessity to change our destinies.

The hardest part of creating is the power to evolve from pain to purpose. The widow's pain became her purpose! The death of her husband, debt, and the threat of losing her children all became the catalyst for her miracle. What part of your life feels the most threatened right now? What area brings you the most pain? More importantly, how will you take that pain and use it as a catalyst for change—not just for yourself, but for your family as well? The truth is that our most profound breakthroughs often arise from our greatest moments of pain.

In these moments, God is preparing us to birth something new. Pain can lead to purpose when we choose to look beyond our circumstances and ask God to reveal what we already have in our hands. In the same way, modern-day Christians can grow by transforming their painful experiences into godly opportunities for something greater and better. Whether it's a business idea, a ministry, or a new direction in life, our challenges often become the birthplace of new opportunities.

I want you to close your eyes for a moment (unless you're driving!) and take a deep breath. Reflect on your struggles. Acknowledge the pain, but then ask yourself: "What is God teaching me through this? How can this experience lead to something that benefits me or others in the long run?" Shifting your perspective from pain to purpose can open doors to unexpected blessings.

We are nothing without our relationships and the spirit of gratitude—two vital lessons we can learn from the story of the widow. When Elisha instructed her to gather jars from her neighbors, it was her relationships with those around her that played a pivotal role in her breakthrough. I am often taken aback when I hear people say, "I am a loner," or "I don't have friends." At any point in life, emergencies can arise—who will look out for them and cover them?

Please, if you have not made it a habit, start today to cultivate the spirit of gratitude for the people God has placed in your life, as they can often lead to unexpected blessings. Here's the truth: building strong relationships over time allows you to seek help when needed without feeling like a burden. Investing in your community, church, and friendships is essential, as they all play a role in your journey toward success. Gratitude opens the door to favor and positions you to receive help when you least expect it. The story of the widow and her oil is more than just a tale of miraculous provision—it's a blueprint for how modern-day Christians can approach their challenges through DIY. Often, what we need is already within our reach, wrapped up in a skill, a talent, or an idea. At first, it may seem rough or insignificant, but when combined with faith and action, it can transform—just like a diamond formed under pressure—leading to extraordinary results.

In moments of desperation, don't focus solely on what you lack—instead, be open to trying something new or different. This might mean revisiting past ideas that others suggested but you once dismissed. Ask God to open your eyes to the possibilities around you, just as He did for Elisha's servant in 2 Kings 6:17.

And when the servant of the man of God arose early and went out, there was an army, surrounding the city with horses and chariots. And his servant said to him, "Alas, my master! What shall we do?" So he answered, "Do not fear, for those who are with us are more than those who are with them." And Elisha prayed, and said, "Lord, I pray, open his eyes that he may see." Then the Lord opened the eyes of the young man, and he saw. And behold, the mountain was full of horses and chariots of fire all around Elisha.
2 Kings 6:15-17

During Elisha's time, his servant felt overwhelmed and afraid when faced with an army, uncertain of what would happen next. But Elisha prayed for his servant's eyes to be opened—to see the endless possibilities that surrounded them. In the same way, we must seek both divine wisdom and practical solutions in our quest for our own "oil jar." Be open to ideas, even when they seem small or insignificant, as you may discover what you thought was nothing might hold the key to your breakthrough.

Modern-day Christians should begin to seek out the hidden treasures within their own homes. There is untapped potential to unlock wealth and create multiple streams of income—without even stepping beyond the four walls of your house. What may seem like ordinary household items could hold lucrative possibilities, just as they did in the widow's story.

Look for the things in your home that can be repurposed or consider leveraging your existing skills—especially those that are currently underutilized. Maximize the ordinary, DIY what you have, and transform it into an extraordinary source of income. With faith, prayer, and a willingness to act, you can change your circumstances and create lasting generational wealth—just as God did for the widow.

CHAPTER 18

BORROWING WITH A PURPOSE

The Widow's Vessel Strategy

So, my brother is into finance, and when I wanted to buy my home, he advised me to build my credit. You see, I had always ignored credit card offers, assuming they weren't necessary. But he explained that if I wanted to buy a house, I needed to demonstrate creditworthiness—which meant getting and managing multiple credit cards responsibly. In essence, he convinced me that getting a number of credit cards was necessary for the purpose of buying the house I wanted. So, I did my research and after much prodding, I listened to him and seven months later I was in my house.

I did not get a bunch of credit cards because I wanted to take an expensive vacation or buy some expensive outfit. I had one purpose in mind, and that was real estate. I was going to borrow with a purpose, and this next chapter is all about the widow's vessel strategy—a plan that required her to borrow with intention. When the widow approached Elisha in desperation, he assessed her situation and instructed her to do something many would have considered counterproductive—he told her to borrow vessels.

Wowwwww! Wait a minute, Prophet Elisha! Did you not hear what she said about her dead husband, crushing debt, and the fact that her creditors would be enslaving her children by 2:00 PM on Sunday after church? And yet, you want her to borrow vessels—lots of them? Let's unpack this together, shall we? Elisha told her to borrow as many vessels as she could gather. This request might seem paradoxical because it was borrowing that had contributed to her precarious situation in the first place.

Yet, there was a stark difference between the two types of borrowing: the widow's late husband's borrowing had led to debt without a plan, while Elisha's instructions were designed with a clear purpose and strategy. It's just like living in America—if you're getting a credit card without a strategic plan to leverage it for building wealth or starting a business, then how are you any different from the widow's late husband? But if you have a clear plan in place, then borrowing with purpose takes on a completely different meaning.

In this chapter, we explore the concept of borrowing as a tool for financial growth rather than a path to financial ruin. Just as the widow's borrowing paved the way for her miracle, modern-day Christians can learn how to use debt wisely by creating financial opportunities instead of falling into the trap of endless financial struggle. To do this, we must first understand the true purpose behind both the widow's borrowing and that of her late husband.

The widow and her late husband's initial debt had no purpose other than to meet immediate needs; perhaps like many people today, they borrowed money for basic survival. However, without a clear strategy or financial plan, borrowing can quickly spiral into an unmanageable burden, threatening a family's well-being. Many married couples, in particular, tend to borrow beyond their means, assuming that having two incomes provides a safety net. In contrast, single individuals often recognize that they alone are responsible for their financial stability, making them more cautious with debt.

While I agree with Scripture that "two are better than one," this mindset can sometimes lead couples to become more financially reckless, assuming that their partner will be there to bail them out. However, financial security requires intentional planning, not just the presence of a second income. Whatever the reason behind their borrowing, the widow and her late husband ultimately found themselves in a precarious financial situation that jeopardized their family's future. This is why Proverbs 22:7 warns us about the dangers of borrowing recklessly.

The poor are ruled by the rich, and those who borrow are slaves of moneylenders.
Proverbs 22:7 (CEV)

However, the borrowing that Elisha instructed the widow to do was fundamentally different—it was specific and purposeful. Rather than accumulating debt without direction, she was told to gather empty vessels with the clear intention of holding the oil that God would miraculously multiply. This strategic act of obedience was designed to yield a bountiful return, not only paying off her debt but also securing a future for herself and her sons.

The first lesson for every modern Christian is that borrowing without a plan leads to a financial **deficit** while borrowing with a purpose can lead to **growth**. Before taking out a loan or borrowing money, it's crucial to have a clear, executable, and attainable strategy in mind. Ask yourself: Are you borrowing to invest in something that will generate returns, or are you borrowing to cover immediate, non-essential expenses? Understanding this distinction is key to using debt as a tool for financial progress rather than a trap leading to financial ruin.

There are different types of loans and borrowing—as my brother will say, "*Sandra, not all debt is bad.*" Some forms of borrowing can actually serve as a stepping stone to financial stability and growth if used wisely.

1. ***Business Loans:*** If you're borrowing to start or expand a business and have a well-thought-out plan, this type of debt can pave the way for financial success. Entrepreneurs often take out loans to fund new ventures, but the key is understanding both the risks and rewards. The widow's act of borrowing vessels can be likened to a business loan—an investment in a strategy designed to generate income.
2. ***Educational Loans:*** Borrowing to invest in education or skill development can provide long-term financial benefits. Gaining knowledge and expertise enhances earning potential and creates new opportunities. However, it's essential to borrow wisely, ensuring that the chosen field of study or skill leads to viable job prospects or business opportunities.
3. ***Home Loans or Mortgages:*** A home loan, when secured with careful planning and financial discipline, is often considered good debt. Real estate typically appreciates in value, and homeownership can contribute to long-term financial stability and wealth creation. However, it's crucial to borrow within your means and avoid overextending yourself.
4. ***Investment Loans:*** Borrowing to invest in stocks, bonds, or other financial assets can drive growth if approached strategically. However, this carries greater risk and should only be undertaken by those with a strong understanding of the market or the guidance of a trusted financial advisor.

5. ***Debt Consolidation Loans:*** These loans enable individuals to consolidate multiple high-interest debts into a single loan with a lower interest rate. While this doesn't eliminate debt, it can simplify repayment and reduce the risk of falling deeper into the debt trap.

By focusing on borrowing that is tied to growth and business opportunities, today's Christians can avoid the pitfalls of debt that lacks a clear purpose or return on investment. This was a significant part of the widow and her late husband's struggle; they borrowed out of necessity rather than with a strategic plan. Borrowing without a clear repayment strategy ultimately led to their financial crisis.

The lesson for modern-day Christians is clear: never borrow without a plan. Whether it's a credit card, a personal loan, or even a favor from a friend, borrowing should always be accompanied by a detailed repayment strategy and, ideally, a financial benefit. Borrowing for consumable goods or to sustain a lifestyle beyond your means—without a clear plan—sets the stage for financial hardship.

In contrast, borrowing for a well-thought-out purpose—such as education or starting a business—can lead to financial stability and success, provided there is a clear plan for repayment and growth. The Bible offers examples of borrowing that resulted in financial stability when approached with wisdom and purpose. In each case, the individuals had a strategy or divine guidance that transformed their circumstances. Let's begin with Nehemiah, the cupbearer who became a builder.

In Nehemiah 2, we read that Nehemiah requested resources from King Artaxerxes to rebuild the walls of Jerusalem. He didn't seek a handout; instead, he asked for specific materials and permissions that would enable him to accomplish a greater purpose.

Furthermore I said to the king, "If it pleases the king, let letters be given to me for the governors of the region beyond the River, that they must permit me to pass through till I come to Judah, and a letter to Asaph the keeper of the king's forest, that he must give me timber to make beams for the gates of the citadel which pertains to the temple, for the city wall, and for the house that I will occupy." And the king granted them to me according to the good hand of my God upon me.
Nehemiah 2:7-8

His borrowing had a clear purpose, which was to rebuild the city, which resulted in the restoration of Jerusalem, demonstrating how borrowing with a plan can lead to overwhelming success. Another prime example is King Solomon, who borrowed from neighboring nations to build the temple in Jerusalem. He understood that the resources he acquired would serve a higher purpose—creating a place of worship for God. His borrowing was strategic and aligned with his long-term vision.

In both examples, borrowing was not done out of desperation or to cover immediate needs. Instead, it was part of a broader vision and plan that ultimately led to success. While one man was a cupbearer with limited means, Solomon was among the wealthiest men of his time. Yet, both borrowed strategically to fulfill an assignment that served a greater purpose. This demonstrates that borrowing is not just for those with limited means but also for those who are financially powerful.

We can learn from these two men who were on two different societal levels and yet both leveraged the opportunity to borrow to fulfill a divine assignment. What do you need to complete that requires a certain amount of borrowing for you to attain your goal? On the flip side, for those experiencing financial distress—what are your current plans for overcoming it? Are you dealing with credit card debt, payday loans, or other high-interest borrowing that has spiraled out of control? What is your strategy for repayment? These are all crucial considerations, whether facing good or bad debt.

Borrowing, when done purposefully and with a plan, can be a powerful tool for growth. The widow's borrowing led to her financial freedom because she followed Elisha's instructions with a clear goal in mind. Modern Christians can learn from this example by ensuring that any borrowing is tied to a well-thought-out repayment plan and a focus on financial growth.

If you're considering borrowing money, ask yourself these key questions:

1. What is the purpose of this loan?
2. How will I repay it?
3. What is the expected return on this investment (ROI)?
4. Am I borrowing within my means?

By answering these questions honestly and seeking divine guidance, you can use borrowing as a tool for growth rather than a debt trap.

In the end, the widow's story provides invaluable lessons about borrowing, debt, and financial wisdom. While borrowing put her in a precarious position, Elisha's instruction to borrow vessels with a clear purpose led to her financial breakthrough. Modern-day Christians can learn from this example by recognizing the importance of borrowing with a detailed plan and using debt strategically to create opportunities for financial growth. By doing so, we can avoid the pitfalls of borrowing without a clear purpose or plan.

Just as the widow's borrowing led to a miracle, borrowing for the right reasons and with a solid strategy can lead to financial success. Whether it's for education, business, or homeownership, borrowing can serve as a tool that opens doors to new opportunities—provided it's done with wisdom and a clear goal in mind. Ultimately, Christians must seek divine guidance in their financial decisions, including when and how to borrow.

By following the lessons of the widow's oil, believers can use borrowing to build a future of financial stability, create generational wealth, and avoid the pitfalls of purposeless debt.

CHAPTER 19

OBEDIENCE IN UNCERTAINTY

Faith Facing the Impossible

Have you ever been asked to do something, and the person telling you what to do says those three famous words, "Just trust me"? And you did—even when it didn't make any sense! Many years ago, after losing everything due to my money being embezzled, I was slowly rebuilding my life and in need of a car. I had attempted several times to get a particular car and kept being denied. It was an early Saturday morning when God woke me up and told me that I was going to get my car that day.

He told me that I should trust Him and walk in faith and not call anyone for a ride to the dealership but call the salesman to pick me up. Of course, I disobeyed God and called everyone, and they all turned me down! Well, when that did not work, I decided to trust God. The salesman picked me up, and as we entered the salesroom, I saw the same salesman who had always turned me away coming toward me. I panicked, but God whispered, "Trust Me and have faith." Immediately, he was called away, and I proceeded to the car, where the finance guy told me that, based on my credit, I couldn't afford the car in question.

I responded, "But God told me that is my car." About 20 minutes later, the entire dealership was celebrating. You see, the salesman had called the head of the finance department for this particular car, and the head of finance told the dealership that, without a co-signer, I couldn't get the car. To which the dealership replied that they would co-sign for me. UNBELIEVABLE!!! I got to pick up my car and drive home in a brand-new vehicle, as a result of my agreement with the dealership. This is what this chapter is all about—obedience in uncertainty is not about foolishness, but rather when you have nothing to lose and are walking purely by faith. Granted I stumbled in the beginning, but in the end, I had faith in facing the impossible moment.

Just like in 1 Kings 4:1-7, when the widow found herself in a place of deep mental struggle due to the weight of her situation—a dead husband, insurmountable debt and her sons facing slavery—it was overwhelming, to say the least. In her moment of despair, the widow seeking help from Prophet Elisha was given a solution that seemed illogical. He suggested she borrow empty vessels, despite the fact that borrowing had already contributed to her precarious financial position. How could borrowing more possibly be the answer to her debt problem?

Nevertheless, she exercised her faith by choosing to obey Elisha even though his plan seemed illogical, and she didn't fully understand it. She obeyed, despite her doubts and confusion, becoming the catalyst for her miraculous breakthrough. Obedience is our focus—just like the widow's—in that when we find ourselves in situations where God requires us to have faith in His plan, we should obey Him even when His instructions don't make sense. It's in these moments of uncertainty that our faith is most powerful.

The widow's situation was one of immense emotional and mental distress as she was at her wit's end, unable to find a way out. Yet, in her darkest hour, God's solution didn't come in a form that made any sense. Elisha's instructions to borrow vessels seemed like a contradictory suggestion, placing her in a mental conundrum. Facing the threat of losing her sons to creditors, how could borrowing more possibly be the answer? She must have had a series of questions, such as:

1. How could borrowing empty jars solve her debt crisis?
2. Where would she get oil to fill them?
3. Wouldn't this just add to her debt and embarrassment?
4. How could she face her neighbors after defaulting on previous loans that got her into this situation?

Yet, in her moment of desperation, she chose faith and obedience over logic and fear. We, too, battle with countless questions in those moments, just like the widow, especially when we consider how others perceive our predicament and how they might judge us. Similarly, in our modern lives, we often face situations that seem insurmountable, and our natural inclination is to rely on logic and practicality. When God's instructions seem to go against what we know or expect, it becomes a battle between what makes sense and what requires faith.

This tension is where growth happens, and it's where God tests our trust in Him. The widow's story teaches us that faith is not about understanding what is happening, but about obedience, even when the path ahead is unclear. Faith is about obeying in the unknown. The widow had every reason to question Elisha's suggestion of why borrowing more vessels would solve her financial woes, yet she refused to give in to doubt and obeyed—borrowing the vessels as instructed. Her simple act of faith unlocked the miracle that would change her life. This lesson applies to us today. Often, God requires us to act in faith, to obey His direction, even when we don't fully understand the plan.

God's instructions may seem impractical, or even counterintuitive, but obedience is the key that opens His door to blessings in our life. Modern-day Christians must learn to trust God's way even when it doesn't align with their worldly wisdom. The widow could have doubted Elisha and remained paralyzed by her situation, but her obedience, despite her mental struggle, led to divine provision. The widow's decision to obey Elisha's seemingly strange request exemplifies what it means to walk in faith when everything looks hopeless. With nothing but a small jar of oil, it would have been easy for her to doubt that God's plan would work. Yet, she chose to trust His word and act in faith by borrowing vessels, not knowing how their being filled would change her life. In the end, her faith was rewarded when the oil continued to flow until every vessel was filled.

Faith is not about believing when things make sense; rather, it's about believing and acting when they don't make sense at all. For modern Christians, this means trusting God even when our circumstances appear bleak and hopeless. Faith isn't truly needed when everything is going well, but true faith is demonstrated in moments of crisis—when you have nothing.

There are many biblical giants who also had their faith tested in the face of immense testing and hopelessness. One such person is the father of faith himself, Abraham, who in Genesis 22 was asked by God to sacrifice his son of Promise, Isaac. How could Abraham's lineage continue if he sacrificed Isaac? Yet, Abraham obeyed without hesitation, and just as he was about to carry out the sacrifice, God provided a ram as a substitute. God showed that He rewards Abraham's faith and obedience. God's ways often go beyond human understanding, but obedience leads to His blessings.

When the Israelites found themselves trapped between the Red Sea and Pharaoh's advancing army without a way out, they panicked. But God instructed Moses to raise his staff over the waters to part the sea, allowing the Israelites to cross on dry ground. This was an act of faith! Had they relied on logic, they might not have seen a possible escape. However, their obedience to God's plan led to their deliverance and the destruction of their enemies, the Egyptians. Faith often takes care of even the unexpected areas of our lives. By the sea, God made a way of deliverance while wiping out their enemies who were following them.

These are examples of when individuals faced what seemed like hopeless and impossible situations, yet by obeying God's word, they experienced miraculous results. Just like in the widow's story, when we walk in faith, God will reward us even when the path is uncertain. We all know the saying, "Faith without action is dead." It's not enough to pray and wait for God's intervention in our lives; we must also be willing to have faith and act in obedience to His direction. The widow could have simply prayed for a miracle, but without her active participation in borrowing vessels and pouring out her oil, no miracle would have occurred.

As modern-day Christians, we often fall into the trap of thinking that faith is just about prayer and letting Jesus take the wheel, but this is not a balanced theology. While prayer is an essential part of Christian living, God also requires us to take steps of faith through our actions. Whether it's starting a new venture, forgiving someone who hurt us, or stepping out of our comfort zone, our faith involves obedience that leads to action.

While the prophet's suggestion to borrow vessels may have seemed irrational to the widow, in following God's instruction through Elisha, she got a miraculous outcome. This teaches us that when we trust God's plan, even when it defies logic, we position ourselves for His supernatural provision. Our greatest struggle as believers is surrendering our understanding to God's higher wisdom and purpose for our lives by taking the necessary actions to demonstrate our faith. The Bible often reminds us that God thinks differently from us as finite individuals.

For My thoughts are not your thoughts, Nor are your ways My ways," says the Lord. "For as the heavens are higher than the earth, So are My ways higher than your ways, And My thoughts than your thoughts.
Isaiah 55:8-9

Just like the widow, we must learn to trust God's ways, even when they seem contrary to our understanding. Noah built an ark without ever experiencing or seeing rain, facing ridicule from his neighbors. In the end, his faith saved his entire family and the animals. He obeyed an illogical instruction, which led to his preservation. The woman with the issue of blood had suffered from a blood disorder for twelve long years and reached out to Jesus' hem by faith.

What I love about her story is that, unlike many others who received direct instructions from God or a prophet, she exercised her faith independently and acted upon it. She had lost all she owned and took a risk by seeking Him out. Her desperation activated her faith and brought about her complete restoration!

Now a woman, having a flow of blood for twelve years, who had spent all her livelihood on physicians and could not be healed by any, came from behind and touched the border of His garment. And immediately her flow of blood stopped. And Jesus said, "Who touched Me?" When all denied it, Peter and those with him said, "Master, the multitudes throng and press You, and You say, 'Who touched Me?' "But Jesus said, "Somebody touched Me, for I perceived power going out from Me." Now when the woman saw that she was not hidden, she came trembling; and falling down before Him, she declared to Him in the presence of all the people the reason she had touched Him and how she was healed immediately.

Luke 8:43-47

From a bleeding disorder of twelve years to complete healing; the woman with the issue of blood's belief in Jesus' power demonstrated her faith in Him. The truth of the matter is that whenever we walk in faith, we should be ready for all the things that will come to try and derail us from walking in obedience—from the widow's mental anguish to Noah's ridicule by his friends. We should expect that, in walking by faith, those who do not share the same faith will not understand our decisions, and it is not for them to. Decide today that you will walk by faith and not by sight, no matter what anyone says!

As always, there are those who will not walk in faith or take the necessary actions to do so. One such example is the young rich ruler in Matthew 19:16-22. The young man wanted eternal life but was not willing to give all he had to the poor in order to obtain it. Sorrowfully, he left because he wasn't willing to make the sacrifice and take the necessary actions. His inaction cost him everything, including the possibility of inheriting eternal life. The story of Lot's wife in Genesis 19:26 is reminiscent of many times when we look back while God is instructing us to move forward. Lot's wife was instructed, along with her family, to flee the city of Sodom and not look back. However, she disobeyed God's instruction by looking back and turned into a pillar of salt.

Her inability to follow through with God's command led to her demise. When we lack faith and obedience, we remain in the past, always looking back at "what used to be" instead of looking forward to "what could be." The sad part of looking backward is that the things we think we are missing are not as great as the new possibilities that lie ahead in the future! Let us learn the lessons of Lot's wife while embracing the endless opportunities and hope that the widow's story offers us all.

There might be things happening in your life right now that are beyond the limits of your understanding or even control, but do not be discouraged! Instead, move forward just like the widow did in her predicament, knowing that God's solutions are always perfect, even when they defy human logic. Trust that through His wisdom, we can experience the fullness of God's provision, protection, and blessings in our lives.

The only way to thrive and resist the temptation of relying on our own understanding is to:

1. Seek God's wisdom through prayer and His Word.

2. Listen for His specific instructions.
3. Obey promptly, even when it doesn't make sense.
4. Trust His outcomes, not our expectations.

That said, many contemporary Christians are facing what seem like hopeless situations. The widow's story offers several practical lessons to take away, and they are as follows:

1. Acknowledge your needs and limitations.
2. Seek godly counsel.
3. Be willing to take bold, faith-filled action.
4. Involve others in your journey of faith.
5. Create space for God to work (shutting the door).
6. Use what you have, even if it seems insignificant.
7. Expect God to multiply your resources supernaturally.
8. Keep "pouring out" until God's provision is complete.

In conclusion, the truth is that God often tells us to step out in faith when His instructions defy human reasoning. Considering the numerous biblical examples, such as Noah building an ark before rain even existed in Genesis 6 (which I consider innovative), do not be afraid when God tells you to do something that no one has ever done before. It means that He sees a pioneer within you. Abraham left his homeland for an unknown destination, seeking to explore new lands, and with that comes new opportunities.

Joshua marched around Jericho's walls along with Gideon, reducing his army from 32,000 to 300 men in Judges 7, speaking to quality over quantity! God often challenges our faith in the very areas that we are struggling in or have failed in the past, but He wants to promote us for our future no matter how bleak our circumstances might be looking at the moment. Understand that obedience activates God's power, as seen in the case of Elijah and the widow of Zarephath, who was facing starvation with her son. Her obedience resulted in her flour and oil miraculously lasting throughout the famine.

Or consider Peter stepping out of the boat in Matthew 14:22-33 in the midst of a storm, obeying Jesus' call to walk on water. Today, he remains the only man, after Jesus, to experience walking on water supernaturally! I also want to mention those like me, and Jonah, who obeyed after a brief stint with disobedience. Jonah was swallowed by a whale for three days before he repented and fulfilled his mission (do not be like us!).

Obey God no matter how difficult it may seem, knowing that faith without corresponding action is insufficient. When we combine unwavering trust in God with prompt obedience to His instructions, we position ourselves to experience His supernatural power. I close this chapter by asking the questions: In your own life,

1. What "empty vessels" is God asking you to gather?
2. What small resource (like the widow's oil) do you need to offer in faith?
3. How can you create space for God to work miraculously?

Remember, obedience often precedes understanding. Also, know that God often places us in situations that stretch our faith. So, take that step of faith today and watch God transform your impossibilities into testimonies of His faithfulness, love, and grace.

CHAPTER 20

BORROWING WITHOUT BORDERS

Transcending Borders

What crossroads of life are you currently facing that require you to step out of your comfort zone? Are you considering moving from an employee to an entrepreneur owning a business? Are you afraid of going away to college, leaving behind the safety of family and friends? Are you single and suddenly finding yourself in love with someone and talking about marriage? Okay, let's pause and take a look at life's crossroads, which can be daunting: should one aggressively choose to have a mastectomy due to a family history of cancer, or wait? Or walk away from an abusive relationship as it begins to affect one's children's mental welfare?

In the story of the widow and her jar of oil, we encounter a powerful lesson about faith that requires stepping outside of our comfort zones and taking bold action to achieve personal breakthroughs. The widow, faced with an impossible situation of crippling debt and the threat of losing her sons, had nothing but a small jar of oil to her name. So, when Elisha commanded her to borrow vessels from her neighbors, she found his direction both perplexing and daunting. Yet, she took a leap of faith and followed the prophet's instructions, pushing beyond the limitations she had likely placed on herself.

Just like the widow, many modern-day Christians often find themselves at life's crossroads when embarking on new ventures. Whether it's a new business idea, a career change, or a personal development journey, the widow's experience teaches us not to allow limitations—whether mental, physical, or circumstantial—to hold us back from success. It is imperative that we learn from the widow's story about breaking free from the boundaries we set for ourselves and stretching beyond our comfort zones if we are to confidently pursue new ventures and embrace life's opportunities.

The truth remains that the widow's initial response to Elisha's inquiry about what she had in her home was quite telling. She stated that she had nothing except a small jar of oil. This is an example of a mentality of lack, where we focus on what we don't have rather than what we do. She was blinded to the potential in the little she possessed because she had already mentally resigned herself to failure. However, the prophet saw beyond her lack and recognized the value in what she already had.

Sadly, many of us contemporary Christians in today's world often dismiss our talents, resources, and abilities because they seem insignificant to us. We tend to focus on what we 'lack' rather than on what we 'possess'. The widow teaches us that even the smallest asset, when coupled with faith and action, can lead to immense breakthroughs! We must learn to realign our focus in order to see potential, not scarcity, which often masks our insecurities. We must see differently if we are going to be blessed differently! Hence the story of Jesus healing the blind man at Bethsaida, where the first time he touched him the man stated that he saw men like trees.

> *Then He came to Bethsaida; and they brought a blind man to Him and begged Him to touch him. So He took the blind man by the hand and led him out of the town. And when He had spit on his eyes and put His hands on him, He asked him if he saw anything. And he looked up and said, "I see men like trees, walking." Then He put His hands on his eyes again and made him look up. And he*

was restored and saw everyone clearly.
Matthew 8:22-25

I love the story of Jesus healing the man because not only could the man not see, but the first time God touched him, he had an inverted vision. This means that the man saw men as trees, which speaks to how he saw himself as well. What I love is that God had already changed his location, God had already touched him, and God had already spoken to him, but he still could not see properly. This was until the Lord touched him the second time and he saw everyone clearly.

I love the widow's story, which starts off almost like the blind man's, but the difference is that she chose to see her debt differently and, therefore, approached it inversely as well. The widow could have been like the blind man, only seeing insurmountable debts as trees, but when she chose to fully trust by faith, she saw clearly what God was trying to achieve in her life—to be debt-free and walk in prosperity.

Modern-day Christians must learn to stop limiting themselves by focusing on scarcity and instead see the potential in what they have, whether it's a skill, an idea, or a passion. Let us realign our focus so that we can clearly see what God has in store for us and our families.

If we are going to walk in the fullness of what God has for us, it will require stepping boldly out of our comfort zones. Elisha's instruction to the widow was clear: *"Go and borrow vessels from all your neighbors—empty vessels; and not just a few"* (2 Kings 4:3). Imagine how humiliated the widow must have already felt by her financial situation; asking her to borrow from her neighbors must have been incredibly difficult.

The widow must have been forced to deal with a myriad of emotions within herself; she must have had to confront her pride as a famous prophet's widow. Then there is the emotion of shame and fear of the possibility of rejection by her neighbor. Think about the embarrassment, doubt, anxiety, insecurity, hopelessness, and even resentment she may have felt towards her late husband for leaving her in such a predicament. All of these emotions could have stopped her from stepping outside her comfort zone and seeking help, but they didn't! Instead, she processed them and stepped out, beyond her comfort zone, discovering her breakthrough.

For modern-day Christians, stepping outside our comfort zones is often where growth happens, and there's no way around it. Just as the widow had to knock on her neighbors' doors to borrow vessels, we, too, must learn to reach beyond our familiar surroundings and embrace the opportunities that lie outside our immediate comfort. This could mean seeking mentorship, asking for business advice, collaborating with people in your community, or even using social media to expand your reach.

In the business world, especially for aspiring entrepreneurs, it's essential to break through personal limitations. Comfort zones can become traps that prevent us from taking the necessary risks to grow. In my book *"Unlocking the Deborah in You,"* I state that "***Yesterday's risk takers are tomorrow's history makers***!" The widow's willingness to step out of her comfort zone and borrow vessels led to a life-saving miracle. In the same way, we must be willing to step into new territories, explore unfamiliar areas, and push ourselves to achieve personal success.

One of the significant lessons from the widow's story is that her breakthrough came when she went beyond the borders of her home: 'Faith Without Border.' The prophet's instruction was that she needed to borrow from her neighbors, meaning that her success wasn't confined to her own home or limited by what she had. It required her to expand her thinking into a transformative mindset in a way that she would be willing to seek help outside of her immediate environment. I am often surprised when people say things like, "I'm private" or "I don't like to ask anyone for help," yet they expect to be successful without interacting with others. Around the world, we've seen countries that open up their borders to interact with neighbors or internationally evolve into greater, more dynamic nations with thriving economies. This happens only when they adopt an elevated perspective.

As Christians, we often restrict ourselves to what feels safe or comfortable; often hesitating to expand our ideas, network, or business ventures because we fear failure or rejection. True growth and success often come from stepping beyond our familiar surroundings. Whether it's launching a product, expanding a business, or exploring a new career, we must be willing to push past our physical and mental borders.

Today, the internet and social media have made it easier than ever to break through these borders. Entrepreneurs and businesspeople can now reach customers worldwide, market their products globally, and collaborate with others from different locations. Like the widow, we must learn to think beyond the confines of our immediate environment and tap into the broader resources available to us.

Having already dealt with the negative consequences of borrowing, the widow was convinced by Elisha to borrow one more time—but this time, with a purpose behind it. She obeyed, and this borrowing was no longer a sign of financial strain, but a tool for her breakthrough! The lesson here is clear: not all borrowing is bad when it is done with a clear purpose and a doable plan. Borrowing, when done strategically, can be the key to financial success!

In modern-day entrepreneurship, borrowing to invest in your business or new venture can be a smart move if it's done with wisdom and strategy. Borrowing to invest in assets that will yield returns such as equipment, education, or marketing can lead to financial growth. Let us examine three powerful stories of individuals who stepped outside their comfort zones and experienced remarkable transformations in the process. We'll begin with the father of faith, Abraham!

Abraham is one of the most prominent examples of a man who stepped out of his borders, both literally and figuratively, when God called him to leave his homeland, his family, and everything familiar to him, and go to a land that God would show him. This was a monumental act of faith. The father of faith, not knowing where he was going or what the future held, trusted God and obeyed.
Genesis 12:1-4

In the process of stepping out in faith, God blessed Abraham immensely. He would not only become the father of many nations, the father of faith, but God promised that through him, all the families of the earth would be blessed. His faith and obedience not only changed his life but also impacted future generations.

Just like Abraham stepped out of his comfort zone, when the widow followed suit, God provided for her and her sons. When we step out in faith, trusting God even when it doesn't make sense, He meets us with abundance and provision. To date, no other man is recorded on earth to have walked on water apart from Peter, who stepped out of his comfort zone by faith.

When the disciples saw Jesus walking on the water, Peter boldly asked if he could join Him. Jesus invited him to step out of the boat and walk toward Him. Peter took the courageous step, leaving behind the safety and security of the boat. Though fear eventually gripped Peter and he began to sink, Jesus saved him, all the while commending his initial step of faith.

And Peter answered Him and said, "Lord, if it is You, command me to come to You on the water." So He said, "Come." And when Peter had come down out of the boat, he walked on the water to go to Jesus. But when he saw that the wind was boisterous, he was afraid; and beginning to sink he cried out, saying, "Lord, save me!" And immediately Jesus stretched out His hand and caught him, and said to him, "O you of little faith, why did you doubt?" And when they got into the boat, the wind ceased. Then those who were in the boat came and worshiped Him, saying, "Truly You are the Son of God."
Matthew 14:28-31

Peter experienced the extraordinary—he walked on water. Though his faith wavered, the act of stepping out in faith transformed him forever. It was a pivotal moment that strengthened his relationship with Jesus, teaching him to keep his eyes on Him. When he lost focus, he began to sink. It not only demonstrated God's power over nature but prepared him for leadership as well. By leaving the security of the boat and stepping into unfamiliar waters just like the widow, he got to experience the supernatural!

Both Peter and the widow faced fear and uncertainty, yet they chose to obey. In both instances, God responded to their faith. For the widow, this meant her small jar of oil was multiplied, meeting her needs and saving her sons from slavery. Peter, on the other hand, learned that even when we falter in our faith, God will miraculously intervene.

After Jesus' resurrection, several of the disciples, including Peter, returned to their old way of life—fishing. They had been out all night without catching anything. When Jesus appeared on the shore, unbeknownst to them, He instructed them to cast their nets on the right side of the boat. Despite their unsuccessful night of fishing, they obeyed His command. When they did, their nets were filled with so many fish that they couldn't haul them in.

I love the story of the disciples fishing, both for the first and last time; they had come full circle. Peter, John, and James were recruited from Lake Gennesaret after fishing all night with no success until Jesus borrowed Simon's boat in Luke 5:1-7. At that moment, they caught a boatload of fish—a net-breaking, record-setting haul.

> *But Simon answered and said to Him, "Master, we have toiled all night and caught nothing; nevertheless, at Your word I will let down the net." And when they had done this, they caught a great number of fish, and their net was*

breaking. So they signaled to their partners in the other boat to come and help them. And they came and filled both the boats, so that they began to sink. When Simon Peter saw it, he fell down at Jesus' knees, saying, "Depart from me, for I am a sinful man, O Lord!"

Luke 5:5-8

And here they find themselves at the seashore, fishing because their leader had been crucified, but they decided to obey the voice at the shore and caught an overwhelming load of fish. I believe this moment was not just about reaffirming the disciples' faith in Jesus and marking a new chapter in their ministry, but also an expression of love to John, Peter, and James—the original three He had first met in ministry.

It was also to solidify their permanent transition from fishermen to fishers of men. No matter how difficult things may get in the future, they will remember the two experiences on the waterfront. Just as the disciples had to cast their nets in a different direction, the widow had to take a different approach by borrowing vessels. Both examples show that when we obey God's instructions—even when they don't make sense to us—He provides abundantly. The widow's oil didn't run out, and the disciples' nets were filled to overflowing. Both stories illustrate the importance of obedience, faith, and stepping beyond the limitations of what seems logical.

One of the greatest challenges people face when starting a new venture is the fear of failure. Some even self-sabotage their own success. Like the widow, many of us struggle with self-doubt, wondering if we have what it takes to succeed. Her story teaches us that faith and obedience are powerful tools for building self-confidence. Even when borrowing vessels must have seemed like a risk, she trusted in the prophet's words, and her faith was rewarded. I would be remiss if I didn't leave you with some tools to help build your confidence as you expand your product or idea. Here are a few to try:

1. ***Identify Your Strengths:*** Just like the widow had a jar of oil, identify what you have; whether it's a skill, talent, or resource. Recognize its potential and how it can be developed into something greater. You can write down all the things you could potentially use, that skill, talent or resource, to create a financial opportunity.
2. ***Seek Wise Counsel:*** The widow sought advice from the prophet, something that modern-day Christians should do, as they should not attempt to do everything on their own. Seek counsel from mentors, experts, or people who have walked the path before you. Their insights can help you navigate challenges and avoid common pitfalls.
3. ***Take Small Steps:*** Expansion doesn't have to happen overnight. Start small and grow gradually. The widow didn't need to fill her house with vessels immediately; she started by borrowing what she could and trusting that each step would lead to greater results.
4. ***Embrace Failure as Part of Growth:*** Not every venture will succeed immediately, and that's okay. Failure is often part of the journey to success. The key is to learn from it and keep pushing forward. In my book *"Igniting Your Vision: Failures and Successes,"* I discuss how there are great benefits in failure,

just as there are limited lessons in success. Embrace the entire experience!

5. ***Rely on Faith:*** Just as the widow trusted Elisha's instructions, trust that God is guiding your steps. Faith in God's plan will give you the courage to take risks and step into new ventures with confidence.

I have met numerous Christians who in their time of trouble complained to me that no one in their circle could help them. When I asked about their circle, it was usually small and often close-minded. I told them they needed to expand their circle, and that's why many of them are stuck. I am a preacher, worship architect, prayer strategist, and prophetess, but my circle is expansive because I am also a friend, coworker, comedian, traveler, and advisor. I have friends ranging from believers to unbelievers! I believe I am to be all things to all people, that I might win some (1 Corinthians 9:22).

The widow's breakthrough didn't come solely from within her own home; it required her to connect with her neighbors and borrow from them. Imagine if your lifeline was with your next-door neighbor, but you had never built a relationship with them. Even the Bible instructs us to keep good relationships close.

Do not forget your friends or your father's friends.
If you are in trouble, don't ask a relative for help;
a nearby neighbor can help you more than relatives
who are far away.
Proverbs 27:10 (GNT)

This is a powerful lesson on the importance of expanding your network. No one succeeds in isolation, and in today's connected world, building a strong network is essential for growth and success. For modern-day Christians, this means building relationships within the community, joining business groups, networking on social media, or collaborating with others in your industry. The people around you may hold the key to your next opportunity.

Just as the widow's neighbors provided the vessels that led to her miracle, the people in your network can provide the resources, connections, or advice that can propel you to success. We must not allow the borders of our minds or physical circumstances to limit our potential. The widow had to expand her thinking, step out of her comfort zone, and borrow vessels from her neighbors to experience her breakthrough.

Likewise, modern-day Christians must learn to think outside the box, take risks, and pursue new ventures without allowing fear, doubt, or limitations to hold them back. In today's world, the borders that once limited us are dissolving through the power of the internet, social media, and global connectivity. We now have the ability to reach new markets, collaborate with people across the world, and grow our businesses in ways that were once unimaginable.

By following the lessons of the widow, we can remove the borders of our minds, step out in faith, and pursue opportunities that lead to both personal and financial success. Her story teaches us that success comes from a combination of faith, action, and the willingness to go beyond our limitations. When we do, we open ourselves to the miracles and breakthroughs that God has in store for us. Like the widow, we must learn to look beyond what we have, borrow wisely, and trust that God will provide the increase.

Just as Abraham, Peter, and the disciples stepped out in faith, so too did the widow. Each one of them allowed themselves to go beyond their comfort zone, and as a result, they experienced God's provision and blessings. Let us modern-day Christians learn from these biblical giants that we too can step out of our comfort zones and experience the same type of success—if we are willing to!

CHAPTER 21

HEAVEN'S STRATEGY, EARTH'S RESOURCES

The Power of Dual Networks

What if I tell you that there are different types of networks in one's life and that you are responsible for identifying early on what network supports you and in what capacity. This is vitally important to lay the proper foundations so that in your time of trouble, you are not left out in the cold. While in the previous chapters, we explored the concept of borrowing as a tool for financial growth rather than a path to financial ruin, here we are going to look at different types of support systems and their importance.

Also, why were the widow's neighbors willing to help her this time but not earlier? It is just as important to understand why people were willing to lend her empty jars of oil, while her husband had to turn to creditors for financial help. Let's examine why they supported her instead of her late husband. From these insights, we can learn valuable lessons to make better life decisions.

To differentiate between the network of Elisha versus the network of the community as it pertained to the widow, let us begin with the first network, which starts with the widow and Elisha. The widow-Elisha network was a spiritual one, where Elisha served as a source of divine guidance, spiritual mentorship, and prophetic insight. He provided the widow with a God-inspired strategy that aligned her faith with her actions. These types of networks focus on spiritual empowerment and alignment with God's will under His divine authority. Elisha's involvement highlights the importance of divine intervention in moments of despair.

Divine networks are essential in the lives of every believer; they are needed every day but especially in our most crucial moments when our faith is being tested. It's these networks that help activate our faith in God to follow His plans. Elisha's strategic guidance provided a clear, actionable plan rooted in divine wisdom, along with supernatural support that, in turn, opened doors to miracles beyond human effort. Without spiritual networks, we would struggle to gain the confidence needed to align our actions with God's will.

While these are great strengths, spiritual networks also come with challenges. Many Christians act as *'spiritual addicts,'* relying solely on revelation without obedience or faith. These individuals seek out 'prophets' or 'prayer consultants' with no intention of following divine strategies, believing instead that they can buy their way into a miracle.

Another drawback of spiritual networks is the belief that a man or woman of God can provide financial assistance. I often hear the frustrations of Christians who assume that their pastor or prophet—who often has limited practical resources—can meet their financial needs. Since spiritual networks do not typically offer immediate, tangible assets, including finances, believers may find themselves in a difficult situation. You find many believers who believe their spiritual network should also be their financial network as well but that is not how it works!

Now let us be clear, if your spiritual network has the ability to help, they should absolutely do so or send you to someone who can help you. Throughout the Bible, you will notice that spiritual networks rarely gave money but performed miracles or provided a prophetic strategy that solved a problem. Elisha didn't give the widow any money; instead, he provided her with a strategy that fulfilled a divine prophecy. This strategy enabled her to leverage her network and attain wealth. Similarly, in 1 Kings 17:8-16, Elijah and the widow of Zarephath were on the brink of perishing due to famine. However, Elijah instructed the widow to first make him a small cake, setting the stage for divine provision. She obeyed and in her last bit of food, a supernatural provision was provided without any material exchange.

And Elijah said to her, "Do not fear; go and do as you have said, but make me a small cake from it first, and bring it to me; and afterward make some for yourself and your son. For thus says the Lord God of Israel: 'The bin of flour shall not be used up, nor shall the jar of oil run dry, until the day the Lord sends rain on the earth.' So, she went away and did according to the word of Elijah; and she and he and her household ate for many days. The bin of flour was not used up, nor did the jar of oil run dry, according to the word of the Lord which He spoke by Elijah.

I Kings 17:13-16

The story of the fallen axe in **2 Kings 6:1-7** exemplifies how a spiritual network, rather than financial resources, can lead to restoration and miraculous outcomes. This narrative underscores the crucial role of spiritual relationships and divine strategies in overcoming life's challenges, even when monetary solutions are not an option. The man didn't cry out for money to replace the axe head, as the solution wasn't to gather resources to buy a new one, as it was borrowed. Instead, Elisha relied on God's guidance to solve the problem supernaturally.

But as one was cutting down a tree, the iron ax head fell into the water; and he cried out and said, "Alas, master! For it was borrowed." So, the man of God said, "Where did it fall?" And he showed him the place. So, he cut off a stick and threw it in there; and he made the iron float. Therefore, he said, "Pick it up for yourself." So, he reached out his hand and took it.
2 Kings 6:5-7

This underscores the value of spiritual networks that offer divine strategies, insight, and intervention rather than relying solely on financial resources or material aid. The axe head was recovered without any exchange of money, demonstrating that restoration can come through faith, divine intervention, and the support of a spiritual community. In the end, our spiritual networks are just as important as our communal ones.

What is a communal network? To me, it represents your practical connections—ranging from business associations and school alumni to community activism and neighborhood support. The widow's neighbors symbolize her human, social, and relational ties within her immediate environment. They provided the physical vessels she needed to carry out Elisha's plan. The purpose of a communal network is to offer resources, collaboration, and support to help fulfill a mission. What does your communal network consist of, and how are you building it for the future?

The greatest strength of a communal network is resource sharing. In the widow's case, this meant access to practical tools (vessels) necessary to achieve her goal. A communal network holds little value without the resources behind it, which rely on relational trust—where goodwill strengthens community bonds. Collaboration is a key component of a communal network, often showcasing how collective effort can help meet individual needs.

Finally, for a communal network to thrive, it must be sustainable. There must be ongoing opportunities for mutual support and reciprocity. In this chapter, we will explore how the widow leveraged this aspect of her community relationships with her neighbors.

There are also a few cons regarding communal networks; the main one is judgment or skepticism, in that some neighbors might have doubted her intentions and thus refused to help her and her family. Another aspect is relational dependency, where an individual becomes excessively reliant on their community to bail them out, leading to unmet expectations and frustration among community members who may feel taken advantage of. When these feelings arise, they can create fragility within the network, causing individuals to withhold resources or limit access—especially if strong relationships have not been built within the community.

Why are these cons very important when it comes to our communal relationships with others? Let me put it this way—have you ever met a married couple and found yourself liking one spouse more than the other? Or perhaps you've said something like, "I would help her if she wasn't married to that loser," or "If his wife weren't so difficult, I'd spend more time with him." The only reason you would make such a comment is if that individual were part of your communal network.

Now, I am not suggesting that the late prophet was a bad man at all, but I think the widow had a greater reputation for financial integrity than her dead husband. Despite her late husband's financial mistakes, the widow may have had a strong personal reputation for honesty and reliability, which encouraged her neighbors to support her. It is also possible that her husband had exhausted the goodwill of his community, leaving him unable to borrow from neighbors or friends—forcing him to turn to creditors instead.

The communal network thrives on communal honesty and compassion, which may be why her neighbors helped her, because they had compassion for her dire situation. The same community that did not help the widow while her husband was alive now empathized with her plight, willingly lending their vessels out of consideration for her and her children. Our communal relationships shape how people interact with us, often differing from spouse to spouse or neighbor to neighbor. Reputation matters in communities and can significantly impact whether those with the resources to help will step in to change your situation.

I also believe that many of the widow's neighbors were aware of Elisha's reputation as a prophet. By leveraging his request, they trusted that his instructions would lead to a miraculous outcome for her and her children. When a community believes in the integrity of a minister, they are more likely to extend kindness to those connected to them. Additionally, many people believe in second chances and may have seen this as an opportunity for the widow to rebuild her life.

I also believe that there are those individuals who felt that loaning one vessel per person would play a small yet meaningful role in a larger miracle, fostering a sense of community participation based on collective contribution. This may have been their way of inspiring hope within the widow, while some may have also feared that by not contributing to her and her children, they would miss out on being part of an extraordinary miracle performed by Elisha, the prophet.

It was also expected that the community would gather around and help a widow in distress as it was considered a moral and spiritual duty, especially where children were involved, out of cultural obligation. I am sure that many people admired the widow's boldness and determination to do whatever it took to save her children. It may have been the first time they saw her in this light, and it could have impressed the community enough to inspire their willingness to help change her circumstances. I firmly believe that many supported her out of personal gratitude for what her late husband had done for the community, seeing this as an opportunity to reciprocate the kindness her family had once shown.

While some may have felt societal pressure to help the widow so as to avoid judgment, others may have been motivated by curiosity—wondering how lending her their vessels might change her outcome or simply wanting to see how her situation would unfold. I also believe that Elisha's involvement enhanced the widow's credibility, which may have further encouraged people to support her.

I also believe that for many people, loaning an empty vessel posed minimal risk while the potential benefit of supporting a neighbor in need was significant. Hence small risk, big impact or reward. Since the widow wasn't asking for money or food but only for empty vessels, it was easier for people to say yes without any financial loss or cost to them. Ultimately, I believe many in the community had faith in the widow's borrowing with a purpose—much like building credit for a home. Her strategy and intention to honor her family's legacy may have inspired others to contribute.

The story of the widow shows us invaluable lessons about faith, provision, and community. The prophet's instruction for the widow to borrow vessels from her neighbors—people familiar with her and her situation—highlights the importance of a communal network. In her time of desperation, Elisha directed her to seek help from those closest to her, individuals who knew her family and understood her struggles. This directive wasn't just about borrowing vessels; it was about leaning on community support in a moment of need.

In modern terms, this story serves as a powerful reminder of the importance of reaching out to our own circle of family, friends, and neighbors when facing challenges. While today's world often emphasizes formal financial institutions like banks, which require collateral in the form of houses or other assets, the widow's story teaches us that there is another, more relational way to seek help—one that begins with the people who know us best.

Elisha's counsel to the widow to borrow vessels from her neighbors wasn't just about providing a practical solution to her problem. He was teaching her about expansion—about the power of community. The people she was instructed to borrow from were those who knew of her husband's death and the debt that threatened to enslave her children. In such a close-knit community, her neighbors would have witnessed her struggles, making them more inclined to help.

Elisha's instruction emphasizes the importance of vulnerability in times of need. The widow wasn't told to seek help from strangers or institutions indifferent to her story. Instead, she was directed to reach out to those who knew her well enough to empathize with her situation. This principle remains just as relevant today. Often, we overlook the help that is available within our immediate circle, fearing judgment or feeling ashamed of our needs.

Today's modern Christian has numerous ways to seek help in times of trouble, including platforms like GoFundMe, Kickstarter, GiveSendGo, ChristianFundMe, and many others that can be leveraged in difficult times. However, these apps do not replace communal relationships; rather, they thrive because of them. The widow's story teaches us that there is power in asking for help from those who already know and care about us; and we should not be ashamed to ask for their help when we are in a tight corner.

How are you leaning on your inner circle? Many people hesitate to ask friends and family for help due to the fear of appearing weak, inadequate, or overly dependent. In a society that celebrates independence and self-reliance, admitting our struggles can feel difficult. However, the widow's story reminds us that seeking support from those closest to us in times of need is not a sign of weakness but of wisdom.

The Bible is filled with stories of individuals who leaned on their inner circle during tough times. For example, when King David fled from Saul, he found refuge and support from Jonathan—Saul's own son and David's close friend (1 Samuel 20). Jonathan protected David at great personal risk, demonstrating the kind of loyalty and support that comes from leaning on those who truly know and care about us.

And as soon as the boy had gone, David rose from beside the stone heap and fell on his face to the ground and bowed three times. And they kissed one another and wept with one another, David weeping the most. Then Jonathan said to David, "Go in peace, because we have sworn both of us in the name of the Lord, saying, 'The Lord shall be between me and you, and between my offspring and your offspring, forever.'" And he rose and departed, and Jonathan went into the city.
I Samuel 20:41-42

Similarly, the widow's neighbors likely understood her situation and were willing to help by lending her the vessels she needed. Rather than judging her for her lack, they became part of the solution to her problem. This teaches us that sometimes the people closest to us are eager to help—but we must first be willing to ask.

One of the greatest barriers to seeking help from those who know us is the fear of judgment. It's natural to feel embarrassed about our struggles, especially when they involve financial difficulties, emotional pain, or failure. We worry that by revealing our vulnerabilities, we may be seen as less competent—or worse, as burdens to those we love.

But the widow's story offers a different perspective: in her moment of desperation, she didn't hesitate to ask for help. She may have felt ashamed to reveal the extent of her debt, yet she followed Elisha's advice and borrowed from those who knew her. In doing so, she discovered that her neighbors were willing to support her without judgment. This demonstrates that when we are open about our struggles, we often find people more willing to help than we expect. Many times, our friends and family are looking for opportunities to show their support, but they can only do so if we allow them to see our needs.

Another valuable lesson from the widow's story is the strategy of borrowing a little from many. Elisha instructed her to borrow "not a few" vessels from her neighbors, encouraging her to reach out to as many people as possible. This approach ensured she had enough vessels to contain the oil God would provide while also distributing the burden of her request across a wider group, minimizing the financial strain on any one person.

Today, this can be compared to requesting small favors or loans from multiple people rather than placing a heavy burden on one or two individuals. Seeking help from several sources can sometimes ease the pressure of relying on a single person for significant assistance. It serves as a reminder that there is strength in numbers and that small contributions from many can collectively provide the solution we need.

The Bible provides numerous examples of individuals who sought help from their inner circle in times of need, reinforcing the idea that God often provides for us through the people already in our lives. John Guare's 1990 play Six Degrees of Separation explores this same concept of interconnectedness, illustrating how individuals are linked through a small number of relationships. It simply suggests that all people are connected to one another by six or fewer social connections.

This is an important theory because throughout the world we do see levels of connectivity and it reminds us how small the world really is. For example, when Moses became overwhelmed with the task of leading the Israelites and judging their disputes, his father-in-law, Jethro, offered wise counsel on how to delegate his responsibilities (Exodus 18:13-24). Moses heeded Jethro's advice, which eased his burden and enabled him to lead more effectively. This demonstrates that a communal network is not just about financial resources—it also provides wisdom and guidance.

The same thing was applicable in the story of Naomi and Ruth; when Naomi lost her entire family, her daughter-in-law Ruth chose to stay by her side, traveling with her back to Israel and working to provide for them both. Ruth's loyalty and willingness to help Naomi during her time of need led her to work in the field of Naomi's relative Boaz. This ultimately led to blessings for both women, including Ruth's marriage to Boaz and the continuation of Naomi's family line (Ruth 1-4). These examples illustrate how God often works through the people closest to us, offering help and guidance through the relationships already in place.

For modern-day Christians, there are several ways to seek support from friends and family when facing challenges, drawing from the lessons in the widow's story. Some of these methods include:

1. ***Financial Help:*** Just as the widow borrowed vessels, there are times when we need financial assistance. Instead of requesting

a large sum from one person, consider asking multiple people for smaller amounts. This approach distributes the burden and increases the likelihood of receiving help.

2. ***Emotional Support***: In times of emotional hardship, don't hesitate to lean on your loved ones for support. Simply sharing your story and requesting prayers can often provide the strength needed to persevere.
3. ***Practical Assistance:*** If you need help with tasks, don't be afraid to ask friends and family for practical support. Whether it helps with childcare, school, transportation, or even advice, people are often more willing to help than we realize.

One of the key takeaways from the widow's experience is the importance of sharing your story with those who are in a position to help. As a consultant in corporate America, I was taught that sharing my story would make me more relatable and help clients feel a deeper connection. The widow also leveraged the power of her story—had she remained silent about her need, she would never have received the vessels required. Similarly, if we don't share our struggles with others, we can't expect them to help us.

It's natural to feel hesitant about sharing personal struggles, but vulnerability is often the key to receiving the help we need. The people closest to us care about us, and by sharing our stories, we give them the opportunity to support us in meaningful ways. From the widow's story, we learn that there is no shame in asking for help from those who know us best. Vulnerability is a crucial ingredient in achieving a breakthrough. The widow's willingness to leverage both her spiritual and communal networks teaches us that without both, she would not have experienced God's miraculous provision, saving her family from ruin.

As modern-day Christians, we too need both spiritual and communal (financial) networks. While money can address immediate physical needs, our spiritual networks provide solutions to deeper, underlying issues that we cannot see. We must remember that miracles aren't bound by finances—God's power operates beyond human resources and transcends monetary limitations.

While in moments of desperation, spiritual networks offer encouragement and guidance, there also lie practical strategies that are applicable to real-life situations as well. We must also embrace the fact we must put in the work expected. While our spiritual networks inspire innovative, God-given strategies to solve problems, our communal networks provide the financial help, emotional support, or practical assistance we need from those who know us best. Remember, God often works through the people in our lives, and by sharing our struggles, we open the door for His provision to flow through them.

CHAPTER 22

THE POWER OF ONE GOOD IDEA

One Idea, One Miracle

What if I told you that all you need is one good idea to change your entire life? Throughout history, countless individuals have taken a single idea and transformed their lives forever. Some even started with one invention, only to pivot when it didn't work as expected—ultimately leading to an innovation used for something entirely different. So, before you decide to abandon your idea, let me share the remarkable story of Alfred Fielding and Marc Chavannes.

In 1957, inventors Alfred Fielding and Marc Chavannes set out to create a three-dimensional plastic wallpaper—but they failed! However, instead of abandoning their idea, they pivoted and discovered that their wallpaper design could be repurposed as a protective packing material. This led to the invention of sealed air, commonly known today as bubble wrap! Now, imagine how a so-called failure turned into a multi-million-dollar concept that we still use today. This teaches us a valuable lesson—just as Elisha didn't need to give the widow money or pay off her debt, sometimes the key to a breakthrough isn't direct provision but a strategy to transform what we already have.

Instead, he gave her a practical idea to take the oil she already possessed and use it in an entrepreneuring way that she had never considered before. The key takeaway from this story is that sometimes, all you need is one idea—whether good or seemingly bad—to transform your life. Many successful businesses and individuals started with a single idea. It wasn't necessarily a grand or complex strategy, but rather a simple concept that was pursued with faith and perseverance. Like the widow, Christians today can learn to seek and recognize that one idea that has the potential to open doors to success, whether in business, relationships, or personal growth.

One of the most important lessons in the widow's story is that the source of her innovative idea came from Elisha, a man of God; more significantly, it came in a way she didn't expect. She approached him with her problem, and he responded with an assignment! Oftentimes, God gives us ideas from unexpected sources, yet many of us miss out on these opportunities because we fail to recognize the value of the idea due to its source. Sometimes, we dismiss suggestions simply because we don't view the person as an expert, or we are too familiar with them to take their insight seriously.

The truth is that God can use anyone to spark an idea that leads to an invention or breakthrough in our lives. Just as the prophet's instruction to the widow didn't seem grand at first, many successful ventures today began with simple, humble beginnings. For example, during the COVID-19 pandemic, while many businesses and individuals faced financial struggles, others seized the opportunity to start new businesses—and thrived.

During the COVID-19 pandemic, my car detailer started his business. He had always loved cleaning his car, and one day, his brother suggested he turn that passion into a mobile car cleaning business. At first, he scoffed at the idea—it didn't seem like a life-changing opportunity. But eventually, he decided to take his brother's advice. He launched his business, and just three years later, he retired from his six-figure government job to run a thriving mobile car cleaning service full-time.

The lesson is clear: be open to ideas, even if they don't come from a *"traditional"* source of wisdom or expertise. Sometimes, all you need is that one idea, regardless of its packaging, to transform your life.

Another big hurdle in life that I have discovered is the inability to overcome personal biases to receive ideas. This is because many people often reject even the best ideas simply because of the person or source from which they come. In the story of the widow, she trusted Elisha's idea even though he had no business background, and his instructions didn't seem logical. She could have allowed her biases to prevent her from following through, but instead, she chose obedience—and was rewarded. The Bible reminds us not to judge others by outward appearances but to seek divine guidance in all things, taking everything to God in prayer.

As Christians, we must be careful not to let familiarity or preconceived notions prevent us from receiving life-changing ideas. Sometimes, we dismiss advice simply because it comes from family members, friends, or acquaintances, assuming their insights aren't valuable. This mindset can be dangerous, causing us to overlook blessings that God has already placed in our path.

I am often reminded of the story of Moses, the prince turned fugitive, who was mistaken for an Egyptian all because he came wrapped up in an unfamiliar package, so the daughters of Jethro just left him at the well after he helped them. The daughters assumed him to be Egyptian due to his clothes and their personal biases. It would be later on that both Jethro and his daughters came to realize that Moses would be the prophet of God, Jethro's future son-in-law and the deliverer of Israel.

When they came to Reuel their father, he said, "How is it that you have come so soon today?" And they said, "An Egyptian delivered us from the hand of the shepherds, and he also drew enough water for us and watered the flock." So he said to his daughters, "And where is he? Why is it that you have left the man? Call him, that he may eat bread."
Exodus 2:18-20

Proverbs 11:14 says, *"Where no counsel is, the people fall: but in the multitude of counselors there is safety."* We must recognize that good counsel can come from various sources—whether from a young child or an elderly person. It's essential to be both discerning and humble enough to accept valuable ideas, even when they come in unexpected ways. When others share their ideas with us, we should treat them with respect and consideration rather than dismissing them outright.

Rejecting someone's idea outright can lead to missed opportunities and even strained relationships. Instead of dismissing ideas too quickly, Christians can take intentional steps to harness and leverage the wisdom shared by others. Here are some practical ways to do so:

1. ***Listen Actively:*** Take the time to fully understand the idea being presented, even if it doesn't seem like something you would normally consider.

2. ***Pray For Discernment:*** Ask God for wisdom and clarity to know whether this idea is something you should pursue.

3. ***Take Small Steps:*** If the idea seems promising but you're unsure, start small. Just as the widow had to start by borrowing

vessels, you can take small actions to test the viability of an idea.

4. *Give Credit:* If an idea leads to success, acknowledge the person who shared it with you. Doing so not only strengthens relationships but also honors the process through which God works, demonstrating your integrity.

The widow's story holds several key lessons that 21st-century Christians can apply to their lives, especially during times of financial struggle when they desperately need a breakthrough idea to overcome hardship.

1. ***Start With What You Have:*** The prophet didn't give the widow something new but told her to use what she already had available—a little jar of oil. Many times, our breakthrough is hidden in the resources we already possess.

2. ***Be Open to Unconventional Ideas:*** The solution to the widow's problem wasn't typical or expected. This means we must be willing to embrace ideas that may seem unconventional, yet doable.

3. ***Act in Faith:*** The widow's obedience to the prophet's idea was an act of faith. Similarly, when God gives us an idea or inspiration, we must be willing to act, even if we don't fully comprehend the outcome.

4. ***Involve Your Community:*** The widow didn't solve her problem alone. She involved her neighbors by borrowing vessels from them. In today's world, success often comes from collaboration and involving others in our journey.

5. ***Trust God's Provision:*** Ultimately, the widow's financial breakthrough came because she trusted God's provision. As Christians, we must trust that when we act on the ideas given to us, He will provide the resources and opportunities we need to bring them to fruition.

Oftentimes, the stories we hear about great single ideas are born out of the most insignificant moments, a place of immense struggle, or even poverty. Regardless of the reasons behind why an individual starts a business, the fact remains that one idea can be life-changing. One great real-life scenario where an individual used a single idea to overcome his financial struggle to succeed is the story of **Howard Schultz**, the founder of Starbucks.

Schultz had the idea to transform Starbucks from a small coffee bean seller into a café that served coffee drinks. This vision revolutionized the coffee industry and made Starbucks a household name worldwide. Similarly, another groundbreaking idea was nurtured by two brothers, Orville and Wilbur Wright—famously known as **"The Wright Brothers."** They believed that powered flight was possible, and their idea changed the course of history. While they didn't invent flying machines overnight, their persistence with this one idea eventually changed the world of transportation forever.

From the biblical era to modern times, individuals with transformative ideas have not only changed their own lives but also impacted those around them. For instance, Jethro taught Moses the concept of delegation, enabling him to lead the Israelites more effectively. Many of today's leaders have embraced this age-old principle, using it to distribute authority within their companies and organizations.

A single idea can also change and shape the lives of individuals such as one Naaman, the leprous Syrian general who got the idea of getting healed from his wife's servant girl. She suggested he go to the prophet Elisha for healing; following the prophet's advice, he was miraculously healed! All of these examples, old and new, show that God often uses people to share ideas that can change our lives and bring about His purpose as well. Our ideas, no matter how small, grant us access to the creative nature of God. It was through an idea and a spoken word that the world was formed, and we continue to live and experience God's power daily.

For modern-day Christians to gain access to life-changing ideas, we must first of all develop the ability to actively listen and then implement the ideas we have been given. Here are some ways to build this habit:

1. ***Stay Open-Minded:*** Be open to considering ideas from anyone, even if the source is unexpected or unconventional. Avoid dismissing an idea too quickly simply because you do not fully understand it or have not taken the time to explore it. Stay flexible.

2. ***Seek Advice:*** Don't be afraid to ask for input from others. Sometimes, the best ideas come from conversations with people who see things from a different perspective.

3. ***Take Action:*** Once you receive an idea, don't let it sit idle: act on it, test it, and see where it leads. Years ago, I had an idea during a trip to London, which I shared with a friend. However, we sat on it for five years, and by the time we were ready to act, it had already gained popularity in the United

States—marking the end of that opportunity. So, make hay while the sun shines!

4. ***Cultivate Gratitude:*** When someone shares an idea that works, shows gratitude and appreciation. This keeps the door open for more valuable input in the future. Cultivate a spirit of gratitude so that people will not only continue sharing ideas with you, but also provide information that can help refine and enhance your ideas.

In conclusion, all the widow needed was one transformative idea—just a spark that would change her life forever. 21st-century Christians must cultivate the habit of recognizing the power of a single good idea and develop the willingness and courage to act on it, no matter how small or unexpected it may seem. By remaining open to ideas from others, taking action, and trusting in God's provision, we can unlock the doors to success and breakthrough, especially in times of financial struggle.

Many of my friends often come to me with numerous ideas, and I always make time to listen—whether it's an opportunity they want to pursue or something they believe will interest me. In return, I remain respectful and gracious, even if I never implement the idea.

The key is to remain humble, teachable, and open to receiving from others. God often uses the people around us to deliver ideas that can change our lives forever. Let us commit to listening, learning, and acting on the wisdom God places in our path, knowing that sometimes, all we need is one good idea to transform our future.

CHAPTER 23

THE WIDOW'S PERFECT PRODUCT

Supply, Demand, and Oil

When you think of a product that you really like, what attracted you to the product? Was it the product itself, or did the packaging play a significant role in how much you liked it? What do you consider a good product with excellent packaging? As an author and publisher, I believe in not only creating a great product but also offering outstanding packaging. Your client's experience with your product should be so positive that they keep coming back for more.

The story of the widow's jar of oil teaches a powerful lesson in the combination of faith, innovation, and practicality. Elisha didn't just give her an idea, but he showed her how to turn what she had into something of ***'value'***. She already had oil, but it wasn't until he instructed her to borrow vessels to pour the oil into that her breakthrough arrived. Perhaps the widow didn't just sell the oil; her true innovation was selling the oil in jars! This gave her product more value than just the liquid inside. The concept of packaging a product in a way that enhances its usability or attractiveness can change everything for a business.

As Christians looking to build successful businesses, the story of the widow teaches us that it's not just about having a great product or idea; it's about how that product is presented and how the idea is executed. We must learn that innovation isn't just about invention; sometimes, it's about taking something ordinary and making it extraordinary through packaging, presentation, and accessibility.

Elisha's idea for the widow was groundbreaking for her era and situation; and would have meant nothing if she didn't have a great product to sell. At that time, people often had to carry along a jar if they needed to transport a product. For the widow, the oil was valuable— it was something people needed, but it was more than just having oil. Imagine a scenario where, every time people wanted to buy oil, they had to bring their own empty jars to fill. Through a godly idea, the widow recognized an opportunity to add value by selling the oil in prepackaged jars.

This small but significant change could have made all the difference. Her product wasn't just the oil—it was oil in a jar! It was convenient, ready to use, and more appealing than what her competitors might have been offering, which was just oil. In today's business world, the lesson is clear: even with a great idea, it needs to be paired with a great product. The product must meet a need, but beyond that, it must stand out from the crowd. It must have a differentiating factor to it, something that gives it an edge over other products like it in the market!

This means that whether through innovation, presentation, or convenience, your product needs to offer something that makes people choose it over other available options. It's important to understand that there are certain key elements to building a successful business, and it starts with innovation, which is at the heart of every great business.

Innovation is at the heart of every great business. It's not always about creating something new from scratch; often, it's about taking something existing and improving it. The widow likely wasn't the only person selling oil, but by packaging her oil in a jar, she could have added ease and convenience for her customers.

Christian business owners need to cultivate a spirit of innovation as just having a product isn't good enough; we must creatively think of ways to make our product user-friendly, easily accessible, and more appealing. It's vitally important to understand that innovation doesn't always mean a groundbreaking invention, but it can mean simplifying a product or a process to make it more efficient.

A good example is the difference between buying coffee beans and buying a cup of coffee; it's essentially the same product, but it's the packaging that adds significant value. Coffee in a cup allows for the convenience of taking it on the go. People are willing to pay more for convenience and ease, and applying this principle to one's business model can lead to success.

The widow gained a profound new respect for the oil as she viewed her situation with a fresh perspective after receiving the prophet's instruction. Previously, she may have seen the oil as just another household commodity in her kitchen, but by the word of the prophet, she began to see her opportunities through the lens of innovation when Elisha told her to borrow empty jars to fill. It was at that precise moment that she caught the vision and began to repackage the oil in a manner that people would want to buy both the bottle and the jar together!

If you're a Christian sitting on any ideas today, think of several ways you can repackage your product to make it more accessible, user-friendly, and appealing. Here are a few suggestions:

1. ***Convenience:*** Make your product easier to use. If there's a way to save your customers time or effort, they will appreciate it and will likely choose your product over others.
2. ***Presentation:*** How your product looks matters. Packaging, branding, and the overall aesthetic can make a significant difference in attracting customers.
3. ***Accessibility:*** Make sure your product is easy to find and purchase. Whether through online platforms, social media, or physical locations, accessibility is key to reaching more people.
4. ***Personalization:*** Tailoring your product to meet the specific needs or preferences of your customers can set you apart from competitors.
5. ***Innovation in Distribution:*** Like the widow going to her neighbors, think about different ways or platforms you can leverage to reach your customers. Don't limit yourself to just one channel—explore multiple avenues for distribution.

With all these recommendations, your product can remain the same, but it's up to you to find innovative ways to present it and deliver it in a manner that makes it more attractive and valuable.

With all these ideas for repackaging your product, an idea means nothing without a great product to back it up! An unapplied idea is like an empty promise—there's no delivery because there's no product! Let me put it in perspective: the widow's oil was valuable, which is why the prophet's idea worked. Similarly, when we have an idea, it's crucial that the product we offer matches the potential of that idea.

Consider this: if you have a great marketing plan but a subpar product, customers may buy it once, but they won't return. Your product needs to deliver on the promise your idea makes. This means putting effort into quality, ensuring that your product does what it's supposed to do, and continually refining it to meet the needs of your customers.

In the modern business world, your product must stand out not only for its utility but also for the experience it offers. Think of companies like Apple, which have mastered the art of combining innovative ideas with great products. Their success lies in the fact that their products match the boldness of their ideas.

While having a great product can be exciting, it's equally important to think about the different ways that the product can complement other offerings or ideas. In the widow's case, selling the oil in jars may have been her way of adding value to her product. Additionally, she could have explored other ways to expand her business. For example, once she became known for selling oil in jars, she could have moved into selling jars and other household items that complemented her oil business, thus expanding her empire.

Christian business owners need to think creatively about how they can add complementary products or services to their offerings. This can lead to additional streams of income without requiring a complete shift in focus, while also expanding their customer base and influence. A prime example would be a baker who specializes in cakes also offering cake-decorating classes or selling cake-decorating kits.

Another example would be a graphic designer who offers website-building services or social media management packages alongside their design work including making logos, business cards, etc. This type of business concept could work just as well for an individual selling essential oils. They could branch out by selling diffusers, and bottles, or even offering workshops on the benefits of using oils. The next step could be expanding into lotions as well. By thinking about how your product can complement other areas, you open up new avenues for income and growth opportunities.

Another aspect of business growth is repackaging your idea or product, which can revolutionize your business if you have the right product. Sometimes we create products that don't work the way we'd like them to, which is why we must learn how to pivot when things need to change. There are real-life scenarios where key individuals repackaged an original product or idea and found great success in the process. Here are a few examples.

1. ***Sara Blakely, Founder of Spanx:*** Blakely transformed the traditional concept of shapewear by reimagining it as more comfortable and user-friendly. By prioritizing ease of use and comfort, she turned her idea into a billion-dollar brand.

2. ***Reed Hastings, Co-Founder of Netflix:*** Netflix began as a DVD rental service by mail. Recognizing the growing trend of digital streaming, Hastings shifted the business model to a subscription-based streaming platform, revolutionizing how we consume entertainment.

3. ***Tupperware:*** Earl Tupper didn't invent food storage, but he elevated it with his innovative airtight plastic containers. He revolutionized the market by introducing a unique

packaging concept and creative distribution methods, such as Tupperware parties.

4. ***Amazon:*** Jeff Bezos launched Amazon as an online bookstore. Seeing the potential in e-commerce, he expanded the platform to sell virtually everything, transforming it into the largest online retailer in the world.

Repackaging didn't just start in the 21st century; it also happened in biblical times. Here are three examples we can draw from those repackaged ideas that led to the success of these individuals, starting with Joseph.

1. ***Joseph in Egypt*** (Genesis 41:33-36): Joseph didn't just interpret Pharaoh's dream; he transformed the common practice of storing grain into a national survival strategy. By proposing the idea of stockpiling grain during the seven years of abundance, he innovated a solution that saved Egypt from devastation during the famine.

2. ***Moses and the Bronze Serpent*** (Numbers 21:4-9): When the Israelites faced a deadly crisis, Moses devised a unique solution by creating a bronze serpent and lifting it on a pole as a symbol of healing. This creative approach introduced a new method to address a critical issue effectively.

3. ***Jael and Sisera*** (Judges 4:17-22): Jael turned everyday household items into tools for victory. When Sisera, the enemy general, sought refuge in her tent, she gave him milk and a blanket to lull him into a false sense of security. Seizing the opportunity, she used a hammer and tent peg—ordinary

tools from her home—to decisively eliminate him and secure victory for Israel.

The truth is that reimagining or repackaging products, ideas, and services has been around for a long time and speaks to one's ability to pivot when necessary. Success in business often comes down to the alignment of three key components: your product, your packaging, and your idea. All three must work together harmoniously to create a great business.

1. ***The Product:*** This is the core of your business. It must meet a need or solve a problem while adding value.
2. ***The Packaging:*** This is how your product is presented. It needs to be attractive, convenient, accessible and user-friendly to your target market. Your packaging should also enhance the product's appeal and usability.
3. ***The Idea:*** This is the concept that drives your business. It's the spark of innovation that sets you apart from the competition, differentiating your product from your competitors.

When these three elements come together, they create a powerful force that can lead to financial success and impact, just as the widow had a great product (oil), the right packaging (jar), and the right idea (collecting empty jars from Elisha). In the biblical account of the widow and the jar of oil from 2 Kings 4:1-7, we see a profound lesson in how a great idea, coupled with a solid product, can lead to extraordinary results.

Prophet Elisha didn't just give the widow an idea; he guided her to see the value in what she already had, which came in the form of the oil.

Yet, it was her innovative approach to packaging the oil that made the difference. This chapter explores why the widow's success wasn't just about having a good idea, but also about the quality of her product and its presentation. It highlights the importance of innovation and proper packaging in turning an idea into a thriving business.

One of the powerful lessons here is recognizing that the widow's successful business venture hinged on having a valuable product. Her oil wasn't just any oil, but one that people needed and wanted. Her innovative idea to sell the oil in jars made it more accessible and appealing compared to the traditional method of buying oil. With the widow, you could just pick up a jar of oil on the **'go.'**

In today's business world, having a great idea alone is not enough; your product must meet a demand and stand out in some way. It must have a differentiating factor, and the widow's was likely the convenience of her oil being housed in jars, adding further value to her product. This lesson applies to modern Christians looking to start or improve their businesses. The quality of your product must align with the promise of your idea; without a great product, even the best idea can fall flat.

Innovation is crucial in any business venture; it's not just about coming up with something entirely new, but also about enhancing existing concepts. For the widow, the innovation might have been in the way she packaged her oil, making it more convenient for customers. Christians need to cultivate a spirit of innovation, which means always looking for ways to improve on what we already have. Here are some innovative approaches to business:

1. ***Identify Pain Points:*** Understand the challenges your customers face and find ways to alleviate them. For instance, if customers have to carry their own jars, offering pre-filled jars could add value.
2. ***Simplify Processes:*** Streamline processes to make them easier for your customers. This could be through better packaging, improved customer service, or more efficient delivery methods.
3. ***Enhance Usability:*** Make your product more user-friendly. This could involve redesigning the product for better functionality or creating complementary products that enhance the main product's value.
4. ***Stay Current:*** Keep up with industry trends and adapt accordingly. Innovation often involves staying ahead of the curve and meeting evolving customer needs.

Innovation is about making your product or service stand out and address needs in a way that others might not have considered or have failed to do so successfully. The story of the widow teaches us that the way we present our product can make a significant difference in how successfully we sell it. By borrowing vessels and selling oil in jars, she made it easier for customers to purchase and use the oil.

Here are several ways Christians can view opportunities and repackage them for better accessibility:

1. ***Design Convenience:*** Make your product or service easier to access. For example, if you sell food, consider offering pre-packaged meals for convenience.

2. ***Improve Presentation:*** Invest in attractive packaging that catches the eye and communicates the product's benefits clearly.

3. ***Offer Bundles:*** Create product bundles that offer added value, such as combining related items at a discounted price.

4. ***Provide Customization:*** Allow customers to customize their purchases to better meet their individual needs.

5. ***Enhance Delivery:*** Offer flexible delivery options, such as subscription services or on-demand delivery, to make it easier for customers to receive their products.

By refining how your product is presented and delivered, you can enhance its appeal and make it more accessible to your target audience. If you're not yet financially ready to scale up, consider incorporating customization and flexible delivery options as future strategies. These services can add value and attract more customers as your business grows.

While a great idea is the foundation of any business, its success depends largely on the quality of the product. The widow's oil was valuable because it met a need, but its presentation in jars added even more value. This likely enabled her to sell her newly jarred oil at a higher price than sellers who only offered unbottled oil. Here's why product quality and innovation are crucial:

1. ***Product Quality:*** Ensures that your product meets or exceeds customer expectations. Poor quality can damage your reputation and reduce customer trust.

2. ***Innovation:*** Helps differentiate your product from competitors. Even if you offer a similar product, unique features or better packaging can set you apart.

Your product should be strong enough to stand on its own merit, but its presentation and innovation can further enhance its attractiveness and marketability. Earlier in this chapter, I discussed the importance of having a complementary product to increase your income. While for the widow, the jar itself may have been an innovation that added value to her oil, today's Christians have many different ways to generate extra income. Here are a few ways to do so:

1. ***Add-On Sales:*** Offer complementary products or services that enhance the primary product. For instance, if you sell coffee, consider selling coffee mugs or brewing accessories.
2. ***Subscription Models:*** Create a subscription service for regular delivery of your product. This ensures steady revenue and builds customer loyalty.
3. ***Workshops or Classes:*** Offer training or workshops related to your product. For example, if you sell cooking equipment, consider offering cooking classes.

By finding ways to complement and enhance your primary offering, you can create new revenue streams and increase overall profitability. In conclusion, the story of the widow has taught us the power of repackaging for success. Joseph's practical idea of storing grain during the years of plenty evolved into a national strategy, demonstrating how innovation can lead to national success. Likewise, Jeff Bezos' online bookstore expanded into various product categories, transforming into a comprehensive online shopping experience worldwide.

When we open ourselves to repackaging an idea, it can lead to tremendous success—whether personally or nationally—provided that the product and its presentation align with market needs. For a business to thrive, the product, packaging, and concept must work together seamlessly to create a powerful formula for success. The widow's story exemplifies how combining these elements can lead to remarkable results. By investing in each aspect—product quality, innovative packaging, and a compelling idea—you set the stage for a successful business venture.

Embrace innovation while enhancing your product's presentation to ensure that your idea is supported by a strong and valuable product. With these elements working together, you can transform your business vision into a successful reality and make a lasting impact in the marketplace.

CHAPTER 24
FROM HEARTBREAK TO HUSTLE

Phoenix Rising

What if I told you that tragedy has often been the steppingstone for certain individuals to find their voice and change the course of history? Let me share the story of Candy Lightner. In 1980, she founded Mothers Against Drunk Driving (MADD) after her 13-year-old daughter, Cari, was killed by a repeat drunk driver. Fueled by grief, she transformed her tragedy into a national movement, advocating for stricter laws to combat drunk driving.

MADD's early efforts led to significant changes, including raising the legal drinking age to 21 through the National Minimum Drinking Age Act of 1984, lowering the legal BAC limit to 0.08%, and implementing measures such as sobriety checkpoints and ignition interlock devices. These reforms have played a crucial role in reducing drunk driving deaths across the U.S.

Today, MADD continues its mission to end drunk and drugged driving, support victims, and prevent underage drinking, leaving an enduring legacy of saving lives and transforming societal attitudes toward impaired driving. While Candy founded a nonprofit, the fact remains that she used her tragedy to discover her calling and change American laws related to drinking.

There are many others, like the widow, who have stepped into entrepreneurship through tragedy, oftentimes unintentionally. Many people have leveraged loss to find a new purpose, just as the widow did. Her tragedy became the birthplace of a new business opportunity. When faced with debt and the threat of losing her children, she turned to the prophet Elisha for help. What she received was more than just a miracle; it was the seedling of entrepreneurship.

This chapter explores how Christians, particularly women, can discover their purpose and calling in the midst of loss, tragedy, or financial struggle. It encourages those currently facing difficulties to view this season as an opportunity to step out of their comfort zones and embark on a new path—perhaps one they never imagined.

The widow's story is a powerful journey from debt to entrepreneurial success. What makes it particularly compelling is that she began her business from a place of deep loss. Having just lost her husband and facing financial ruin, she found the courage—at her darkest moment—to follow the prophet's advice and start her own business. Had her husband not died, she might never have discovered her entrepreneurial potential. It makes me wonder how many of us are sitting on untapped potential simply because we've never faced a tragedy strong enough to push us beyond our comfort zones!

This teaches us an important lesson: sometimes, adversity is the catalyst for discovering our true purpose and hidden identity. The widow could have been paralyzed by fear or self-pity, but instead, she embraced an unexpected opportunity to step into a role she never envisioned for herself. She went from being a housewife with no marketable skills to a successful businesswoman. All along, she carried within her the power to create wealth—her true identity was more than just a housewife; she was a business mogul in the making!

What is your true purpose? What hidden identity lies dormant within you, buried beneath routine and familiarity? Will it take adversity to bring it to the surface, or will you uncover it on your own? It has been noted that challenges drive entrepreneurship. As the saying goes, "Necessity is the mother of invention." This proves that many times, struggle is the perfect catalyst for stepping out on your own. While it may seem counterintuitive, times of hardship and loss can actually be the ideal moments to consider entrepreneurship. Here are several reasons why:

1. ***You're Already Out of Your Comfort Zone:*** Struggle forces you to step out of the 'familiar' and when you are already uncomfortable, it's often easier to take risks, because the fear of failure seems less daunting than remaining in a painful situation.

2. ***New Perspective:*** Pain and loss often give you a new perspective on life. You start to value things differently, which can lead to creative solutions and new ideas. This can even lead you to pivot into a new career or line of business.

3. ***Necessity Breeds Innovation:*** When faced with a financial struggle, people often become more resourceful. You start looking for ways to solve problems, and this mindset is the foundation of entrepreneurship.

4. ***Motivation to Succeed:*** Financial pressure or the desire to change your situation can be a powerful motivator. In multi-level marketing, you are told to find your **"WHY."** The widow's *'why'* was saving her children from slavery, fueling her motivation. When we find our why, it's when we discover who we really were meant to be. The widow was meant to be a business mogul, yet it took a loss to push her to act.

5. ***Discovering Hidden Talents:*** Sometimes, it is only through adversity that we uncover talents or interests we never knew we had. The widow never envisioned herself as a businesswoman, but her circumstances revealed her entrepreneurial potential.

For modern-day Christians who find themselves in similar circumstances, this can be the perfect time to reflect on the new paths God may be calling them to explore. While we do not celebrate loss or tragedy, many people often discover purpose through pain. It is important to recognize that God can use difficult situations to reveal new purposes in our lives.

The widow's tragedy became the starting point for her entrepreneurial journey. She had no idea that her small jar of oil would become the foundation of a successful business, but God used her pain to guide her toward a new path. I also want to acknowledge that sometimes, God has been calling us to step out onto the water, but fear holds us back. Then, when tragedy strikes, we suddenly become open to new ideas and opportunities.

Contemporary Christians facing loss or hardship can look to the widow's story for inspiration. Could it be that God is using your current situation to reveal a new calling? Is it something you may never have considered or perhaps only toyed with in the past? Here are some ways to nurture your hidden potential:

1. ***Reflect on Your Interests and Passions:*** What activities or skills have you always enjoyed but never pursued? This could be a clue to your next calling or opportunity.

2. ***Look for Unmet Needs:*** Just like the widow filled a market need by selling oil, you can look for gaps in your community or industry and see how you can meet them.

3. ***Seek God's Guidance:*** Pray for clarity and guidance during this time. Ask God to reveal the opportunities He has for you in this season of life.

4. ***Talk to Others:*** Sometimes, others see our potential more clearly than we do. Reach out to trusted friends or mentors and ask them for their perspective on what you might be called to do.

5. ***Take Small Steps:*** You don't have to start big. The widow didn't open a large store; she simply borrowed vessels from her neighbors and began filling them. Start with what you have, and let God multiply your efforts.

As Christians, we draw strength from knowing that God often uses our darkest moments to bring about new beginnings. In times of loss or hardship, consider these steps to transform your situation into a divine opportunity:

1. ***Start Small:*** Don't despise small beginnings (Zech 4: 10). The widow started with a tiny jar of oil, and God multiplied it. Start with the resources and skills you already have.

2. ***Be Willing to Learn:*** If you've never considered entrepreneurship, take the time to educate yourself. There are countless free resources online, as well as local organizations that offer support for start-ups and small businesses.

3. ***Network and Connect:*** Reach out to others for advice and support. The widow leaned on her community to borrow vessels. You can lean on your community by networking with other entrepreneurs or joining a business group.
4. ***Stay Focused:*** It's easy to get overwhelmed when starting something new. Stay focused on your goal, and trust God to provide the resources and opportunities you need. You must approach your business with laser focus and see its importance so that you do not get off track (Nehemiah 6:3).
5. ***Trust God's Timing:*** The widow didn't know how her situation would resolve, but she trusted the prophet's instructions. Similarly, trust that God's timing is perfect, and He will open doors for you at the right time.

It is essential that women are empowered to find their voices through entrepreneurship. In my book, "*Woman, God Has Given You Your Voice Back,*" I emphasize that the power of your voice will create your platform. The widow's story is a testament to the impact of women in business—women who use their voices to transform their circumstances. I have met numerous businesswomen who, more often than not, pursued entrepreneurship out of passion or a desire for independence.

As a faithpreneur, I have spoken with many Black American businesswomen, and a common theme among them is that the loss of employment often pushed them into business ownership. I find this deeply relatable, as I pursued entrepreneurship and authorship after an unexpected layoff. The refusal to pay me my bonus—combined with the experience of working while battling COVID—made me even more determined to find a way to own and secure my financial future.

Many women, just like the widow, refuse to allow their circumstances to define them. Instead, the widow found a way to support herself and her family through entrepreneurship. For many Christian women, societal, racial or cultural expectations may limit their potential. Women are often chided to focus on their roles as wives or mothers. They are often discouraged from pursuing their entrepreneurial aspirations. But the widow's story encourages us to break free of these limitations and pursue the opportunities God has for us.

Here are some home-based businesses that women have started and turned into million-dollar companies:

1. ***Chichi Eburu (Juvia's Place):*** This Nigerian-born entrepreneur started her business with just $2,000 in savings, operating from her home to create bold, high-pigment makeup products that celebrated African heritage and catered to deeper skin tones. Today, this multi-million-dollar venture has global dominance and recognition.
2. ***Sara Blakely (Spanx):*** What started as a simple idea of cutting off the feet of her pantyhose turned into a billion-dollar company. Blakely worked from home in the early days and grew her business from the ground up.
3. ***Sophia Amoruso (Nasty Gal):*** Amoruso started selling vintage clothes from her apartment on eBay. Today, Nasty Gal is a multi-million-dollar company.

4. ***Jessica Alba (The Honest Company):*** Actress Jessica Alba co-founded The Honest Company, focusing on eco-friendly, non-toxic household and personal care products. It has grown into a trusted brand for parents and families.

Just like their 21st-century counterparts, the Bible is full of stories of women who through tragedy or difficulties found new purpose and success. Here are a few of them.

1. ***Ruth:*** After losing her husband, Ruth could have returned to her homeland, but she chose to stay with her mother-in-law Naomi and work in the fields. Her diligence and loyalty led her to Boaz, and she became the great-grandmother of King David.
2. ***Esther:*** Esther's rise to royalty came through a difficult and dangerous situation. Her bravery in approaching the king to save her people changed the course of history.
3. ***Deborah:*** In a time of national crisis, Deborah, a prophetess and judge, rose to lead Israel to victory. She didn't let the limitations of her gender hold her back but stepped into leadership when her people needed her.

These examples show that women, even in the midst of adversity, can step into new roles and make a lasting impact. This is especially important for the modern-day woman—whether Christian or not—because the ability to pursue entrepreneurship for financial independence is something no woman should fear. If you're a Christian woman considering entrepreneurship, here are some practical steps you can start taking today.

1. ***Join Organizations That Encourage Business Growth:*** Many organizations offer resources and support for women in business. Look for local or online groups that provide networking opportunities, mentorship, and business advice.

2. ***Find a Mentor:*** A mentor can provide guidance, encouragement, and wisdom as you navigate the challenges of starting a business. Even if you don't have a business idea yet, finding a mentor in the business world can help you prepare for the future.

3. ***Start with What You Have:*** Just like the widow used her small jar of oil, start with the resources and skills you already have. You don't need a large investment to begin—just a willingness to take that first step.

4. ***Build Your Confidence:*** Entrepreneurship requires confidence and courage especially when facing uncertainty. Pray and surround yourself with people who will encourage and support you.

5. ***Trust God's Leading:*** Ultimately, entrepreneurship is a journey of faith. Trust that God will guide your steps and provide what you need to succeed.

In conclusion, the widow's story reminds us that women can have it all—that entrepreneurship is not reserved for a select few. It is a path open to anyone, especially those facing the most challenging circumstances. As Christians, we can discover our voice, purpose, and calling through entrepreneurship, no matter where we begin. The key is simply to start!

For Christian women—especially those who may feel limited by societal, religious, and cultural expectations—the story of the widow offers hope and inspiration. God can use your current situation—whether it's loss, hardship, or financial struggle—to reveal a new purpose and give you the courage to step into entrepreneurship. Whether you are just beginning to explore business ideas or ready to take a leap of faith, remember to seek out supportive communities.

Find yourself some great mentors, and trust that God's plan for your life is bigger than your current circumstances. Just as the widow found her calling through tragedy, you too can find your voice and purpose in entrepreneurship.

CHAPTER 25

FAITH, FRIENDS AND FINANCE

Faith-Filled Strategy

How is your faith-o-meter? What if I told you that your faith is the foundation for starting anything of substance? Like everyone else, I have had my faith tested, stretched, and at times, even crushed. One year, I was determined to purchase a home—then my car started acting up. Everyone advised me to buy the house first and wait six months before getting a new car.

But I knew it was time to replace my car. So, I went to God in prayer and asked whether I should buy the house first and wait before replacing my car. His response was clear: "Yes, their advice is correct, but are you like everybody else?" Realizing what God was telling me, I stepped out in faith. Within three weeks, I had purchased both my car and my house—but I had to take that first step of faith!

The widow's first step was one of faith. Despite facing crushing debt and the threat of slavery, she turned to Elisha for guidance. His response stirred enough faith in her to obey his instruction—allowing a small jar of oil to become the key to transforming her future. Here are the ways faith played an essential role in her decision-making process:

1. ***Faith in the Word:*** The widow trusted in the word spoken by the prophet of God, that God will do what He promised.
2. ***Faith in the Unseen:*** The widow trusted that the small jar of oil would be multiplied and that the vessels she borrowed would be filled.
3. ***Faith in God's Provision:*** Even though her circumstances were dire, she believed that God, through the prophet, would provide a way out.

4. ***Faith in the Process:*** She didn't know how everything would work out, but she trusted that by following the instructions, a solution would emerge.

For modern-day Christians, faith is the cornerstone of any entrepreneurial endeavor. Starting a business often requires stepping into unfamiliar territory, trusting that God will guide you and provide what you need—even when resources seem insufficient.

Though the widow had faith, she was also practical. She understood that her small jar of oil was her only asset, highlighting the importance of budgeting and resource management. She didn't waste what she had, nor did she overextend herself. Instead, she took stock of her current resources and made the most of them. Here's how the concept of budgeting impacted her strategy:

1. ***Starting Small:*** The widow began with what she had—a small jar of oil. She didn't go beyond her means but worked within her limits.

2. ***Incremental Growth:*** As the oil was multiplied, she was able to sell it and pay off her debt. This allowed her to grow her business gradually, without taking on unnecessary financial risk.

3. ***Frugality and Resourcefulness:*** While she didn't have access to a large amount of capital, she was resourceful with what she had.

The Bible has often instructed us to count the cost before embarking on a venture or journey. At first, this might seem contradictory to faith, but counting the cost does not indicate a lack of faith. Instead, it teaches us the importance of resource management, budgeting, and accountability—all with a clear goal in mind.

> *For which of you, desiring to build a tower, does not first sit down and count the cost, whether he has enough to complete it? Otherwise, when he has laid a foundation and is not able to finish, all who see it begin to mock him, saying, 'This man began to build and was not able to finish.' Or what king, going out to encounter another king in war, will not sit down first and deliberate whether he is able with ten thousand to meet him who comes against him with twenty thousand? And if not, while the other is yet a great way off, he sends a delegation and asks for terms of peace.*
> *Luke 14:28-32*

How can you tell the difference between a budget and faith? It's simple. With a budget, you have time to plan and the opportunity to weigh all your options before making a decision. Faith, on the other hand, often comes into play when you are at your wit's end, with nothing more to lose. It can feel like a gamble—taking a chance on yourself. Consider what the Scriptures say about building a tower: before construction begins, one must sit down and deliberately count the cost. This highlights the importance of budgeting and resource management.

The second key principle is having a clear goal in mind. You don't want to find yourself stuck in the middle of your project, unable to finish what you started. For aspiring Christian entrepreneurs, budgeting is crucial—you don't need a large amount of capital to start a business. Instead, begin with small, manageable resources and grow from there.

The widow wisely combined her faith with the belief that she would receive provision, blending her spiritual convictions with practical budgeting strategies. By doing so, she positioned herself for success without compromising her beliefs. Her story teaches us the importance of planning wisely and stretching our resources for maximum impact.

I'm sure you've heard the saying, "Location is everything!" This couldn't be truer, as location played a crucial role in the widow's business success. While she lacked the resources to establish a shop or reach distant markets, she strategically leveraged her immediate community by borrowing vessels from her neighbors.

By doing so, she positioned her business within a familiar, trusted environment—among people who knew her and her family. She was able to gain support primarily due to the proximity and familiarity of her situation with her neighbors. Location is a powerful tool in business strategy, and here are its benefits as they relate to the widow's business venture:

1. ***Proximity to Customers:*** The widow's oil was sold locally, likely to those who knew her or lived nearby, making it easier to sell her product.
2. ***Community Support:*** Her neighbors were willing to lend her vessels, and they may have also been her first customers. Starting locally allowed her to build a support system within her community.
3. ***Trust and Relationships:*** People are more likely to buy from someone they know. Her neighbors likely trusted her, which gave her an advantage in selling her product.

For modern entrepreneurs, the key lesson here is to start locally within your community—unless you have an online store. By borrowing vessels based on her financial and local limitations, the widow wisely leveraged her immediate environment, first building a home-grown network. This strategy allowed her to maximize two critical factors simultaneously: location and relationships. As believers, it's essential to introduce your product within your immediate network. This is where you'll find valuable support, trust, and the power of word-of-mouth marketing!

While I do not believe in building relationships solely for business gain, relationship-building is a vital aspect of business growth, and one must be intentional when engaging in business. The truth is that friendship and community played a crucial role in the widow's success. Elisha's instruction to borrow empty vessels was not a random command—it was strategic business advice that required her to rely on the relationships she had built with her friends and neighbors.

Without their willingness to lend her the vessels she needed, her business venture would have failed before it even began. Her friends and neighbors became her first investors, providing her with the essential tools to transform her small jar of oil into a thriving enterprise. Here are three key benefits that friendship and neighborly support provided for the widow:

1. ***Support Network:*** The widow's neighbors supported her in her time of need. In business, having a strong support network is essential, especially during the early stages.

2. ***Collaboration:*** Rather than viewing her neighbors as competitors or outsiders, the widow collaborated with them. This spirit of collaboration can lead to business partnerships and opportunities that might not exist otherwise.

3. ***Trust and Loyalty:*** Her friends were likely loyal customers, helping her business grow through their purchases and word-of-mouth recommendations.

The role of friendship in business is profound and has often made a significant difference, particularly in collaborative spaces and shared responsibilities. While the widow operated her business independently, many successful ventures have been built on friendships rooted in collaboration. These partnerships have led to thriving businesses, such as the examples below:

1. ***Larry Page and Sergey Brin:*** Co-founders of Google, they met as graduate students at Stanford University. Their friendship and shared interest in organizing information on the Internet led to the creation of one of the most successful companies in history.

2. ***Ben Cohen and Jerry Greenfield:*** Founders of Ben & Jerry's, the iconic ice cream brand. Lifelong friends since middle school, they turned their passion for quality and creativity into a global brand known for its delicious flavors and social activism.

3. ***Evan Williams, Biz Stone, and Jack Dorsey:*** Co-founders of Twitter. As friends and colleagues, they collaborated to create

one of the most influential social media platforms, shaping how people communicate in the digital age.

For modern entrepreneurs, friendships and relationships can be among your greatest assets, whether you're selling a product or pursuing a joint business venture. Networking, collaboration, and community support are crucial to any business endeavor. Surrounding yourself with people who believe in you and your vision can be the defining factor between success and failure.

This section focuses on budget, bonds, and belief, exploring the four pillars of smart borrowing. These essential factors—faith, finance, location, and friendship—had to be successfully harmonized to ensure that the widow's borrowing led to growth rather than increased debt. By aligning these elements, she was able to determine how, where, and whom to borrow from within her circle.

The Four Pillars of Smart Borrowing

For modern-day Christians aspiring to become entrepreneurs, understanding why the four pillars of smart borrowing are deeply intertwined in the widow's story is essential for setting themselves up for success. Here's how to practically bring them together for a strong foundation:

1. ***Faith to Take the First Step:*** You don't need to have everything figured out before you start. Just like the widow, you can begin with a small step of faith, trusting that God will provide the resources and guidance you need as you move forward. Start with prayer and reflection—seek God's direction for your

business idea, pray for wisdom and clarity, and trust that He will lead your steps.

2. ***Budget to Manage Your Resources Wisely:*** Don't wait for large amounts of capital before starting. Be resourceful and maximize what you have. The widow began with just a small jar of oil and built her business step by step. As a contemporary Christian entrepreneur, take stock of what you already have and create a simple budget. Ask yourself: How much can I invest? What resources do I have access to? Map out a budget that allows you to start small and grow gradually.

3. ***Location to Leverage Your Immediate Environment:*** Start where you are. Your community, neighborhood, or online network can be a valuable asset in growing your business. Identify your local resources quickly—whether it's your neighborhood, online community, or social network—and look for ways to leverage your immediate environment. Can your friends and family support your business? Can you offer your product or service locally to build a customer base?

4. ***Friendships to Build a Strong Support System:*** Relationships matter. Surround yourself with people who will support you, lend resources, and help you grow. Just as the widow's neighbors lent her vessels, your friends and community can provide valuable support for your business. Cultivate relationships with those who can uplift you on your entrepreneurial journey. Join a small business group, network with like-minded individuals, and seek out mentors who can offer guidance and encouragement.

By mapping out a realistic plan and incorporating the four pillars of smart borrowing, you can lay the foundation for a successful business. Recognizing these key areas early is crucial, as they will continue to shape your growth. From the church pews to the neighborhood streets, we have the power to build a Christian-based lending network—one that works in our favor and strengthens our spiritual community.

We must encourage 21st-century Christians to strategically leverage both their spiritual community and local environment to gain the support needed for their business ventures while fostering growth within the community.

These four areas are essential, especially in the early stages of any business, as they lay the foundation for long-term growth and sustainability. Faith provides the courage to take the first step and the strength to remain steadfast through challenges. Budgeting ensures wise resource management, allowing for responsible scaling and preventing financial overextension.

Location helps you determine where to start and how to connect with your audience. As your business grows, your community and market will expand, opening doors to new opportunities. **Friendships** and **relationships** serve as valuable support systems, offering essential connections that foster growth. Over time, these relationships will deepen, providing ongoing support, collaboration, and potential partnerships for future success.

By integrating these elements, you develop a well-rounded strategy that empowers you to step out of your comfort zone and confidently pursue your entrepreneurial calling. These foundational principles also drive expansion—just as they did for the widow, enabling her to grow her business sustainably. She successfully leveraged her network without incurring financial strain or jeopardizing her relationships.

The widow's relational ties provided her with resources she might not have otherwise accessed, serving as a powerful model for business owners today. She strategically leveraged the hidden power of intentional borrowing, demonstrating a plan rooted in her unique context, friendships, budget, location, and faith. In conclusion, the widow's story serves as a compelling blueprint for entrepreneurship. Her faith, resourcefulness, and relationships were the driving forces behind her success. Modern-day Christians can draw valuable lessons from her example by applying the same foundational principles—faith, budgeting, location, and relationships—to their own business ventures.

By effectively intertwining the four areas mentioned, one can step into new opportunities, grow a business, and create a sustainable path forward with strategy and intention. No matter your starting point—whether you have limited resources, a small budget, or a tight-knit community—remember that God can multiply your efforts.

This is not just about the purposeful navigation of debt but about providing a framework for Christian entrepreneurs seeking to mirror the widow's approach—mixing faith, finances, location, and relationships before borrowing. In the end, let us all remember that the widow's vow to borrow 'not a few' vessels was driven by faith, shaped by necessity, guided by a wise strategy, and enabled by local friendships.

I want to remind you that you can build a successful business and step into the purpose God has for your life. Just like the widow, God can take what little you have and transform it into something extraordinary. Embrace your faith-filled strategy today!

CHAPTER 26

SITUATIONAL-DRIVEN STARTUPS

The Unplanned Entrepreneur

What if I told you that not every great business idea is birthed from a warm, special feeling? It's time to be honest with aspiring entrepreneurs and faithpreneurs— not every successful business concept comes with the sound of angels singing in our backyard! For some of us, we simply have a knack for spotting financial opportunities in every situation.

For other people, they birthed a great idea because they were able to follow instructions to the letter! I started a couple of businesses when I was unemployed a couple of times, and it wasn't because I had a passion for them! I didn't hear the heavenly hosts or have this overwhelming passion; it was simply a case that I needed to make money.

I believe we do people a great disservice when we tell them to simply follow their passion without providing a clear roadmap on how to do so. Part of that guidance means being honest—sometimes, they may have to do work or start businesses they aren't necessarily passionate about. However, if they work hard enough to make what they have—even if it's just a little—successful, they will eventually be able to build the business of their dreams.

In this chapter, we will explore the dual nature of the widow—someone with no prior business experience who also did not tie emotions to the business she was starting. She simply followed Elisha's instructions and became successful! Elisha gave her four simple instructions: gather empty vessels, close the door, pour the little oil she had into them, and sell the oil to pay her debts.

What's remarkable about this miracle is that she followed his instructions, without any personal feelings or emotional attachment to the task. Unlike many of today's entrepreneurs who are encouraged to *"follow their passion,"* the widow's business was born out of necessity. With a dead husband and sons slated to be taken as slaves, all she had left was a small jar of oil. In her obedience and practicality, she uncovered a way out of her tragedy and created a path towards financial stability.

This chapter explores the concept of building a business not from passion, but from necessity—and how Christians can learn to embrace opportunities that may not always evoke emotional attachment but still meet a vital need. We will discuss the importance of trusting divine guidance, stepping out of our comfort zones, and finding the balance between passion-driven and necessity-driven ventures.

In previous chapters, we addressed tragedy and necessity, but here, the widow's story serves as a clear example of a business born not from passion, but from sheer necessity. Her survival and the future of her sons depended on her ability to take quick action and follow the prophet's instructions without hesitation. There will be times in life when one must set emotions aside in order to create a business venture from a passionless place.

Building a business from necessity is sometimes how the greatest entrepreneurial moves are born, from a place of complete detachment and situational urgency, rather than passion. The *"no attachment requirement"* move can cause you to thrive in a business that you never dreamed of. Yes, real success can emerge from scenarios you didn't initially desire or feel passionate about. This was such for the widow, whose business journey was far from the typical narrative of pursuing one's passion. Instead, these were the three things that motivated her:

1. ***Immediate Need for Financial Security:*** The widow's primary concern was not finding her dream job or building a business she loved but securing the financial future of her family. The sale of oil was a means to an end, paying off her debts and saving her sons from slavery.
2. ***Practical Obedience:*** The widow had no previous experience in selling oil or running a business. She simply followed the instructions she was given, trusting that it would work, even if it didn't seem logical or emotionally fulfilling at the time.
3. ***Necessity as a Motivator:*** Her business venture wasn't driven by passion but by the urgency of her situation. Her motivation was survival, and her success came through her willingness to act quickly and pragmatically.

Many modern-day Christians may find themselves in similar situations where starting a business is not about fulfilling a lifelong dream but about meeting an immediate need. The widow's story reminds us that businesses born from necessity can be just as successful as those driven by passion—perhaps even more so—because they are often fueled by determination and resilience.

The reality of starting a business from a place of tragedy is more common than one might think, though it comes with unique challenges and opportunities. When life presents difficult circumstances, we often have to make tough decisions and find new ways to move forward. For some, entrepreneurship becomes a pathway to recovery and restoration. Here are a few key realities of building a business in the midst of tragedy:

1. ***Loss as a Catalyst for Change:*** Sometimes, it takes a major loss to push us out of our comfort zones. The widow's business only came about because of her husband's death. If he had still been alive, she may never have had to explore entrepreneurship, and they would have continued being in debt! Similarly, many people find themselves starting businesses after losing a job or a loved one or experiencing a significant life change.
2. ***Strength in Adversity:*** Building a business out of necessity often requires a level of strength and resilience that isn't always needed when pursuing a passion project. Tragedy can force us to tap into hidden reserves of determination, creativity, and perseverance.
3. ***Turning Pain into Purpose:*** One of the most superb aspects of necessity-driven entrepreneurship is the ability to turn pain into purpose. Just as the widow's oil business provided her with a way out of her financial distress, many people who start businesses in difficult times find that their new venture gives them a renewed sense of purpose and direction.

The widow's story is not the only example of someone transforming a difficult situation into a business opportunity. Both the Bible and the modern world are filled with stories of individuals who found success by building businesses out of necessity. Let us explore a couple of examples:

Biblical Example: Joseph in Egypt

Joseph's journey is another biblical example of someone who, despite facing significant hardship, found a way to thrive. Sold into slavery by his own brothers and falsely accused of rape, he was wrongfully imprisoned—yet he eventually became the second-most powerful man in Egypt. His ability to interpret Pharaoh's dreams and implement a strategy to save Egypt from famine transformed him from a prisoner into a leader. His 'business,' so to speak, was born out of necessity—the urgent need to provide agricultural solutions for food during a time of crisis.

Modern Example: Sara Blakely, Founder of Spanx

Sara Blakely, the founder of Spanx, built her billion-dollar business out of necessity. She was working a job she didn't enjoy while trying to solve a personal problem—how to create a smoother silhouette under her clothes. Blakely didn't have a passion for fashion or a background in business, but she saw a need and filled it. Today, Spanx is a global brand, and Blakely is one of the most successful female entrepreneurs in the world.

Starting a business out of necessity often requires a different approach than starting one from passion. It means separating your emotions from the strategic decisions needed to establish your business. Sometimes, the most effective business strategy involves setting aside personal attachments to focus on immediate opportunities. In life, circumstances may push us into new business ventures—even when we lack passion for them. Here are key strategies to consider when pursuing a business out of necessity:

1. Focus on the Need; Not your Emotions

When starting a business out of necessity, it's essential to focus on the need rather than getting caught up in emotions. This was true for the widow; her primary goal was to meet a financial need, not to pursue a lifelong dream of selling oil.

Entrepreneurs who find themselves in similar situations must learn to separate their emotions from the task at hand. While passion can fuel creativity, it can also *cloud judgment*, leading to poor business decisions. By focusing on the practical aspects of the business such as meeting a demand or solving a problem, you can move forward with clarity and purpose.

2. Use What You Have

The widow's business success came from using what she had—a small jar of oil. Similarly, necessity-driven entrepreneurs often have to start with limited resources. Instead of waiting for perfect conditions or sufficient capital, focus on what you already have—whether it's a skill, a product, or a service that meets a need.

3. Stay Flexible and Open to Change

When your business is born out of necessity, you may not always feel emotionally attached to it—and that can be an advantage. It allows you to remain flexible and open to change. If the business needs to pivot or a better opportunity arises, you'll be more willing to adapt without the emotional attachment that can sometimes hold back passion-driven ventures.

4. Build Mental Toughness

Starting a business from a place of tragedy or necessity requires mental resilience. There will be challenges, setbacks, and moments of doubt, but building mental toughness will help you stay the course. This toughness often comes naturally in necessity-driven situations because failure is not an option.

5. Stepping Out of Your Comfort Zone: Embracing the Unfamiliar

The widow had no experience as a businesswoman, yet she stepped out of her comfort zone and followed the prophet's instructions. Many modern-day Christians hesitate to start a business because it feels unfamiliar or lacks an emotional connection. However, stepping out of your comfort zone is essential for growth. By applying these five strategies, you can begin your journey of starting a business without emotional attachment—allowing you to focus on making money and, if desired, exit when the time is right.

Not every business venture will give you a 'fuzzy and warm' feeling, and that's okay. It's important to set realistic expectations. Some businesses are simply about meeting a need or solving a problem. You must let go of the notion that every business is born out of passion. A successful business can thrive without deep personal attachment—as long as it provides value to others and meets your financial needs.

There may come a time when you find yourself becoming too emotionally involved in your business. When this happens, it's important to step back and assess your situation objectively. With the right level of detachment, you can build a stable and thriving business. Pausing your passion doesn't stifle creativity, as some might believe.

In fact, desperate moments often ignite the best ideas, leading to successful business concepts—even without deep personal passion.

Quite frankly, as a Christian entrepreneur, you must approach your business as though you are in the business of survival. Without necessity or desperation, there is no driving force to encourage you to be resourceful or creative. You must prioritize objectivity over emotions. There is great benefit in launching a venture with a clear, unclouded mindset, free from sentimental constraints.

While passion will always be an important motivator, necessity-driven businesses have their own advantages. A successful business doesn't always have to stem from a deep emotional connection. In fact, balancing both passion and practicality can lead to even greater success. There are several advantages to running a necessity-driven business, and they are as follows:

1. ***Practical Focus:*** When building a business out of necessity, you're more likely to make decisions based on what works, rather than what feels good. Sound decision-making is the hallmark of a temperate and stable business owner.

2. ***Resilience:*** Necessity-driven entrepreneurs tend to be more resilient because their business is often a lifeline. In such businesses, there is not much wiggle room for failure, you must be 100% all in to succeed.

3. ***Meeting Real Needs:*** Businesses built from necessity are often more attuned to the needs of the market because they're born out of a direct response to those needs and the desperation to succeed at all costs.

It is possible to find purpose in a non-passionate project. Just because you're not passionate about a business when you start it doesn't mean you can't find purpose in it later. The widow likely didn't feel a deep emotional connection to selling oil, but through her obedience and hard work, she found financial stability and a way to support her family. There are also those who never find their passion for a successful project, yet in the end, may sell it for a hefty profit. And there is no need to feel guilty if that becomes your ultimate decision.

It is very possible to thrive in a business that you never intended to start; by following strategic instructions, you can find success even if the business idea doesn't initially thrill you.

In conclusion, starting a business out of necessity is nothing to be ashamed of. In fact, many successful businesses were born out of difficult circumstances. Whether your business comes from a place of passion or a place of tragedy, what matters is your willingness to step out in faith and embrace the opportunity.

Christians should feel empowered to explore new business opportunities, even if they don't feel a strong emotional connection to them at first. Whether your business is meeting a need, solving a problem, or simply providing for your family, it holds value. Do not let anyone guilt-trip you into thinking otherwise! By trusting God's guidance, setting realistic expectations, and balancing passion with practicality, you can build a successful business and unapologetically fulfill the purpose God has for your life.

CHAPTER 27

GO BEYOND ENOUGH

Effort vs. Rewards

What if I told you that your 'commitment level' will shape your financial miracle, which is your harvest? Partial or half-hearted commitment will never yield significant financial returns. You must adopt the mentality of going beyond just enough to unlock exponential returns, and that requires putting in extra effort. One early morning, my father called to tell me about how much effort my baby sister was putting into securing a new job right out of college.

My father told me that my sister had applied for a job but was told she was too inexperienced. So, one day, she called the company back and asked if they had hired anyone yet. They informed her that they had two candidates they were considering for the position. Despite this, my sister got dressed, went in, and convinced the company to hire her over the two other candidates.

The employer told her that her persistence reminded her of when she was younger and would not take no for an answer. Her commitment became a testament to who she is as an individual. The moral of the story is that her persistence, effort, and commitment earned her the reward of a job she would work at for six years! This chapter is about encouraging you not to settle for the minimum, but to push further to yield the greatest possible outcome, just as the widow's abundant effort yielded abundant oil.

Partial commitment leads to limited returns, while full engagement invites more significant breakthroughs. The truth is that no one ever reaps a great financial windfall without being fully committed or engaged in the process. In the widow's desperate situation, with

Elisha's specific instructions: '*Go, borrow vessels from everywhere, from all your neighbors, empty vessels; do not gather just a few' (2 Kings 4:3)*, the significance of this instruction goes far beyond simply gathering vessels.

Elisha's guidance was a direct challenge to the widow's faith, as he wasn't merely telling her what to do; he was testing the limits of her belief in God's provision. The truth is, the more vessels she gathered, the more oil she would have. The less she collected, the less she would receive. Her willingness to follow these instructions to the letter is a powerful example of how obedience, effort, and faith are deeply interconnected in the journey toward success.

This chapter explores the widow's decision to borrow a large number of vessels and what it teaches us about effort, faith, and the principle of abundance in business. It's about the importance of putting in the right amount of effort to achieve success. It's the difference between working smarter versus harder, and how modern-day Christians can learn the invaluable lesson of following divine instructions precisely.

One of the most important lessons we can glean from the widow's story is the direct connection between her effort and her return. If she had gathered only a few vessels, her oil supply would have been limited, and would not have paid off her debt in full. This principle holds true in every area of our lives, particularly in business. The reality is that **little effort equals little return,** which is often a sign of insufficient faith or fear. When we fail to put in the necessary work, or when we allow fear or doubt to dictate our actions, our potential for success diminishes greatly.

The reason why little effort yields little return comes from a fear of failure. Many times, we hesitate or procrastinate in putting in the work because we're afraid it won't pay off, and in doing so, we limit our own potential. This also ties into the concept of self-sabotaging behavior; it occurs when people intentionally (or subconsciously) act in a manner that hinders their own success. While it may seem surprising, some people undermine their own progress or work.

Another vital lesson is a **lack of clear vision** or belief in the possibility of success, it's easy to put in minimal effort, which is work without cost. Just as the widow had to believe that God would fill every vessel she gathered, Christian entrepreneurs must believe in the possibility of their own success if they are to put in the effort required to achieve it.

In business, as in life, the principle is simple and remains the same: if you don't believe in the abundance that is available to you, you won't put in the work required to receive it. Just like the widow, we must gather as many vessels as we can in our lives while putting in the maximum effort to experience the fullness of God's provision.

There are people who find it acceptable to put in some effort and receive some return; this is often the result of limited faith. Just imagine if the widow had decided to gather a moderate number of vessels. She may have felt it was a **'safe'** approach, ensuring that she wasn't overextending herself, but this would have resulted in only a partial blessing.

The danger of **some effort versus little effort** is that with some effort we're often hedging our bets, and it is not because we do not have what it takes. It is rather about just *'settling'* on barely enough. The lack of full commitment is devastating because oftentimes the person has the power to be fully committed but chooses not to follow through.

Playing it safe is a familiar trap that many people fall into because they just do just enough to avoid failure but won't take the extra steps needed to achieve significant success. This can be frustrating for those around them who can see their full potential. The servant who buried his one talent played it safe and lost in the end in the book of Matthew.

He also who had received the one talent came forward, saying, 'Master, I knew you to be a hard man, reaping where you did not sow, and gathering where you scattered no seed, so I was afraid, and I went and hid your talent in the ground. Here, you have what is yours.' But his master answered him, 'You wicked and slothful servant! You knew that I reap where I have not sown and gather where I scattered no seed?
Matthew 25:24-26

The widow could have played it safe, just like the servant with the talent, by gathering a few vessels, but she chose to go all in by collecting as many as possible. And because she put in all the effort, she reaped the full reward! When we operate with limited faith, we may see some return, but it will always fall short of the abundance that is available to us. Partial effort leads to partial blessings; you cannot commit halfway and expect a bountiful harvest.

We have addressed little effort and some effort, but let us learn how the widow's story teaches us that great effort leads to multiple returns, which ties into the principle of abundance. By gathering as many vessels as she could, the widow positioned herself for an abundance of blessings. The more vessels she collected, the more oil she received, and it showed!

Whenever we demonstrate **faith in abundance**, we also get to reap blessings in abundance as well when we have put in the right amount of effort. The widow's actions were a demonstration of her faith in God's provision. She believed that God would fill every vessel she collected, and so she made the effort to collect as many as possible. The abundance of our faith must match the abundance of our efforts as well. There are no shortcuts, and sadly, a great majority of Christians exploit the term 'grace' to avoid putting in the necessary effort to be successful.

As a bi-vocational minister who preaches globally, writes, publishes, and has had several businesses on the side, I have always believed in the power of preparedness and effort. My brother would visit me for several months at a time, and one day he told me how, when he left for work, I would be diligently working on my job. And that when he returned from work, I would be on my personal computer. He told me that my efforts were commendable. People are judging you by the amount of effort you are putting into that which you say you believe in.

A sign of great effort is your level of preparedness for your blessing. The widow's willingness to gather many vessels showed that she was prepared for God's blessing. In business, when we put in great effort, we are demonstrating that we are ready for great success. This means that we believe in the abundance that is available to us if we simply position ourselves and do the necessary work.

The lesson is clear: **the amount of effort you put into a business venture will either diminish, equal, or exceed your future returns**. In economics, the widow demonstrated a series of different principles, such as diminishing returns, equal returns (linear growth), and the one everyone would love to achieve—exceeding returns, dealing with the compounding effect and scaling. (Who knew my economics class would come in handy when writing a book?) The widow's success was directly tied to her willingness to put in the work, and the same is true for anyone who is pursuing a business or entrepreneurial venture.

One of the most important distinctions in the modern business world is the difference between working smarter and working harder. The widow's story wasn't just about working hard; she worked strategically. She didn't waste her time trying to create more oil; instead, she simply followed the instructions she was given and allowed God to do the rest. This phrase is credited to Mr. Morgenstern, a 1930s industrial engineer who developed work simplification methods aimed at increasing efficiency without unnecessary effort. By the 1980s, it became a widely used phrase in business and self-improvement literature. Let us explore the vast difference.

Working Harder

More labor, less return: Working harder often means putting in more physical effort but not necessarily seeing greater returns. This can lead to burnout and frustration, especially if the strategy behind the work isn't sound or sustainable.

Working Smarter

Efficient effort, greater return: Working smarter means using your time and resources strategically to maximize your return. For the widow, working smarter meant trusting Elisha's instructions and focusing her efforts on gathering vessels, rather than trying to figure out how the oil would multiply. She also applied the principle of delegation by having her sons gather the empty vessels. Had she attempted to do everything herself, she would have been working harder without seeing a substantial return on her investment (ROI).

The widow avoided the pitfalls of a limited vision in her business venture. She refused to quit too soon or collect too few vessels. She emphasized consistency and took decisive action to secure maximum benefit for her and her children. Because she had no small plans, she turned her abundant effort into market-breaking results!

In business, it's not always about how hard you work, but how strategically you work. By thinking and acting on a larger scale, you can foster the best returns, just as the widow's forward-thinking approach did. As believers, by following divine instructions and focusing your effort where it counts, you can achieve far greater success than simply working harder without a clear plan.

One of the challenges we face in business and life is determining how much effort is enough. For one person, gathering 100 vessels might seem like a lot, while for another, 1,000 vessels might be their standard of abundance. You have to decide, 'What's your enough?' This is not about greed or stepping on others to get ahead. It's not about comparing yourself to others either. Instead, you must ask yourself the question, '*Is my effort matching my enough?*

It's easy to let fear—whether of failure or success—hold us back. The widow didn't allow fear to dictate her actions; instead, she trusted that God would provide for her based on her level of faith. The greatest thing we can do as believers is set high expectations for ourselves, trusting that God's provision is abundant. Rather than asking, 'How much is enough?' we should ask, 'How much can I believe for?' The amount of effort we put into a venture should reflect our faith in God's provision. If we limit our efforts out of fear or doubt, we limit the blessing we can receive.

While many people fear failure, there is also a powerful obstacle called the **'fear of success.'** Some individuals hesitate to put maximum effort into their business ventures because they fear what success might bring. True success means responsibility, expectations, social consciousness, global ambassadorship, and even the pressure to sustain one's profitability and achievements. The pattern of fearing success and repeatedly sabotaging one's own efforts is commonly referred to as 'Success Inhibition' or 'Fear of Success Syndrome.' Below are several examples:

Signs of Fear of Success (Achievemephobia)

1. ***Procrastination On Important Tasks:*** Delaying or avoiding tasks that could lead to success is a huge sign that they might be afraid of greater responsibility, higher expectations or even too much recognition.

2. ***Self-Sabotage Opportunities:*** Engaging in behaviors that undermine progress, such as missing deadlines or failing to complete important work that leads to success. Oftentimes such people associate success with stress or losing control.

3. ***Avoiding the Next Step:*** People often commonly associate this with people getting wedding jitters, but it is more than just that. They resist moving forward because they are afraid of the unknown or the responsibilities that come with the next step.

4. ***Comfort-Zone Mentality:*** Staying in a safe, familiar place rather than pushing for greater success. This is for people who do not want to stretch themselves further.

5. ***Trusting in God's Plan:*** Success is part of God's plan for us. Just as the widow had to trust that God's provision would be enough, we must trust that He will equip us for the success He has in store.

6. ***Pushing Through Discomfort:*** Success often requires us to step out of our comfort zones. The widow didn't know how much oil she would receive, but she trusted enough to gather many vessels. We, too, must push past our fears and take bold steps toward success.

Everyone desires success, but many struggle to achieve it due to fear and insecurity. However, this doesn't mean success is out of reach. These challenges can be overcome. Do not allow triggers or limiting beliefs to steal the opportunity for success.

The ability to listen and follow instructions is often the cornerstone of success for those who are willing to embrace it. The widow's story underscores the importance of following guidance. Elisha's directive to gather as many vessels as possible was specific and her success depended on her willingness to follow these instructions precisely.

In business, as in life, following **instructions is the foundation of success.**

In 2 Kings 13:14-19, we read the story of a young king who was instructed by Elisha to strike the ground with his arrows. The king struck the ground only three times, and Elisha rebuked him, saying that if he had struck it five or six times, he would have completely defeated his enemies. This story, much like the widow's, teaches us that **partial obedience results in partial success**. When we fail to follow instructions fully, we limit the blessings that could be ours.

> *And Elisha said to him, "Take a bow and some arrows." So, he took himself a bow and some arrows. Then he said to the king of Israel, "Put your hand on the bow." So, he put his hand on it, and Elisha put his hands on the king's hands. And he said, "Open the east window"; and he opened it. Then Elisha said, "Shoot"; and he shot. And he said, "The arrow of the Lord's deliverance and the arrow of deliverance from Syria; for you must strike the Syrians at Aphek till you have destroyed them." Then he said, "Take the arrows"; so, he took them. And he said to the king of Israel, "Strike the ground"; so, he struck three times and stopped. And the man of God was angry with him, and said, "You should have struck five or six times; then you would have struck Syria till you had destroyed it! But now you will strike Syria only three times."*
>
> *I Kings 2:15-19*

King Joash would never attain a complete victory over his enemies because he did not follow Elisha's final instructions with precision.

Time and again, I have told individuals that following instructions is the key to preventing a situation from spiraling into a massive damage control incident.

Following instructions is crucial as it brings clarity of purpose by equipping us with the tools necessary to navigate a clear path to success. Elisha's instructions to the widow provided her with exactly what she needed to do to succeed. By following both divine and practical instructions, we stay focused on the steps we need to take. It also speaks to our personal level of commitment.

Rarely are we guaranteed success if we fail to follow the instructions given to us. Instructions not only keep us focused but also align us on a proven path to success. The widow's oil continued to flow as long as there were vessels to fill, and our blessings will keep flowing as long as we remain obedient to the instructions we've been given.

For us to be successful, we must not settle for the bare minimum, but push further to achieve the greatest possible outcome—just like the widow's abundant effort yielded abundant oil. I often wish the widow had maxed out her vessels because, much like any modern-day investment, the more we invest, the greater the reward. It is crucial that, as believers, we give our best, paralleling the widow's willingness to collect numerous vessels, ensuring a larger overflow.

It is essential to understand the difference between minimal, medium, and maximum effort. These three levels highlight the direct correlation between input and output. By giving our full commitment to any task, we often experience the bountiful harvest that follows.

When we operate with the mindset of exceeding expectations, only then will we gather more than enough to secure our future.

Inspiring entrepreneurs and believers must learn to push past their basic needs and remind themselves that achieving life's big windfalls requires a higher level of devotion and engagement. It is here that the overflow begins to make a significant difference. In conclusion, the widow's story is a powerful example of how faith, obedience, effort, and following instructions come together to create success. By following Elisha's guidance and putting in the right type of effort, the widow strategically positioned herself for abundant blessings.

This proves that the amount of effort we invest in a venture directly impacts the returns we receive. This holds true whether in business or in life, as success often comes down to how well we can listen to and follow the instructions we've been given. As modern-day Christians, we can learn from the widow's story by applying the same principles to our own lives. This is the key to unlocking the abundance that God has in store for us. By working smarter, putting in the necessary effort, and following divine instructions, we can position ourselves for multiple returns, just like the widow.

So, the next time you're faced with an opportunity, ask yourself: Am I gathering enough vessels? Is my faith driving my effort? If it is, you'll be amazed at the abundance that follows. The truth is, the bigger the buckets, the bigger the blessings. The widow's effort directly equaled her outcome. The more vessels she gathered, the greater her returns, reminding us that the measure of our ambition directly impacts our results. She was able to unlock exponential returns due to her extra effort. What has God placed in you that is waiting to be discovered?

CHAPTER 28

DEPRESSION VS. DRIVE

Pain and Profit

It was the early 1990s. I had lost everything—my inheritance had been embezzled, my house and car were gone, my education was on hold, and the relationships I once cherished had disappeared. I was left with nothing but grief and despair. For weeks, I lay in depression, feeling as though life had stripped me of everything that made me whole. At my lowest, I even considered ending it all. But as I sat with that thought, one image stopped me—the pain it would cause my family. At that moment, I made a decision: If I couldn't find the will to live, I would at least find the will to work. And through that, I discovered something unexpected—my pain became the very thing that pushed me into purpose.

This chapter is for anyone who has ever felt stuck in their struggle. Sometimes, loss is the very thing that propels us forward. Like the widow in 2 Kings 4:1-7, who faced financial devastation after her husband's death, many today find themselves in desperate situations when tragedy strikes. Whether it's the loss of a loved one, financial collapse, or an unexpected life change, these moments force us to make a choice—stay buried in grief or rise with determination.

Often, we are told to simply wait, pray, and hope for things to get better. Encouragement is important, but what if our pain isn't just something to survive—but something to use? What if adversity isn't meant to break us, but to awaken something within us? Sometimes, God allows struggle to push us out of complacency, forcing us to maximize what we already have. Hardship strips away excuses, leaving us with one viable option: push forward.

This chapter is a wake-up call for the forgotten—for those who feel like they're at their wits' end. It's for the ones who look around and see nothing but disaster and mayhem. If that's you, know this—you still have a story to tell, and your greatest breakthrough may come from your darkest moment. Pain can be paralyzing, or it can be a launching pad. The choice is yours. This chapter will show you how to take depression and turn it into drive, transforming pain into purpose, struggle into strategy, and tragedy into triumph.

This holds especially true for women who are home providers. If they lose their husbands—the primary breadwinners—they are often left to face financial struggles, emotional turmoil, and the challenge of stepping into a new role. Here, we will focus on how modern-day Christian housewives or husbands may find themselves forced into the workforce after a personal tragedy and how they can navigate this new reality with faith, determination, and balance.

There is no biblical indication that the widow with the jar of oil was lazy or unskilled. In fact, her actions suggest the opposite—her willingness to work, combined with sheer determination, set her apart. Her story is a powerful reminder that, as believers, we must be prepared to take immediate action when tragedy comes knocking. Oftentimes, misfortune forces us to reevaluate our options, including the possibility of working or starting a business.

In today's world, many Christian women find themselves forced into the workplace due to unforeseen tragedy. The most common scenario is the sudden loss of a spouse, leaving the wife to provide for her family in whatever way possible. Another reason a woman may need to become the primary provider is divorce or separation. A marriage breakdown can often result in financial hardship, especially if the woman is not the primary earner.

A third circumstance that may push a woman back into the workforce is the unexpected illness or disability of a spouse or loved one. When a husband becomes incapacitated, his wife may need to step up as the sole provider while also taking on the role of caregiver. Financial collapse can also force housewives to return to work. When a family's financial stability is shattered due to job loss, bankruptcy, or an economic downturn, women may find themselves re-entering the workforce, even if they are considered unskilled.

While these life events are deeply painful, they also create an opportunity to rebuild with new purpose and strength. The widow's story shows us that even in the most difficult circumstances, God can provide through our work.

Balancing grief and responsibility is never easy. As I write this book, a close friend of mine has just suffered a death in her family. I took time to be with her, trying to make her laugh, even if only for a few hours. The weight of grief can feel overwhelming, especially when the loss is sudden and unexpected. It is difficult to balance the need to mourn with the practical responsibilities of providing for one's family. However, the widow's story illustrates that faith and action can coexist, even in times of great sorrow.

Stepping up after a major setback can be difficult, especially when trying to find new strength in the midst of unexpected loss. Sometimes, we must use our mourning as a catalyst for motivation—pushing ourselves to take on additional responsibilities while exploring new possibilities.

When faced with the challenge of balancing work and grief, there are steps we can take to navigate this difficult season, such as the following:

1. ***Seek God's Guidance:*** The widow turned to Elisha, a prophet of God, for guidance in her time of need. Likewise, when we face difficult decisions, we should seek God's direction through prayer and scripture.
2. ***Take Small Steps:*** It's important to pace yourself and not try to do everything at once. The widow began by collecting vessels—one small, manageable task at a time—which eventually led to her success.
3. ***Find Support:*** Surround yourself with family, friends, and church members who can support you through difficult moments. Don't take pride in being a loner—because when it matters most, you'll realize that we all need somebody.
4. ***Rest and Recharge:*** Don't neglect self-care during this time. Take time to rest, heal, and allow space for grieving even as you work to meet your obligations.

Grieving and working can coexist. The widow channeled her grief into action, allowing her work to become a means through which God provided healing and provision. This is not a new phenomenon—throughout scripture, we see individuals who, in the face of personal tragedy, were compelled to work and provide for themselves and others. Let these stories serve as encouragement for modern-day Christians navigating similar circumstances.

Ruth: Working Through Widowhood

Ruth's story is a powerful example of a woman who, after losing her husband, took action to provide for herself and her mother-in-law, Naomi. Her willingness to glean in the fields of Boaz not only sustained them but also paved the way for her marriage to Boaz and her place in the lineage of Christ. Even in the face of personal tragedy, Ruth's work ethic was a testament to her faith and resilience.

Joseph: Rising from Slavery to Leadership

Joseph's story in Genesis is one of betrayal, slavery, and ultimate triumph. After being sold into slavery by his brothers, he remained diligent in every role he held—from managing Potiphar's house to overseeing the prison. His unwavering work ethic, combined with his trust in God, led to his rise as second-in-command in Egypt. Joseph's perseverance through hardship became the foundation of his success.

Likewise, many people today have discovered their purpose and achieved success after enduring personal tragedy. These stories serve as powerful reminders that, with the right mindset and faith, we can transform our pain into purpose.

U.S. 46th President Joseph Biden: From Personal Loss to Becoming the President of the United States

Grief and work can coexist, as seen in the life of President Joe Biden. After losing his first wife and daughter in a tragic accident, and later his son Beau to cancer, he pressed forward with resilience, channeling his pain into decades of public service. His perseverance ultimately led him to serve as the 46th President of the United States.

Like the widow in scripture, who found sustenance through her work and the oil that never ran dry, Biden turned his personal losses into a driving force, demonstrating that purpose can emerge even from profound sorrow.

Nigeria's 15th President Muhammadu Buhari: From Personal Loss and Failed Elections to Becoming one of the Greatest Nigerian Presidents

Grief and purpose can walk hand in hand. President Muhammadu Buhari is a testament to that truth. In the face of heartbreaking personal loss—first the death of his daughter, and then the passing of close confidants—he did not retreat. Instead, he stood tall, holding steady to his duty and vision for Nigeria.

From his days as a military ruler to his rise as a democratically elected president, Buhari's journey is one of unshakable resolve. Like the biblical widow whose last jar of oil flowed by faith and obedience, Buhari allowed his grief to become fuel, pouring himself into the difficult work of reform, governance, and national restoration.

His story reminds us: even when sorrow knocks the wind out of us, we can still rise. We can still lead. And we can still be used for something greater than ourselves.

Oprah Winfrey: Overcoming Childhood Trauma

Oprah Winfrey faced extreme adversity in her early life, including poverty and abuse. Despite these challenges, she pursued her passion for media and communications while also overcoming racism and gender bias in the workplace. Through perseverance, she rose to become one of the most successful and influential figures in the world. Her story is a powerful testament to the resilience needed to transform tragedy into triumph.

One of the greatest gifts we can give our children is the ability to navigate adversity with grace and faith. As Christian parents, it is essential to model resilience and trust in God when unexpected trials arise, teaching them that challenges can be stepping stones to growth and purpose.

Lessons We Can Teach Our Children

1. ***Faith in God's Provision:*** Just as the widow trusted God to provide, we can teach our children to trust that God will meet our needs, even in difficult times.
2. ***The Value of Hard Work:*** By working diligently, even when faced with tragedy, we show our children that perseverance and effort are key to overcoming challenges.
3. ***Coping with Loss:*** It's important to model healthy coping mechanisms for grief and loss, demonstrating that mourning is natural, but that we can also move forward with faith and hope. As parents and role models, we have a responsibility to equip our children with the necessary tools to navigate grief in a productive and healing way.

The truth is that the key difference between pain and profit lies in our ability to recognize and embrace our duty when circumstances demand it. There will be times in life when necessity compels us to work in ways we never anticipated. During these difficult moments, we must allow our work to guide us—not only toward success but also toward healing. Often, it is under these extraordinary conditions that we discover our ability to thrive under pressure, using it as a formula to overcome obstacles. In moments of intense hardship, our resolve is sharpened, our vision becomes clearer, and our capabilities are refined, allowing us to excel beyond expectation. Like the widow in Scripture, we must demonstrate a willingness to work and persevere, regardless of the pain or cost, knowing that our efforts play a crucial role in our breakthrough.

One of the greatest gifts we can give ourselves is preparing for a rainy day—investing in skills and resources that can help us succeed. A key lesson from the widow's story is the importance of having something to work with in times of need. In her case, she had a small amount of oil, which God multiplied to provide for her. In modern times, this serves as a reminder to always have skills or investments to fall back on. Your greatest investment will always be in yourself.

There are many ways to prepare for a rainy day, and it begins with developing marketable skills. Stay-at-home parents, for example, should strive to keep their skills sharp and relevant—whether through education, side projects, or part-time work—so they are prepared to re-enter the workforce if needed. Another important aspect of preparation is having financial investments, ensuring stability in uncertain times. Having investments, whether in savings, real estate, or other financial assets, can provide security in times of tragedy.

In my book *"Unlocking the Deborah,"* I talk about networking. Your network is your net worth, so it is important that you build the **RIGHT** type of network. Different networks are supposed to provide different things in your life, but first, you have to build one and also it is critical to maintain it as well. Maintaining strong relationships with friends, family, and church members can provide a safety net during difficult times. It's important to have a support system that you can rely on.

When hard times hit, self-sufficiency becomes essential, and having the right network can make all the difference. The widow's journey may have begun with her relying on others, but it ultimately led to her working to provide for herself and her children. Her story serves as an inspiration to believers worldwide, reminding them that they, too, can overcome personal tragedies and find a way forward.

As much as tragedy might bring great people together, it also can bring the worst out of people who want to take advantage of those who find themselves vulnerable. We must all learn how to guard against exploitation in our vulnerable moments by taking the following precautions:

How to Protect Yourself During Difficult Times

1. ***Be 'Super' Cautious when Making Financial Decisions:*** When grieving or facing a crisis, it is crucial to avoid making hasty financial decisions. Seek guidance only from trusted family members, friends, or financial advisors before making any major choices. Sometimes, the wisest decision may simply be to step back and walk away until clarity returns.

2. ***Watch Out for Opportunists:*** Sadly, some may seek to exploit your loss for their own gain. Be cautious of those who appear helpful but are more interested in what they can take from you. Watch out for individuals who speak quickly and try

to pressure you into making an immediate decision. When in doubt, step away or let them know you need to consult a trusted family member before proceeding.

3. ***Lean on Trusted Individuals:*** Rely on those who have proven themselves trustworthy over time and are good with handling money. In moments of vulnerability, it's crucial to have people around you who genuinely care for your well-being and will not take advantage of you or your situation.

For many housewives, especially those fully dedicated to their families, it can be easy to let work skills fade over time. However, maintaining strong work ethics and skills is essential—even for stay-at-home mothers—because you never know when those abilities may be needed. Fortunately, there are many ways to retain and sharpen your skills. Here are some effective strategies:

1. ***Taking Online Courses:*** There are many free and low-cost online courses available that allow you to continue learning at your own pace while expanding your skillset.
2. ***Volunteer or Freelance:*** Volunteering in your community or taking on small freelance projects can help you stay sharp, connected to the workforce and build new networks!
3. ***Start a Side Business:*** Starting a small business from home, whether it's selling homemade products or offering a service, can keep you engaged and maintain your entrepreneurial spirit.

In conclusion, the widow's story is a powerful testament to how faith, hard work, and resilience come together in the face of tragedy. Modern

Christian housewives and women experiencing personal hardships can draw strength from her example. It is essential to recognize that God often provides through our willingness to work and our trust in Him.

The widow's roadmap to financial redemption was birthed out of her decision to work, despite her circumstances. And it was that decision that became the turning point in her life that led to lasting financial stability. As Christian women, we must all prepare for the unexpected, both spiritually, financially and practically. By developing skills, building a support network, and maintaining our work ethic, we can face whatever challenges come our way with faith and confidence. It is here that we get pushed into our purpose using the crisis as a means to ignite our entrepreneurial fire.

The widow's oil serves as a powerful reminder that God can multiply our efforts when we are willing to work and trust Him. Even in the face of tragedy, we can find purpose, provision, and the strength to move forward. Let us embrace the truth that adversity can sometimes be the unexpected catalyst through which God reveals or fulfills a deeper calling in our lives.

CHAPTER 29

ESTABLISHING HEALTHY BOUNDARIES

Drawing the Line

A few years ago, I found myself driving across town to yet another church event. I had been invited to speak, but something in my spirit felt unsettled. I arrived, went through the motions, and left feeling drained—like I had wasted precious time that could have been spent resting, working on my assignment, or simply being with God. It wasn't the first time I had felt this way, but it was the first time I stopped to ask myself: Why am I doing this?

Then, in November 2024, the Lord spoke to me clearly: Beware of Christian distractions. He revealed that some of His most faithful servants had been sidetracked by commitments He never sanctioned—running from one religious event to another, saying yes to programs that added no value, and pouring their energy into things unrelated to their divine assignment. Then He said, "The devil has found it easy to keep My people busy with distractions because they do not see the value in what I have entrusted to them." That was a wake-up call!

The truth is that failing to establish healthy boundaries can drain you emotionally, spiritually, and even physically. Many of life's greatest struggles arise from our inability to draw the line and say, "No, this is not for me." Nehemiah understood this well. In Nehemiah 6:3, when he was repeatedly invited to a meeting that would pull him away from his work, he refused—every single time. He knew his mission was too important to be disrupted by meaningless distractions.

In this chapter, we'll explore how to set boundaries in both ministry and life—recognizing when to say yes and when to unapologetically say no. Not every opportunity is from God, and not every invitation is worth your time. Learning to discern the difference is key to protecting your purpose and staying aligned with what God has truly called you to do.

In what ways have you learned to shut the door in your life—just as the widow did when the prophet Elisha instructed her to shut the door behind her and her sons while she poured oil into borrowed vessels? This act carried a deeper significance than merely closing off the room for privacy. Shutting the door symbolized a spiritual, emotional, and physical reset for the widow, setting the stage for her miracle. It also serves as a powerful lesson for modern-day Christians, especially in times of tragedy, transition, or uncertainty.

In this context, shutting the door can hold multiple meanings—from establishing boundaries to fostering protection and personal growth. This chapter will explore the different interpretations of this act and how it can be a transformative practice for believers today. The truth is that shutting the door is one of the most profound symbols of closing an old chapter and stepping into something brand new.

For the widow, shutting the door symbolized the end of her former life—one marked by debt and despair—and the beginning of a fresh start through obedience and faith. The transition from old patterns or ways of living happens when we intentionally shut the door in our own lives. It is a powerful act of closing off harmful cycles, toxic relationships, or limiting mindsets that have held us back.

Shutting the door is essential for any Christian seeking growth and healing—two key components of moving forward. It positions us to embrace new opportunities, as closed doors separate us from the past so we can step into the future God has prepared for us. For the widow, this signified a new beginning, one where she could create wealth and provide for her family. Spiritually, shutting the door allows God to step in and transform our circumstances. It starts with releasing what no longer serves us or aligns with His purpose for our lives.

Shutting the door is about more than just embracing a new opportunity—it marks a major shift in one's life. It represents a pivotal moment of transition or change, as seen in the life of the widow. In an instant, she went from a helpless, grieving widow to a resourceful entrepreneur. By closing off the external world, she was able to focus entirely on the one task that would change her life forever.

Likewise, we must be willing to close certain doors in our own lives to establish healthy boundaries and step into new beginnings. Setting boundaries can be particularly difficult for women, yet it is essential if we want to make a fresh start while preventing outside demands and distractions from taking over. I have often found it interesting when young people, after ending bad relationships, feel the need to remain friends as a sign of maturity. In reality, I see it as a waste of time. Refusing to shut certain doors often reveals that we have yet to learn the power of simply saying, "No."

Your inability to say no reveals your inability to protect your own household. What if the widow and her late husband had fallen into debt not through reckless spending, but because they struggled to refuse certain requests—from friends, family, or even fellow believers? What if their financial hardship was the result of failing to establish healthy boundaries, simply because they could never find the words to say "No"? I urge modern-day believers to adopt firm boundaries that safeguard their families. It starts with having the courage to say no when something threatens to cost you and your loved ones everything.

When we shut the door to the outside world, we create space for success in private. Then, when the time is right, we can publicly display our victories. Shutting the door allows us to quietly address our failures without the fear of judgment or condemnation from others. It gives us the freedom to experiment, grow, and pivot within the safe walls of our own homes.

The widow's act of literally shutting her door symbolized both emotional and practical protection for her family. It serves as a reminder that we must be intentional about limiting access to our lives, especially during critical moments. If we want to experience lasting success and secure long-term victories, we must learn to guard our space wisely.

Establishing boundaries requires continual practice, and embracing change—especially transitioning from one stage of life to another, as it is often uncomfortable. Whether it's a single man stepping into the responsibility of providing for a new family or an individual shifting into an entirely different career, change can feel daunting. Much like the widow, we may not feel ready for the challenges life brings, especially in the wake of tragedy. However, closing off outside noise and distractions allows us to embrace our new season with unwavering focus and determination.

Shutting the door requires a higher level of faith and a willingness to embrace change. The widow had no idea that her small jar of oil would solve all her problems. Yet, she shut her door in obedience and chose to trust the process—allowing transformation to unfold. In the same way, shutting the door prevents us from seeking alternative routes that could delay the process, or the blessings God has already set before us.

Modern-day Christians must learn to embrace moments of transition, no matter how strange or difficult they may seem. We must trust that God is working behind closed doors to bring about growth, healing, power, and provision. Though we may feel uncertain because we cannot see what is happening, we must hold firm in our faith—knowing that our Father in Heaven has our best interests at heart and is working everything out for our good.

The widow's story is as much about God's provision, obedience, and divine instruction as it is about the importance of establishing healthy boundaries. Her previous lifestyle—one in which her husband accumulated debt—may have stemmed from a lack of clear, enforceable boundaries. In many cases, debt is not just a financial issue but a reflection of our inability to say no to certain pressures, demands, or unhealthy life habits.

When learning from the widow's past, one major lesson is the cost of poor boundary setting, in which I believe she and her late husband may have struggled at both setting financial and emotional boundaries. **The cost of poor boundaries** may have led to their overwhelming debt crisis. As believers, without clear boundaries, it is easy to fall into unhealthy patterns, whether in personal finances, relationships, or even spiritual practices.

Another truth is that **boundaries act as a sign of protection**. When Elisha instructed the widow to shut her door, it was to create a boundary between her and the outside world. This separation allowed her to focus on the task at hand, shielding her miracle from distraction and interference. For today's Christians, establishing healthy boundaries is essential—not only for avoiding burnout and health crises but also for protecting one's purpose and maintaining clarity in both life and business.

Shutting the door is about more than just opportunities, transitions, or protection—it is a safeguard against negative influences, destructive thoughts, and discouraging words that could hinder our progress. When the widow shut her door, she didn't just close off a physical space; she also blocked out doubt, fear, and the judgment of others who may not have understood her divine assignment.

How many times has God given you an assignment, only for you to run off and share it with someone who had no understanding of what He entrusted to you? Before you knew it, doubt crept in, and you began questioning whether you should even proceed with what God had commanded in the first place. The lack of proper boundaries not only affected your faith but also disrupted your assignment. One of the greatest benefits of shutting the door is that it protects your faith.

The story of Jairus arriving with Jesus at his house is one of the greatest examples in the Bible of the power of shutting the door to outside noise and distractions. In Mark 5:37-42, Jairus's deceased daughter was surrounded by commotion and wailing. When Jesus arrived, He immediately addressed the chaos—removing the crowd and allowing only the girl's parents and His disciples to remain in the room with Him.

> *He went in and said to them, "Why all this commotion and wailing? The child is not dead but asleep." But they laughed at him. After he put them all out, he took the child's father and mother and the disciples who were with him and went in where the child was. He took her by the hand and said to her, "Talitha koum!" (which means "Little girl, I say to you, get up!"). Immediately the girl stood up and began to walk around (she was twelve years old).*
> *Mark 5:39-42 (NIV)*

We must learn to shut the door just as Jesus did in the book of Mark because there will always be commotion—and there will always be those who mock what we are trying to accomplish. It is our responsibility to shut out any distractions that could weaken our faith in God and hinder His process. By shutting the door, **we safeguard our faith.** Just as the widow shut out the world, we too must close the door on negativity and doubt—anything that has the power to sabotage our faith and assignment.

Shutting the door is crucial, especially when embarking on a new venture or major life change. It is imperative to shield your vision from those who may not understand or support it—including, at times, members of your own family and church. The widow needed privacy to complete her task without interference or obstruction. For modern-day Christians, shutting the door serves as both spiritual and physical protection, ensuring that we remain focused and undistracted in moments of obedience and action.

The secret process of filling vessels in private—away from public scrutiny—allowed the widow to work without external interference. In the same way, innovative businesses protect their research and development (R&D), recognizing the value of strategic, behind-the-scenes work. This principle reminds us that some of the greatest breakthroughs and divine transformations happen in hidden places, long before they are revealed to the world.

As Christians, just like the widow, we must learn to protect our space by shutting down outside requests during our season of growth and expansion. We must take a page from the widow, who shut her door according to the prophet's instructions. Sometimes, we need to isolate our environment in order to nurture new ventures and build healthy family dynamics.

The story of Nehemiah powerfully illustrates the importance of isolation when embarking on a new assignment. As the former king's cupbearer, Nehemiah was in the midst of rebuilding when he began receiving distracting messages from those who should have understood the significance of his work—but didn't. What did Nehemiah do? He refused to come down and entertain them, even though they were supposed to be ministers of the Gospel! His unwavering focus ensured that he completed the work God had given him.

Then Sanballat and Geshem sent a message, asking me to meet with them in one of the villages in Ono Valley. I knew they were planning to harm me in some way. So I sent messengers to tell them, "My work is too important to stop now and go there. I can't afford to slow down the work just to visit with you." They invited me four times, but each time I refused to go.
Nehemiah 6:2-4 (CEV)

Your greatest distraction won't come from ordinary people. When you are building something incredible, it will often come from those within the household of God—including ministers you know! Nehemiah was discerning and deeply focused on his assignment, refusing to entertain anything that could prevent him from completing it—even if that meant declining to meet with ministers of the faith.

He told them that his work was too important to be interrupted. On four separate occasions, he shut the door on their requests. Learn to recognize when to shut your door—even when the request comes from those within the household of faith—until you have completed the assignment God has given you and are walking in the fullness of His blessing.

The widow learned the power of order by allowing God to deliver her from the **spirit of over-commitment**. The truth is that people who struggle with overcommitment often find it difficult to say, "No" or "That's enough." I believe the widow and her late husband fell into debt for a variety of reasons—one of which was overcommitment. As ministers, we are often inclined to help everyone, even at great personal cost. It is possible that, in his devotion to ministry, the prophet took on responsibilities beyond his human capacity.

Overcommitment could have led to him borrowing without a clear payment plan; also, it could have possibly impacted his health as well. With the death of her husband, the widow must have learned how to say "no" and in the process of her transformation, she educated herself on how to refuse excessive external pressures by ensuring her family's wellbeing was her major priority, which in turn produced family stability.

The widow shutting the door created an opportunity for **solitude and quiet reflection**. The widow needed time alone with her sons to pour the oil—symbolizing a period of personal reflection and deep soul-searching for life's greater meaning and purpose. I often take time for my own soul-searching at the end of the day, asking myself questions like: What did I do right today? What areas do I need to improve in? I also make it a habit to write down things I am grateful for each day.

Taking the time to shut the door in your life—whether for solitude or reflection—creates a valuable opportunity for self-examination. It allows you to consider your journey, your calling, and where God is leading you. For the widow, this moment of seclusion was not just about privacy—it was a sacred time to witness and reflect on the miracle unfolding before her.

In our quiet moments, we have the opportunity to slow down and truly hear from God. Too often, the noise and distractions of the world drown out His voice, making it difficult to receive His guidance. Shutting the door in moments of solitude allows us to tune in to His presence, gain clarity, and align our actions with His plan. Solitude is an essential part of the Christian journey—it fosters insight, strengthens our faith, and helps us stay on the path God has set before us.

Another powerful lesson from the widow's experience is the wisdom of guarding information and not sharing prematurely. When Elisha instructed her to shut the door, he wasn't just telling her to create a private space—he was also advising her to protect the sacred process of her miracle. Had she shared her plan too soon, she might have faced doubt, discouragement, or even interference from others who didn't understand or believe in what God was doing in her life. By sealing out any distractions or chaos, the widow not only prioritized her family's wellness over any public demand but also preserved the sanctity of her miracle by not sharing her ideas as well.

Timing is crucial when guarding information, as premature sharing often invites interference. Revealing too much too soon can lead to doubt, jealousy, or opposition from those who may not have your best interest at heart. The widow needed to keep her task private until it was complete. By setting clear boundaries and shutting the door, she safeguarded both her resources and relationships.

When we set boundaries and uphold them, we create space to focus on what truly matters—our family's well-being and personal obligations. God often works in the Secret Place; His greatest miracles unfold behind closed doors, in moments we least expect. The process of birthing a miracle or breakthrough is delicate and must be well-protected.

Young Joseph learned this lesson the hard way. By prematurely sharing his dreams with his brothers, he nearly lost his life and was sold into slavery. However, years later, as second-in-command to Pharaoh, he exercised wisdom—choosing not to reveal his position prematurely, even to his own brothers. Timing is crucial, and modern-day Christians must discern when to share their plans and when to guard them until the right moment arrives.

Shutting the door also symbolizes making peace with the past and the mistakes you may have made. It represents a commitment to personal growth. For the widow, this act marked the closing of a chapter filled with debt and uncertainty, allowing her to step into a future of opportunity and victory. It was a turning point in her life's journey.

Unfortunately, many people never take the necessary steps toward personal growth and transformation. These are the individuals who remain trapped in anger, bitterness, and resentment—those who lash out, exhibit road rage, or snap at children and teenagers. Instead of acknowledging their past mistakes and seeking healing, they continue to see the world through a lens of frustration and hostility.

The widow could have chosen to be bitter about the hand that life had dealt her with the loss of her husband and the potential slavery of her two sons, but instead, she decided to grow from the experience. The first thing the widow did was to **acknowledge her past mistakes.** The widow had to come to terms with her husband's debts and how they both contributed to their situation; she recognized where they fell short and did not lay the blame even at her husband's feet. She took full responsibility, and God provided a way out of her situation because of her response. We must also acknowledge the areas of our lives where we have fallen short, take ownership and work towards making things right instead of blaming others.

One of the hardest things in life is **forgiving oneself and moving forward.** Forgiving ourselves and others is crucial for personal growth. The widow had to make peace with her circumstances in order to move forward in faith. This act of forgiveness positioned her to receive the miracle God had in store for her and her children. Forgiveness is a key component in receiving blessings from God. It also helps eliminate imposter syndrome—the feeling of unworthiness that can hinder us—by allowing us to embrace God's grace and move forward with confidence.

The only true way for one to grow requires us to let go of what does not serve us anymore. **Embracing change** is much like shutting the door on past pain or failure. When we accept change, we allow God to do something new in our lives—opening doors to fresh relationships and new perspectives. True transformation happens when we embrace change, positioning ourselves to step into our destiny. Modern-day Christians must understand that personal growth often begins with making peace with the past, learning from it, and using those lessons to move forward, fueling our passion and our future.

Several biblical figures experienced the transformative and miraculous power of God by shutting their doors—both literally and figuratively. In doing so, they discovered something new about themselves or their circumstances, emerging changed, and their personal experiences left a lasting impact on the world. One powerful example is found in Genesis 7 when God instructed Noah to shut the door of the ark before the flood. This act signified both the end of an old world and the beginning of a new covenant. Much like the widow's experience, closing the door was a moment of protection and transition. Both Noah and the widow stepped into new realities—Noah into a renewed world and the widow into a transformed life as a businesswoman.

Jesus Christ throughout the Gospel frequently retreated to quiet places to pray in solitude. By constantly shutting the door on the noise and distractions of the world, He connected with His Father, walked in numerous miracles and prepared Himself for the challenges that lay ahead. **Solitude and prayers** were keys to His ministerial success back then, just as they are equally important for us as believers today.

For Christians looking to shut the door on past pain, distractions, or worldly negative influences, there are ways to rise up to a more authentic version of oneself. Here are a few step-by-step guides to get you started:

Step 1: Identify What Needs to be Shut Out

- Write down areas of your life where boundaries need to be set.
- Reflect on past experiences that you need to let go of.
- Identify the areas that people in your past told you to change and begin exploring the possibilities.
- Decide to forgive yourself and those who might have hurt you as well.

Step 2: Seek Solitude for Reflection

- Set aside time for prayer and quiet reflection.
- Disconnect from distractions and external influences; this could include social media, cellphones, etc.

Step 3: Protect your Vision at all Costs

- Be cautious about sharing your goals too soon.
- Focus on building your ideas in a private, protected space.

Step 4: Set Boundaries

- Establish clear emotional, spiritual, and physical boundaries.
- Learn to say no to distractions or unhealthy habits.

Step 5: Embrace the Transition

- Recognize that change is part of growth.
- Step forward in faith, trusting that God is guiding you.

In conclusion, the widow shutting her door was the exact moment that set her on the path to financial success. She learned the importance of limiting external influences and demands, perhaps along with affirmation that every knock need not be answered; she probably also learned why some doors must remain closed in order to move forward!

By closing herself off from distractions, negative influences, and doubts, the widow was able to focus on the task that led to her financial breakthrough. I also believe she gained a valuable lesson in navigating overcommitment, recognizing that her past failure to set boundaries contributed to her financial crisis. Through this experience, she likely developed a deeper sense of self-love, learning the importance of setting limits to avoid similar pitfalls in the future.

The widow's obedience to the prophet's instructions, along with her willingness to shut the door, prepared her mind and heart for what God was about to do for her and her sons. By closing the door to the world, she opened the door to God's miracle. This is why learning to shut our doors and establish healthy boundaries is so important. Shutting your door could be the difference between remaining in the same place or stepping into His grace.

For modern-day Christians, the act of shutting the door carries great significance. Whether it's setting boundaries, protecting your vision, or seeking quiet reflection, this simple yet powerful practice fosters personal growth, renewed purpose, and divine success. As we learn from the widow's story, shutting the door is not about isolation—it's about creating space for God to work in our lives, families, and businesses.

CHAPTER 30

RAISING MONEY-SAVVY KIDS

Next-Gen Entrepreneurs

If you are a parent, in what ways are you turning everyday household chores into financial lessons to ensure your children become money-savvy? While I am not here to tell you how to raise your children, I will say this—if you are not teaching them the value of money and financial responsibility, you may be leaving them at a disadvantage. I recall that at the age of eight, my father opened a bank account for me—and it wasn't a joint one. I was solely responsible for depositing money into it each month.

I had a couple of wealthy uncles, and whenever I saw them, my father would tell them not to give me money. Of course, that never worked—they would generously give me cash, which went straight into my savings account. I remember being 13 years old, standing on our family property in Akwa Ibom, facing the vast Atlantic Ocean. I turned to my father and said, "We could build a hotel resort right here on the beach." He laughed and told me that he was confident I would make it one day.

The moral of the story is this: Either you teach your children the importance of money while they are at home, or they will learn it the hard way—through the harsh realities of the world, where there will be no safety nets or parents to rescue them. The story of the widow's oil is profound, not only because of the miracle that took place but also because of the powerful lessons it teaches about financial responsibility and the importance of passing financial knowledge on to our children.

In the midst of her tragedy, the widow went to great lengths to ensure that her sons learned invaluable lessons about handling finances, work ethics, and accountability. What a great disservice we do to our children when we hide our life's mistakes in an attempt to appear perfect. Sharing our own failures in a vulnerable and honest way—when done appropriately—sets our children up for success rather than failure. This is exactly what the widow did for her sons.

Once the widow understood Elisha's instructions, she didn't handle everything herself—she got her sons involved in the process. In other words, she put them to work. This act of inclusion turned her tragedy into a teachable moment, laying the financial foundation for her sons to avoid the same mistakes that had led their family into debt.

For modern-day Christian parents, the widow's story provides a clear blueprint for turning financial setbacks and other life challenges into invaluable teaching moments for their children. This chapter will explore how parents can use their own mistakes to train their children in financial responsibility, work ethics, and personal accountability—ensuring the next generation is better equipped to handle life's obligations.

One of the most common mistakes parents make is trying to shield their children from their past failures—either by denying them or avoiding the conversation altogether. However, one of the most powerful ways to teach children is through openness, using personal shortcomings as learning tools. This is the first step in breaking cycles of poor financial decisions and unlearning past mistakes.

Just as the widow involved her sons in gathering vessels and witnessing the miracle, modern-day Christian parents must actively engage their children in understanding the consequences of mistakes—particularly financial ones.

How to Use Your Mistakes as Lessons

1. ***Acknowledge Your Mistakes Openly:*** The first step in teaching children is acknowledging that we, too, have made errors in judgment. The widow likely had to come to terms with her husband's poor financial decisions and explain the reality of their debt to her sons and the possible consequences of what would happen if the issue remained unsolved.
2. ***Teach Them How to Avoid Repeating Those Mistakes:*** Use your experiences as examples of what not to do. Whether it's debt, overspending, or lack of financial planning, share those mistakes and show them how to do better.
3. ***Model Better Behaviors:*** It's not enough to simply tell children to do better. You must model it. The widow showed her sons that while they had entered a season of debt, they were capable of working hard to resolve the problem. She modeled diligence, faith, and responsibility.

By taking an active role in teaching our children how to handle mistakes—using our own lives as examples, just as the widow did—we instill in them the value of accountability and the importance of making things right.

Teaching children about fiscal responsibility should begin early, and there are effective strategies to do so. The widow involved her sons directly in securing vessels, which taught them valuable lessons about work ethic, responsibility, obedience, and commitment. In the same way, today's Christian parents can adopt a similar approach to instill financial responsibility in their children.

Steps for Teaching Financial Responsibility

1. ***Introduce Financial Concepts Early:*** As soon as children can understand the basics, start teaching them about money. This can be as simple as introducing concepts like saving, spending, and budgeting.

2. ***Teach Them about Earning Money:*** Just as the widow's sons participated in the process of gathering vessels, teach your children the value of work. Whether it's chores, a part-time job, or earning an allowance, children need to understand that money comes from effort.

3. ***Involve Them in Financial Decisions:*** Let your children see how you manage household finances. Whether it's paying bills or setting up a budget, involve them in the process so they can see how money works in real life.

4. ***Use Real-Life Examples:*** Share stories from the Bible, like the widow's oil, to show how diligence and financial responsibility can lead to miracles and breakthroughs. Also, share modern stories about people who overcame financial struggles.

Use biblical examples such as the Parable of the Talents (Matthew 25:14-30), where Jesus tells the story of three servants entrusted with their master's wealth. The two who used their talents wisely were rewarded, while the one who buried his out of fear lost everything.

Stories like this illustrate to children the importance of using money wisely and the consequences of not doing so. There can be no true learning about fiscal responsibility without first laying a foundation in work ethics. Understanding the value of diligence and wise decision-making is essential for financial responsibility.

While I believe the widow's late husband had a strong work ethic, his efforts unfortunately did not demonstrate the tangible rewards that come with diligent and consistent work. Why is this important? Because in this case, the widow was able to teach her sons the value of hard work that yielded visible rewards—not just spiritual ones! Her sons didn't sit back while their mother did all the work; they were actively involved in gathering the empty vessels needed for their miracle.

This teaches us that work ethic isn't just about doing tasks for the sake of it but about actively contributing to solving life's challenges. As crucial as it is to instill strong work etiquette, we must also model it for our children, starting by setting **expectations early.** Just like the widow, parents should assign their children tasks that require responsibility and effort. Whether it's schoolwork, chores, or a job, children must learn that diligence and perseverance lead to real rewards.

Next is **rewarding their efforts, not just results**: Celebrate the efforts your children put into their work, not just the outcomes. This teaches them how to develop resilience and perseverance, two critical aspects of a strong work ethic. **Teach them to be proactive**: The widow's sons didn't wait for others to bring them their empty vessels; they proactively went out and did the work themselves. Teach your children to take initiative and be proactive in solving problems while building critical thinking skills as well.

The widow's story is about more than just miraculous provision—it also carries a powerful lesson on accountability, a principle often overlooked or dismissed, to our great detriment. The truth is that the widow was in debt and needed to find a way to pay it off. By involving her sons in the process, she taught them the importance of facing their obligations head-on rather than avoiding responsibility or relying solely on prayers and religiosity while doing nothing. Modern Christian parents have a duty to teach their children this vital lesson: accountability matters.

If you truly want to prepare your children for the real world, start by teaching them about debt and accountability. This begins with being honest about your own financial situation, showing them firsthand how to manage debt and financial responsibilities. When children understand that debts must be paid, they develop a strong sense of financial accountability. It's also essential to teach them the dangers of debt through real-life examples of its consequences. Show them how to use credit cards responsibly, emphasizing that credit is a tool, not free money.

Many parents avoid discussing finances, but understanding how debt works is crucial for children to avoid future financial pitfalls. As a parent, it's your responsibility to instill in them the importance of paying off obligations—just as the widow worked to settle her family's debts. Help them see the benefits of being debt-free, such as financial freedom and peace of mind.

One of the greatest traits the widow displayed was flexibility. When faced with tragedy, she didn't resist the unusual instructions given by Elisha; instead, she adapted and involved her sons in the process. This flexibility allowed her to turn a seemingly impossible situation into one of victory. This brings us to how we can teach our children flexibility. It starts with teaching them to be open to change—life is unpredictable, and circumstances will inevitably shift. The widow showed her sons that learning how to pivot was essential for both survival and success.

Encourage problem-solving skills: One of the best things you can do as a parent is allow your children to face challenges on their own while guiding them toward solutions. The widow didn't have a roadmap for how her oil would multiply, yet she trusted the process. By doing so, she allowed her sons to witness the miracle unfold. Instill a spirit of teachability: There can be no flexibility without a willingness to learn. The widow had to be open to receiving and following instructions. Teaching children to embrace learning is crucial for success in every area of life.

One of the greatest examples of the Bible is the story of David and Goliath in 1 Samuel 17, in which he was offered the opportunity to face the giant with typical battle clothing, and at first, he agreed.

> *So Saul clothed David with his armor, and he put a bronze helmet on his head; he also clothed him with a coat of mail. David fastened his sword to his armor and tried to walk, for he had not tested them. And David said to Saul, "I cannot walk with these, for I have not tested*

them." So, David took them off.
I Samuel 17:38-39

This demonstrated David's flexible nature, in that though he had never worn war garments, he was teachable in the moment to work with that he had been given. Another part of flexibility is to know when to pivot, which he also did right afterward when he realized that he could not fight with armor or a sword and chose five smooth stones.

Then he took his staff in his hand; and he chose for himself five smooth stones from the brook, and put them in a shepherd's bag, in a pouch which he had, and his sling was in his hand. And he drew near to the Philistine.
I Samuel 17:40

By being teachable, flexible, and willing to pivot in a single moment, David demonstrated his ability to adapt to the unfolding situation—choosing to use a sling and stones. It was this flexibility in strategy that led to his victory and secured triumph for Israel.

Tragedy brings pain, grief, and disappointment, but it can also become a life-changing, teachable moment. One of the most powerful aspects of the widow's story is how she transformed her calamity into an opportunity to save her sons. Rather than succumbing to despair, she used the very crisis she faced to instill values that would guide them for the rest of their lives. This is a critical lesson for Christian parents navigating their own tragedies—challenges can be turned into moments of instruction that shape the future.

This raises an important question: How do we turn tragedy into a teachable moment of opportunity? It starts with using **adversity as a**

learning experience. The widow didn't shield her sons from the reality of their situation; instead, she involved them in the solution. Likewise, when facing personal challenges, there are times when involving your children in finding real-life solutions can be invaluable.

This raises an important question: How do we turn tragedy into a teachable moment of opportunity? It starts with using adversity as a learning experience. The widow didn't shield her sons from the reality of their situation; instead, she involved them in the solution. Likewise, when facing personal challenges, there are times when involving your children in finding real-life solutions can be invaluable. Life's challenges are inevitable, but how we respond to them teaches our children resilience and perseverance. These are the very traits the widow demonstrated by turning to God and following His instructions through the prophet Elisha.

One of the greatest takeaways from tragedy is the ability to transform short-term struggles into long-term lessons. Just as the widow used her circumstances to teach her sons about financial responsibility, you too can turn hardships into valuable teaching moments. Often, the struggles we endure impart more wisdom than our successes ever could.

In today's world, there are many resources available to help parents teach their children about finances, work ethics, and accountability. Here are a few helpful websites:

1. ***Dave Ramsey's Financial Peace:*** This program offers tools and resources for teaching financial responsibility at any age. (www.daveramsey.com)

2. ***Junior Achievement:*** Provides educational programs to help children understand entrepreneurship, work readiness, and financial literacy. (www.juniorachievement.org)
3. ***Smart Money, Smart Kids:*** A resource for parents to teach their children about money from a biblical perspective. (www.smartmoneysmartkids.com)

In conclusion, it is entirely possible to turn debt into a legacy of financial responsibility, as the widow's story does not end in failure or defeat. Instead, she used her tragedy as an opportunity to teach her sons valuable lessons about financial responsibility, work ethics, and accountability. For modern-day Christian parents, her example serves as a powerful reminder that even in adversity, we can teach our children to navigate life's challenges with wisdom, flexibility, and grace. By involving our children in the process of handling our mistakes, we create opportunities to teach them about finances early. This allows them to model flexibility and resilience, equipping them for the future. By turning tragedy into a teachable moment, we not only help our children grow but also transform our own struggles into opportunities for personal growth and renewed purpose.

In the end, the widow's legacy was not just about oil, it was also about the financial lessons she imparted to her sons. As Christian households, we can teach our children early how finances really work, while guiding them on how to build strong work ethics as well. By doing so, we teach the next generation about accountability and integrity by turning everyday tasks into teachable financial moments for our children. This allows our children to shoulder vessels that they can manage while equipping them early.

As Christian parents, we can use tragedy to teach our children how to turn life's challenges into opportunities for success, ensuring they are equipped to handle whatever comes their way. We have the chance to show them how faith and finance work hand in hand and that being teachable and flexible allows God to do the miraculous after they have put in the hard work. And that is how we raise future entrepreneurs!

CHAPTER 31

FAITH-FUELED EXPANSION

From Jar To Market

I remember meeting a woman who started a small homemade skincare business from her kitchen. At first, she made just a few jars of body butter for family and friends. As demand grew, she began selling at local markets. However, despite the increasing interest, she hesitated to expand. She feared what it would require—more inventory, a larger production space, and the risk of failure.

One day, a major retailer approached her with an opportunity to stock her products in their stores. She was thrilled but overwhelmed. She told me, "I don't think I'm ready. I just started this for fun." I asked her, "Do you think God opened this door just so you could sit back and admire it? Or did He open it so you could walk through it?" That conversation changed her mindset. The last time we spoke, she was expanding her operations to get her skincare line on shelves nationwide. I certainly wish her the greatest success!

The widow in 2 Kings 4 faced a similar moment. She could have stopped when her jars were full and celebrated the miracle of provision. But she didn't. She took what she had been given and turned it into a thriving business—a distribution center. She didn't just survive; she expanded. This is the essence of Faith-Fueled Expansion.

In this chapter, we will explore how faith and action must go hand in hand. The widow's journey teaches us the power of scalability, the dangers of failing to grow when the opportunity arises, and how Christian entrepreneurs can balance faith-based principles with the resources needed for expansion. Whether your calling lasts a lifetime or just a short season, you can make an impact by using the gifts and opportunities God provides. Faith may fill your jars, but your willingness to take them to market determines your true success.

When Elisha instructed the widow to pour her remaining oil into borrowed vessels, he set the stage for a remarkable miracle. But the true beauty of the story lies in the widow's response after the oil miraculously multiplied. She didn't stop at the provision; rather, she took the next step and turned it into a business. She sold the oil, paid off her debts, and lived off the proceeds. In essence, she took what started as a jar of oil in her home and transformed it into a distribution center.

The widow went from a desperate situation to becoming a businesswoman. By involving her sons in gathering empty vessels and distributing the oil, she taught them valuable lessons in entrepreneurship, scalability, and responsibility. This story emphasizes the importance of scaling our operations when God blesses us with an increase.

What is scalability? It is a business's ability to grow and handle increased demand without compromising performance. The widow's business scaled when she moved from a single jar of oil to numerous vessels filled with oil. Had she stopped at just a few vessels, she would have limited her potential. But by borrowing as many vessels as possible, she positioned herself for greater increase—and the oil multiplied accordingly.

Scaling one's business has many benefits and we see this through the actions of the widow, such as:

1. ***Increased Revenue:*** By scaling her business, the widow generated enough income not only to pay her debts but to live off the surplus.
2. ***Job Creation:*** The widow involved her sons in the process, teaching them skills that would serve them in the future. Scaling her business allowed her to provide for her family—not just for the short term, but for the long term too.
3. ***Legacy:*** The lessons the widow's sons learned through this process would have impacted their work ethic, responsibility, and future endeavors.

From the beginning of creation, God has given humanity a biblical mandate to be fruitful and expand. In Genesis 1:28, He issued a fivefold command: be fruitful, multiply, fill the earth, subdue it, and have dominion. This isn't just a biological directive but a principle that applies to every area of life, including business. As Christian entrepreneurs, we are called to expand our influence, multiply what we've been given, and exercise dominion over the areas God has entrusted to us. And it all begins with God's blessing, which empowers us to fulfill the mandate He has given us.

Then God blessed them, and God said to them, "Be fruitful and multiply; fill the earth and subdue it; have dominion over the fish of the sea, over the birds of the air, and over every living thing that moves on the earth."
Genesis 1:28

Taking the lead from God's fivefold creation mandate, we can apply Genesis 1:28 to business needs, starting with:

1. ***Be Fruitful:*** Just as the widow was fruitful in her business by producing oil, Christian entrepreneurs must seek to bear fruit in their businesses, whether that be through providing excellent products or services or making a positive impact on their communities.
2. ***Multiply:*** The widow multiplied her oil, and in the same way, Christian business owners should seek different ways to multiply their revenue streams, expand their customer base, and increase their influence.
3. ***Fill the Earth:*** This speaks to expansion by taking your business to new markets, regions, or even internationally.
4. ***Subdue:*** As business owners, we must learn to overcome challenges, manage resources, and bring order to the operations of our companies. In certain cases, streamlining the processes for more efficiency and effectiveness.
5. ***Have Dominion:*** This is about leadership, setting a high standard in your industry, and operating with integrity, excellence, and purpose that becomes an integral part of your brand or service.

Many successful businesses today owe their growth to scalability. They recognize the need to expand their operations to meet demand and maximize profits. Several well-known companies have successfully scaled their enterprises, demonstrating the power of strategic growth.

- ***Amazon:*** What started as an online bookstore grew into a global e-commerce giant. Amazon's scalability is legendary, as it continuously expanded its product offerings, distribution networks, and technology to dominate the market.
- ***Starbucks:*** Starbucks scaled its business by creating consistent customer experience across the globe. What began as a single coffee shop grew into a worldwide franchise because of its ability to replicate its model in diverse markets.

Just as many businesses owe their growth to scalability, others have failed to scale and become extinct as a result. No business is too big to scale, and history has shown that companies that fail to adapt often pay the ultimate price. Several American businesses serve as cautionary examples of the consequences of lacking scalability.

- ***Blockbuster:*** Blockbuster's failure is a classic example of a business that did not adapt or scale with technological changes. As the digital age dawned, Blockbuster failed to innovate and was eventually overtaken by companies like Netflix, which understood the importance of scaling through streaming services.
- ***Kodak:*** Kodak was a leader in photography but failed to scale its business in response to the rise of digital photography. Its resistance to change led to its extinction.

Scaling a business not only benefits the owner but also positions it as a distribution center—a place where others can access products, services, and opportunities. In the widow's case, she became a hub of oil distribution, meeting the needs of her community while providing for her family. The impact of scalability and becoming a distribution center can be profound, bringing benefits such as employment, community growth, and increased sales. Some key advantages include:

1. ***Community Impact:*** A distribution center doesn't just serve its own interests, but benefits its own community by providing products, services, and in many instances job creation as well.
2. ***Increased Reach:*** As a distribution center, your business gains the ability to reach more people, thus expanding your influence, and exposing your brand while making a positive community impact.
3. ***Innovation:*** Being a pioneer in your field can lead to new products or services, giving you an edge over competitors and attracting more customers.

If the widow was known for scalability, Joseph, on the other hand, became famous for establishing the greatest distribution system of his time in Egypt and the surrounding nations during the famine. Through God's wisdom, he stored grain during the years of plenty and distributed it during the years of famine (Genesis 41). His foresight and scalability not only saved Egypt but also positioned him as a key leader in the region.

The widow transformed her modest jar of oil into a thriving distribution center by embracing faith and strategic planning. Joseph, meanwhile, leveraged his gift of dream interpretation, wisdom, and strategic planning—demonstrating that while God provides different resources, how we use them determines how we scale. By borrowing countless vessels and multiplying her product, the widow recognized the importance of abundance and seized the opportunity to grow her business exponentially!

The widow exemplifies the scripture that urges us not to despise the days of small beginnings. She transformed a seemingly insignificant start into a thriving business through a simple act of obedience. That one decision paved the way for exponential growth, demonstrating that with steadfast faith, even the smallest resource can become the foundation of a powerful distribution network.

For who has despised the day of small things? For these seven rejoice to see the plumb line in the hand of Zerubbabel. They are the eyes of the Lord, which scan to and fro throughout the whole earth.
Zechariah 4:10

Through innovation and business scaling, we create opportunities to build a lasting legacy for our children. One of the widow's most exceptional attributes was involving her sons in the process of gathering vessels. There was a time when business owners ensured their children learned the trade from the ground up. This not only taught them the intricacies of the business but also how to navigate and establish relationships. Unfortunately, today, many children graduate from college, and we immediately want to make them CEOs and partners.

By involving her sons from the ground up, the widow taught them humility, as well as how to innovate and scale a business. She set a precedent for her children and future generations. Through their mother's actions and their own participation, they witnessed the power of diligence, creativity, and stewardship.

Where there is scalability, creativity often follows. When children see their parents taking risks and embracing innovation, it inspires them to think outside the box and pursue their own ideas without fear or hesitation. Work ethic is also built through the process of scaling a business. As the widow's sons watched their mother work hard, they learned discipline, diligence, and perseverance. There is no shortcut to scaling a business—it requires commitment, responsibility, and the ability to manage resources while serving others. Parents have the opportunity to instill these values in their children early.

While the Bible offers timeless wisdom for business owners, Christian entrepreneurs must also be open to learning from secular sources. Many of the most successful business strategies come from secular examples, and integrating these principles with biblical truths allows Christian entrepreneurs to maximize their potential. One of the greatest advantages of utilizing secular resources is gaining access to experts who provide invaluable insights into business growth, marketing, and scalability. Being open to learning from courses, business books, and mentors can help entrepreneurs stay competitive in the market.

Having worked as a woman in technology, I understand the huge benefits that technological tools can offer in helping small and medium-sized businesses scale. There are many tools such as digital marketing platforms, customer relationship management (CRM) systems, as well as automation tools, which are developed by secular companies to ensure the success of companies. Undoubtedly, the Bible provides the foundation around integrity, stewardship and hard work, and God has created secular resources to provide the practical steps needed for us to be successful on the earth. The practical application of these principles in the modern-day business context is what will make the difference in whether our businesses thrive or die.

Scalability doesn't happen overnight; it requires recognition and intentional preparation. As a Christian business owner preparing for growth, it's essential to follow key steps that will set you up for success. I strongly encourage seeking professional services and experienced experts who can guide you through the process and support you along the way. Here are five steps to help you prepare for scalability:

1. ***Identify Growth Opportunities:*** Are you able to recognize where there is potential for growth in your business? What are the new markets, products, or services that you can explore to make that happen? How are you keeping current on the market trends and what is happening in your field?
2. ***Invest in Infrastructure:*** Scaling requires some level of investing, so before you start scaling, ensure that your business infrastructure can handle the growth. There is nothing worse than a company that once had exceptional service but now starts failing because it did not scale properly. This means that you might need to invest in new technology, hire staff or expand your facilities.
3. ***Create a Scalable Business Model:*** Design your business so that it can grow without compromising quality or performance. For example, using automation or streamlining processes can

help ensure that your business can handle increased demand while still providing exceptional service.

4. ***Monitor Key Performance Indicators (KPI):*** Pay close attention to signs of scalability, such as increased customer demand, higher profits, or growing market opportunities. Use these indicators to inform your decisions about when and how to scale your business or service.

5. ***Remain Open to Change:*** As you scale, be open to evolving your mindset and strategy. Just like the widow had to adapt to her new reality, you too must be flexible and willing to adjust to new challenges and opportunities.

While I wrote this book to encourage and ignite the fire of entrepreneurship within you, this is just the beginning—a first step to getting your feet wet. There are many resources available for Christian business owners who want to learn how to scale their businesses. Some useful websites and books include:

- ***Entrepreneur.com:*** Offers articles, advice, and strategies on scaling businesses.
- ***Harvard Business Review:*** Provides expert insights on business growth and leadership.
- ***Biblical Entrepreneurship (www.nehemiahproject.org):*** A resource for Christian entrepreneurs that blends faith-based principles with business strategies.

Every good entrepreneur must have a strong supply chain that effectively connects people to what they need. The widow's miracle was about more than just oil—it was about engaging with her community by borrowing vessels and selling her product to those who needed it most. Scalability goes hand in hand with having a robust supply chain. A well-built supply chain links your product to the people who require it, creating a network of mutual support and commerce.

For modern Christian business owners, establishing a reliable supply chain means nurturing relationships and fostering partnerships and collaborations, while ensuring that your distribution channels are efficient. This interconnected approach not only increases your profitability but also creates a sense of community and shared purpose. Your business becomes a conduit for God's blessings, spreading provision far and wide.

As the widow continued to obey Elisha, her story evolved from a divine act of provision into a powerful lesson in both scalability and entrepreneurship. By recognizing the potential for business growth and acting on it, she transformed her life and left a lasting legacy for her sons, turning her business into a distribution hub within her community. In doing so, she delivered value to the very people who had supported her while also advancing God's kingdom—unknowingly continuing the vision of her late husband's ministry.

For modern Christian business owners, the call to scale is about more than just profit—it's about stewardship, impact, and legacy. Preparing for scalability while integrating both biblical and secular resources demonstrates an openness to innovation. This mindset enables us to build businesses that not only survive but thrive.

This chapter also challenges us to see things from a new perspective. Consider how the widow's product—something she once took for granted—became the catalyst for a profitable and scalable business. All she did was reimagine a simple resource, oil, and transform it into a powerful tool for market disruption. What everyday resource do you have in your home that needs reimagining—one that could elevate your business or profitability? If you align your business strategies with God's plan, He can turn what seems like a crisis into an opportunity for exponential blessings!

As we seek signs of scalability, let's trust God's guidance, remain diligent in our work, and always be ready to invest in the opportunities He places before us. Stepping beyond our comfort zones—just as the widow did—is essential. She began by bringing her problem to Elisha, then took action by borrowing empty vessels, and finally, she sold the oil back to her community. We must not be afraid to walk on water if we want to transform our businesses into distribution centers of blessing and impact for the kingdom of God. In the end, the widow's blueprint for business growth was her ability to scale with purpose, using clear and purpose-driven strategies that led to sustainable success.

In conclusion, the widow's journey—from a single jar of oil to a thriving distribution center—offers timeless lessons in faith, innovation, scalability, and entrepreneurship. As you move forward in your own business ventures, remember to run with your product, recognize its value, and stay committed to the mission God has placed before you. Let the widow's example inspire you to embrace each season of your enterprise with courage, determination, faith, flexibility, and a heart fully surrendered to God's plan.

CHAPTER 32

COLLECT, RESERVE AND REINVEST

No Touch Zone

How disciplined are you? No, really—how disciplined are you? Many years ago, I dated a young attorney who lived in London, a wonderful young man. During one of my visits, he told me he didn't have time to go to the bank to deposit money in his account because he was dealing with a client's issue. He asked me to hold onto the money and remind him to deposit it later. Every day, he would come home tired and exhausted, and I would remind him that he needed to go to the bank.

On a couple of occasions, he even requested some money from what he was supposed to deposit at the bank. Then one day, he decided to take the day off. He stayed home and asked me to give him all the money he was taking to the bank that day. I obliged. About twenty minutes later, he came to me and asked if I was okay. I responded that I was, to which he said, "Sandra, all the money is intact, why—you took nothing for yourself?" I replied, "But you asked me to hold onto it for you to take to the bank?" He looked at me in amazement, then handed me all the money and told me to buy myself anything I wanted.

I can't say whether he was testing me, but the fact remained that the money, to me, was a "No Touch Zone." He had emphasized the importance of the money he had entrusted to me, and there was no way I was going to jeopardize that trust. I demonstrated restraint and discipline—two things he hadn't expected, I guess. The moral of the story? You must know when to exercise discipline and restraint if you want to succeed in business, especially when there seems to be an abundance of money, perhaps more than you've ever seen or experienced before.

This chapter is about the **"No Touch Zone,"** a principle the widow exemplified through remarkable discipline by setting aside her full vessels of oil. This is a crucial lesson for both Christian business owners and new entrepreneurs. Despite her immediate financial need to pay off her debtors, the widow demonstrated the power of restraint. As she followed Elisha's instructions, she poured her last bit of oil into borrowed vessels, and miraculously, the oil kept flowing until every vessel was full. But there's an often-overlooked part of the instruction that once a vessel was full, it was to be set aside.

This simple act of setting aside full vessels carries a profound lesson for new entrepreneurs. Despite her desperate situation, the widow did not immediately use or prematurely sell the oil. Instead, she exercised discipline, waiting until all the vessels were filled before taking any further action. In this section, we will explore the importance of discipline in business, especially for those just starting out. We will examine why setting aside resources, profits, and early successes is crucial for long-term sustainability and growth.

Elisha's instructions to the widow were clear: pour the oil into the vessels and set aside those that were full. This means there were two sets of vessels—those that contained oil and those that were completely full. The instruction was to set the full ones aside. The phrase **"set aside"** means to reserve, save, keep back, spare, hold in emergency, or stockpile. The truth is that the widow could have been tempted to start selling the oil immediately after the first few vessels were filled, especially given the weight of her debts and the desperation of her circumstances. But she didn't. She waited until all the vessels were full, and even then, she still did not sell but instead sought further instructions from Elisha. This was unbelievable! Let's be honest, how many of us would have waited to consult a mentor before taking our next step? Very few. Yet, her actions teach us a critical lesson in what I would call Business 101.

Here is the lesson: J*ust because you're seeing some measure of success doesn't mean it's time to start spending or using your profits.* Instead, recognize when it is the right time to utilize what you've accumulated. Here are a few reasons why you want to practice the art of **"setting aside"**

1. ***Preservation of Resources:*** In a business, especially in the early stages, setting aside profits or resources ensures that you have reserves for future growth or emergencies.
2. ***Strategic Planning:*** Waiting until the right time to use your resources allows you to plan wisely and avoid rash decisions based on short-term success or immediate needs.
3. ***Avoiding Burnout:*** By pacing yourself and setting aside your gains, you avoid exhausting your resources or overextending yourself too early in the process.

The truth is, for many new entrepreneurs, the first signs of success can be both exhilarating and exciting; it is much like writing your first book and finally holding it in your hands. After months or even years of hard work, seeing profits roll in is a thrilling experience. However, the temptation to start spending that money immediately, whether it is on paying off debts, reinvesting in the business, or covering personal expenses, can be intoxicating and overwhelming at the same time. And this is where discipline becomes essential.

The widow's discipline is astonishing! Despite her desperation to pay off her creditors, she exercised remarkable restraint. She didn't sell the oil the moment all the vessels were full, nor did she touch what had been set aside. Her story teaches us that even in moments of urgency, discipline can prevent us from making premature decisions that could hinder long-term progress and negatively impact our success.

Lacking discipline can have dire consequences in business and it starts by experiencing **rapid burnout** which often comes with new entrepreneurs who are sometimes undisciplined. Without discipline, these newly minted entrepreneurs may deplete their profits too quickly, leaving them without the necessary capital needed to sustain their growing business.

When new entrepreneurs spend their early business gains, they **miss out on opportunities for growth**: This often is the missed opportunity to reinvest strategically in their business which can limit their scalability and in some special cases productivity altogether. **Increased financial pressure** is oftentimes the aftermath of a business owner whose lack of discipline has led to financial mismanagement, increasing the likelihood of taking on more debt or facing financial crises later on.

This is why both mentorship and discipline in business are critical to your overall success. For Christian entrepreneurs, discipline isn't just a good business practice, it's a biblical principle! Proverbs 21:5

reminds us, "The plans of the diligent lead surely to abundance, but everyone who is hasty comes only to poverty."

In the early stages of business, practicing both restraint and patience is crucial to avoiding the pitfalls that come with premature success. The truth is, the **"No Touch Zone"** is about resisting the urge to deplete early gains. By leaving the full vessels untouched, the widow exemplified restraint and self-control, ensuring that her blessings were fully realized over time. Business owners must recognize when it's time to seal the jar while exercising good judgment even at the height of their productivity.

The widow recognized the exact moment when all her vessels were full, identifying when her work had been completed. She then took the next step, ensuring the preservation of the resources she had so diligently labored for. Modern-day business owners and leaders must develop proper business acumen along with a spirit of discernment to know when to conclude one phase and prepare for the next, ensuring sustained productivity.

A good business owner must embrace strategic intelligence, just as the widow demonstrated through her choices. She showed that finishing tasks thoughtfully, with adherence to a structured method, leads to achieving entrepreneurial goals in a smart and effective way. By sealing the vessels, she exhibited sharp judgment in marking transitions, an essential skill for both aspiring and veteran entrepreneurs. Recognizing when a venture is complete and guarding successes through restraint and discipline ensures future growth and opportunity.

We have seen the cost of indiscipline; now, it is time to explore the benefits of exercising discipline. The first major benefit is **sustainability**, which comes from practicing restraint early in business. New entrepreneurs must ensure that their businesses are built on a solid, sustainable foundation to allow for steady growth rather than a boom-and-bust cycle. **Flexibility** is another advantage of setting aside profits or resources wisely. It provides the ability to pivot or adapt to changing market conditions without running out of capital.

Long-term vision is actualized through discipline. Restraint helps entrepreneurs stay focused on their long-term goals rather than being sidetracked by short-term gains, quick schemes, or gimmicks. This focus is essential for building a business that lasts. Many companies have been hailed for their discipline in the global market, and one of the greatest examples is Apple. Its worldwide presence and dominance are a direct result of the discipline of its founding leaders.

They refused to expand rapidly or release unfinished products, ensuring Apple's unwavering focus on quality and long-term vision, allowing it to dominate the tech industry. Another company known for exercising significant discipline in its earlier years is Walmart. Through strategic pricing and reinvesting its profits back into the company rather than spending recklessly, Walmart expanded methodically, eventually becoming one of the largest retailers in the world.

Without discipline, businesses, particularly new ones, are at serious risk of failure. According to numerous business studies and data from the U.S. Bureau of Labor Statistics (BLS), 50% of small businesses fail within five years. The reasons range from lack of market demand to poor financial management, issues that can largely be attributed to a lack of discipline or knowledge. The early stages of a business are fragile, much like caring for a newborn. Entrepreneurs who prematurely deplete their profits or resources can find themselves in a worse financial position than when they started.

New entrepreneurs should avoid the temptation of seeking short-term satisfaction. The undeniable rush of seeing profits and spending them immediately, whether for personal enjoyment or business reinvestment, should be restrained. It is crucial for new business owners to understand that the initial growth spurt, where reinvestment is common, is often unsustainable if not carefully managed. Without a strategic plan, early reinvestment can lead to overextension, burnout, and resource depletion.

Developing the skill to recognize when to set aside resources is critical for long-term success. Just as the widow set aside her full vessels of oil, Christian entrepreneurs must exercise the same discipline with their profits, talents, and opportunities. First things first, in the early stages of success, set something aside immediately rather than reinvesting everything into the business.

Cultivate the habit of evaluating your resources before making any major investments. Take the time to assess what you need for future growth and set aside a portion accordingly. Additionally, seek counsel from your mentor, financial advisor, and accountant before reinvesting all your profits back into the business. If you feel the temptation to use your resources prematurely, it is often a sign that it's time to pause and set them aside until you can make a more measured, strategic decision. Maintaining composure during times of rapid success can be challenging—but just as the widow demonstrated restraint under pressure, so should we. Learning to channel your energy into delayed gratification will help you build a stable and prosperous future.

The pressure the widow must have felt was immense, and we all know that desperation can cloud judgment, making it difficult to exercise discipline. In her case, desperation could have led her to sell the oil too soon, potentially limiting her earnings. However, by following Elisha's instructions and exercising restraint, she was able to pay off her debts and sustain herself with the remaining oil. What does restraint mean to you? If your choice today is between selling too soon or exercising discipline, which path will you take?

For new entrepreneurs, desperation and temptation often go hand in hand. Whether it's the temptation to spend early profits or the desperation to reinvest too soon, it's easy to make decisions that seem right in the moment but have long-term negative consequences. One of the greatest dangers of acting out of desperation is making rushed decisions. Desperate entrepreneurs often make hasty choices that are not in the best interest of their business. These actions tend to create a domino effect, leading to financial instability where one desperate act triggers further financial mismanagement, deeper debt, or even business collapse.

Short-term gains, when pursued out of desperation, often come at the expense of long-term success. A business owner driven by urgency may squander valuable opportunities simply because they are too focused on immediate relief rather than sustainable growth.

Whether you are a seasoned business owner or an aspiring entrepreneur, take a moment to ask yourself: What are your priorities? Is your primary goal to pay off debts as quickly as possible, or would you rather build a business that not only clears your debts but also ensures long-term financial stability? The widow's story teaches us that with discipline, we can achieve both. But without restraint, we risk losing everything. Here are some key questions to reflect on as you consider the best path forward:

Reflective Questions:

1. What debts do you want to pay off?
2. Is it more important to pay off your debts quickly, or to build a sustainable business that will provide for you and your family for years to come?
3. How can you practice discipline in your business decisions today?
4. What resources or profits do you need to set aside to ensure long-term success?

The widow's story is a powerful testament to the importance of discipline as a cornerstone of business success and sustainability. By setting aside full vessels and waiting for the right moment to sell her oil, she was able to pay off her debts and secure a prosperous future. Whether you are a new entrepreneur or a seasoned business owner launching a new venture, it is crucial to exercise the same level of restraint and discipline. Experiencing success does not mean it's time to start spending or reinvesting all your profits prematurely!

For those struggling with debt or navigating the challenges of a new business, remember that discipline is key to overcoming financial pressures. Success isn't just about paying off debts; it's about building a business that will sustain you and your family for years to come. Take the widow's example to heart, and remember that with discipline, anything is possible.

CHAPTER 33

THOUGHT REVOLUTION

Mindset Reset

Let me ask you a question: How is your thought process? How have your thoughts evolved over the years? Are you more progressive or more conservative? Are you flexible, or do you remain unbending in your views? Have you become a risk-taker, or are you now more cautious about change? Have you had a thought revolution? And why does this matter—in both life and business? There are things I once believed twenty years ago that I no longer hold as truth. Certain experiences have reshaped my mindset, altering the way I approach challenges, opportunities, and even my faith. Growth demands evolution, and the ability to rethink and adapt can mean the difference between stagnation and success.

At my core, I am Sandra Ekpenyong, the daughter of Jonathan and Genevieve Ekaete. Yet, over time, my experiences and exposure have shaped me in profound ways. Throughout my journey, I have encountered what I call "thought revolutions." Thought revolutionists are individuals who actively seek personal growth without harming others—unlike cults, racism, tribalism, or gender inequalities, which diminish and destroy lives. A thought revolutionist is someone who is constantly evolving—a person who challenges conventional thinking, disrupts outdated paradigms and introduces transformative ideas that shift perspectives and inspire change.

This chapter is about the power of a changed mindset, and how the widow's perception shifted as she started her own business. Thought revolutionists don't just accept the norm but often question it with "whys and what ifs." They are often the people in the room who introduce new ideas and perspectives. These are the people who inspire change among us that can be uncomfortable, often leading to societal, cultural and personal mindsets. They are often unapologetically bold, unafraid to challenge the status quo—even when it makes them unpopular (think of Jesus). Most importantly, they are vision-driven. Their goal is not rebellion but transformation. Those who cling to the past often struggle to work with such individuals, which is why education is crucial. Education has always been the catalyst for true thought revolutions, pushing us to question established norms—especially when they prove ineffective.

In 2 Kings 4:1-7, the widow's journey from desperation to entrepreneurship is a powerful testament to how both tragedy and necessity can force a shift in mindset. She went from financial despair to a successful businesswoman, but this transformation wasn't just external. More importantly, her internal perspective had to change as she stepped into her new role. Her decisions, the responsibilities she took on, and the pressures she faced required her to rethink her approach to life, money, and responsibility. And she had to do it quickly as she raced against time.

Starting a business, especially as a Christian, can profoundly transform how you see yourself and the world around you. It often requires letting go of old mindsets, stepping away from relationships that no longer support your growth, and embracing new responsibilities that may feel overwhelming. In this section, we'll explore how the widow's mindset shifted as she launched her business and how Christian entrepreneurs today can navigate similar changes while staying true to their values.

The Widow's Forced Mental Shift

Let's be absolutely clear—the widow did not step into the business world by choice. It was her husband's death, the mounting debts, and the looming threat of losing her sons to slavery that forced her into entrepreneurship. She found herself at a crossroads, with no option but to take action and find a solution. While it was Elisha's instructions that set her on this path, true success required more than mere obedience. She had to transform her perception of herself, her circumstances, and, most importantly, her future.

She could no longer afford to see herself merely as a victim of tragedy, as this did not diminish or dismiss her reality. Instead, she had to embrace a new identity: the head of the household, the sole provider, a business owner, and a steward of God's provision. The widow was forced into a profound mental shift. In many ways, her experience reflects that of countless new entrepreneurs who enter the business world out of necessity. Whether due to job loss, financial hardship, or the pursuit of a better life, many are thrust into entrepreneurship, and with it comes the challenge of transforming their mindset.

There are three key things that happened for the widow to reset her way of thinking and they are all things that Christians can learn from; they are as follows:

1. ***From Survival to Strategy:*** The widow's first concern was survival; she needed enough oil to sell and pay off her debts. But as her business grew, she had to think strategically about how to sustain that level of success.

2. ***From Consumer to Producer:*** She went from being someone in need of resources to someone responsible for producing and managing a product. This is a very important part of mindset reset: what you are producing rather than what you are consuming.

3. ***From Dependency to Independence:*** No longer dependent on others, she became an entrepreneur who could provide for her family. This changes the dynamics of power as well, since not having to be at the mercy of others is very important.

Starting a business doesn't just transform your financial situation—it reshapes your entire perception of yourself and the world around you. Entrepreneurs often find their priorities shifting as their businesses grow. Relationships evolve, and their perspectives on money, time, and responsibility change. For Christian entrepreneurs, these transitions come with the added challenge of staying true to their faith and values while navigating the demands of business.

Here are some key mental shifts you need to embrace to develop an entrepreneurial mindset:

1. ***From Employee to Owner:*** As an entrepreneur, you are no longer just working for someone else's vision but now you are working on your own. Every decision you make moving forward directly impacts your business, your income, and your future.

2. ***From Spending to Investing:*** Entrepreneurs approach money differently. Instead of just spending, they often consider

every expense as a form of investment into the future of their business.

3. ***From Scarcity to Abundance:*** Many new business owners have to fight the mentality of scarcity; the fear that resources will run out. A successful entrepreneur learns to think in terms of abundance, trusting that with the right strategy, more resources will come.
4. ***From Immediate Gratification to Long-Term Success:*** Running a business often requires embracing delayed gratification. Entrepreneurs must stay focused on their long-term goals, resisting the temptation to take shortcuts or chase immediate success.

As with all things in life, every decision comes with its pros and cons. This is especially true for business owners, as there is often a natural resistance to change. Whether it's the fear of losing friends and family or the reluctance to let go of familiar ways of thinking, the transition can feel overwhelming. For some, the need to maintain control while resisting the necessary mental shifts of entrepreneurship can become a major obstacle. However, embracing a mindset shift comes with significant advantages.

One major benefit is **adaptability.** True entrepreneurs must be willing to shift their mindsets, remaining flexible to meet the evolving demands of their business. Innovation is a key component of success—without a curious and open mind, new opportunities may go unnoticed. Many companies have faded into obscurity simply because they lacked adaptability. The reality is that flexibility unlocks new ideas and innovations that can propel a business forward. Another invaluable advantage of a mindset shift is its impact on relationships. How is this possible? A positive shift in perception can lead to improved communication, strengthening relationships within both business and family. As business owners learn to manage their time and energy more effectively, they often find that their connections with others become more meaningful and fulfilling.

As in all things in life, there are certain cons in resisting a mindset shift and these are dangerous and can cost you everything. The first thing that happens is **stagnation**. Entrepreneurs risk becoming stagnant and **outdated.** The old ways of thinking may prevent the business from growing or adapting to new market demands and emerging technologies needed to take your company forward.

Another major risk is **strained relationships**, which can arise when we cling to outdated perceptions. This often leads to tension, especially when a business owner's priorities shift, but their loved ones struggle to understand the changes. The impact extends to business partnerships as well. A notable example is Christopher Little; the literary agent who helped launch the now-famous children's author J.K. Rowling's career when no one else would give her a chance. However, as Rowling's success grew, she eventually parted ways with him, illustrating how shifting priorities and differing mindsets can affect professional relationships.

It is believed that many of his former partners walked and sadly, his agency would close after his death in 2021. What a monumental loss for the literary community and the writing world as a whole; it is important that we maintain strategic relationships all the while being adaptable.

One of the most significant cons in one's refusal to change their mindset is **missed opportunities** that often happen when we cling feverishly to an old mindset. Many business owners have missed out on opportunities for growth and expansion just because they were unwilling to take the necessary risks or step into new responsibilities.

One of the greatest challenges in business is the danger of a stagnant mindset. Beyond **egotistical CEOs,** a major issue is the refusal to pivot and adapt their business model. While many struggle with change, Christian entrepreneurs face an added burden—the fear of losing their **values or compromising their faith** when making critical business decisions.

Dangers of stagnation do not just end due to outdated ideas, missed opportunities or strained relationships, as there is also a financial component as well. It is called **financial failure** when a business owner refuses to adapt to changing circumstances; they face financial ruin because they are unable to compete with more innovative and forward-thinking companies.

Here are five major companies that became extinct due to their refusal to embrace a shift in thinking. Their failure to adapt to technological advancements, industry shifts, and changing consumer needs allowed competitors to replace them or set a new standard in their industry.

1. Blockbuster (1985–2010)

Blockbuster was once in every city across America, but its downfall came when it refused to embrace the digital streaming revolution and online rentals. The company missed a massive opportunity to buy Netflix for just $50 million, dismissing the idea of streaming movies online. The lesson here is clear—adapt to new technology or become obsolete.

2. Kodak (1888–2012)

Kodak had been around since 1888 but fell because it ignored the rise of digital photography—despite inventing the first digital camera in 1975. The company missed its chance to continue dominating the photography industry, remaining inflexible and stuck on film, convinced that digital would never replace it. The lesson here is clear: innovate or become obsolete. And like many before them, Kodak faded into history.

3. BlackBerry (1984–2016)

I must confess—I loved my BlackBerry. But the truth is, they failed because they refused to evolve beyond physical keyboards and embrace touchscreen technology. While Apple and Android revolutionized smartphones, BlackBerry lagged behind. They grew too comfortable, relying on their status as the government's preferred cellphone provider. The lesson here is clear: user preferences dictate the market—not nostalgia or even government contracts. BlackBerry missed an entire market due to complacency, and ultimately, they became obsolete.

4. Yahoo (1994–2017)

I still can't understand how Yahoo ignored the opportunity to become a search and social media giant, especially after AOL's decline. They passed on the chance to buy Google for $1 million and Facebook for $1 billion—decisions that could have secured their place as a dominant force in the market. The lesson here is clear: a lack of visionary leadership can bring down even the greatest giants. Poor leadership is often the root cause of a company's downfall.

5. Toys "R" Us (1948–2018)

While I loved walking into their stores, the truth is they ignored e-commerce and relied too heavily on physical locations. Their downfall came from failing to invest in online shopping, allowing Amazon to dominate their specialized market. This lesson is a painful one: digital transformation is often not optional, it's essential for survival and growth.

Can you think of other companies that failed to pivot and the consequences they faced in the marketplace? The internet boom signaled a strategic shift for many industry giants, yet some failed to seize the opportunity and suffered a painful decline. Let's learn from these past giants and avoid repeating their mistakes in our own lives and businesses.

Beyond becoming obsolete, **moral compromise** is often a sign of a flawed mindset. Christian business owners, in particular, may feel pressured to compromise their values to keep up with secular practices, ultimately leading to a loss of integrity and trust. When customers no longer trust you, both your business and income suffer.

Isolation has also been the downfall of many companies and individuals. Entrepreneurs who resist change risk cutting themselves off from valuable relationships and opportunities both professionally and personally that could have propelled them to greater heights.

These concerns are valid; however, it is possible to change your perception without losing who you are in the process. The key is to remain flexible in your approach to business while holding firm to your core values. True success comes from adapting without compromising your identity. You must also be willing to walk away from opportunities that contradict your values and beliefs and be at peace with your decisions.

There are powerful examples, both biblical and secular, of transformational mindset shifts. One of the most striking is the Apostle Paul. Before his conversion, he was a Pharisee who persecuted Christians, even witnessing the stoning of Stephen at the height of his fanaticism. Yet, after his encounter with Jesus on the road to Damascus, his entire worldview shifted.

This once-hardline radical became one of the most influential apostles, writing much of the New Testament. Paul's story proves that a radical change in perception can lead to a life of purpose and impact. It also teaches that true radicalism does not seek to harm but to understand, influence, help, love and inspire others.

We cannot discuss 21st-century leaders who have made a tremendous impact without mentioning the late Steve Jobs of Apple. In the secular world, Jobs is a prime example of someone who had to change his perception to achieve success. After being fired from Apple, he learned invaluable lessons about leadership and business. When he returned, his renewed mindset transformed Apple into one of the most successful companies in the world, leading in communication and technological innovation.

Changing your perception as a business owner does not mean compromising your faith or values. In fact, a shift in mindset can deepen your relationship with God and strengthen your commitment to biblical principles. The key is to remain anchored in your faith while being open to new ways of thinking about money, business, and responsibility.

It starts firstly by you staying rooted in the Scriptures. Regularly studying biblical principles about money, stewardship, and business ensures that your mindset aligns with God's will. There is nothing more important than surrounding yourself with wise counsel or mentors. Seek out mentors and advisors who share your values but also challenge you to think differently about business. Just like marriage and work life require balance, so do innovation and integrity as well.

While it is important to be open to new ideas and innovations, it is equally essential to ask: Do these changes align with my core values and faith? Prioritize accountability. Intentionally seek an accountability partner who will hold you to your word and your tasks. Whether it's friends, family, or fellow business owners, surround yourself with people who will keep you grounded in your values as you grow your business.

One of the most powerful aspects of the widow's journey into business was her transformation through perspective—a direct result of her mindset shift. She moved from despair over limited resources to recognizing the potential in her small jar of oil. Instead of dwelling on what she lacked, she embraced prophetic wisdom, allowing it to propel her forward. A critical shift in her journey was moving from a scarcity mindset to an abundance mindset. She no longer saw her limited oil as a deficiency but as the seeds of abundance. This shift set in motion a transformative journey, securing a prosperous future for her and her sons. By following Elisha's prophetic guidance, she redefined her narrative, shedding old limitations and embracing new opportunities. Her story is a testament to how perception shapes reality—scarcity can be reinterpreted as an opportunity for growth and renewal.

She recalibrated her perspective, rising above past constraints with a renewed outlook that unlocked new possibilities and immense potential. Viewing life through a fresh lens can shift our perspective, paving the way for breakthroughs that transform our circumstances for the better. By adjusting her mindset, the widow saw her situation in a new light and realized that her once modest supply of oil held the power to multiply beyond measure.

With this fresh perspective, the widow found the inspiration to take bold steps and actions, emphasizing that breakthroughs begin when we dare to see our circumstances differently. Like the widow, our turning point comes only when we rewire our thoughts in a way that empowers us to transform our future. The moment the prophet instructed the widow to fill every vessel marked a pivotal shift in her life. It compelled her to reframe her mindset from fear to faith, setting her on a path of radical transformation while demonstrating the power of decisive change.

While shifting your perception is essential for business success, it's equally important to be mindful of adopting a purely secular mindset. Some entrepreneurs, in their pursuit of success, start mirroring the world—prioritizing profits above all else, compromising ethics, or neglecting personal relationships and spiritual responsibilities.

Embracing a completely secular mindset can have significant negative consequences, often with far-reaching effects.

Oftentimes, when Christian business owners adopt secular business practices, they tend to embrace the negative aspects like compromising integrity, damaging their reputation, and ultimately suffering financial loss due to unethical decisions. An unhealthy obsession with success at any cost can strain personal relationships, creating distance from family, friends, and fellow believers. Furthermore, prioritizing business over faith can lead to spiritual decline. When a Christian entrepreneur places their business above their relationship with God, they risk moral and spiritual deterioration.

One biblical example is King Saul, who lost his way by adopting a worldly mindset. Instead of trusting in God, he became consumed with power and control, which ultimately led to his downfall, the death of his children and the loss of his kingdom to David. Christian business owners must remain vigilant against the temptation to follow the world's way of doing business at the expense of their faith and family.

One of the greatest challenges Christian business owners faces is balancing business growth with spiritual development. As one's business expands, the demands on time and resources increase, making it tempting to prioritize work over faith. However, true success lies in maintaining a healthy balance between the two through a few simple yet practical steps. The first step is to schedule time for God. Just as you set aside time for business meetings and tasks, prioritize prayer, Bible study, and fellowship with other believers.

Another key practice is incorporating faith into your business without alienating those who do not share your beliefs. This can be done through ethical decision-making, integrity, and generosity. For example, while I never preached on the job, I treated people with such respect that they recognized my faith, especially when I refused to engage in gossip.

Make it a priority to rest once a week, as God has commanded. Taking time to recharge both physically and spiritually is essential for overall well-being. In the end, true success requires breaking through the barriers in our minds to create lasting change. More often than not, these mental barriers are what keep us bound, stagnant, and in despair. The widow's journey in 2 Kings 4 reminds us that shifting our perception is often a vital step toward growth in both business and in life.

As Christian entrepreneurs, we are called to embrace these changes without losing sight of our core values. By staying rooted in faith, surrounding ourselves with wise counsel, and remaining accountable, we can navigate the mental shifts that come with entrepreneurship while still honoring God.

Remember, changing your mindset does not mean compromising your faith. It means growing in wisdom, responsibility, and stewardship. The widow's success came not only from following the prophet's instructions but also from her ability to adapt to new circumstances while keeping her heart aligned with God's will. What made the widow a thought revolutionist was her decision to think radically and beyond conventional limits, which propelled her from a place of hopelessness to a miraculous breakthrough. Here are six core principles that defined her as a thought revolutionist:

1. The Widow Who Refused to Accept Defeat:

In her society, a widow without a husband or financial means was expected to succumb to her circumstances, but instead of resigning herself to fate, she sought a solution from the prophet Elisha.

Core Takeaway: Thought revolutionists do not accept their circumstances but seek to change or transform them.

2. The Widow Who Engaged in Unconventional Thinking:

When Elisha asked what she had in her house, she didn't see the small jar of oil as valuable. Yet, she trusted the process when Elisha told her to gather empty vessels.

Core Takeaway: She shifted her mindset from scarcity to abundance, embracing an unfamiliar but divine new economic/business model.

3. The Widow Who Activated Her Faith Through Action:

Instead of questioning the absurdity of borrowing vessels and without knowing what would happen, she took bold action, and it resulted in success.

Core Takeaway: A thought revolutionist is not just a thinker but a doer; one who moves forward despite fear and uncertainty.

4. The Widow Who Leaned on Her Community:

She borrowed jars from neighbors, showing that community engagement was a part of her breakthrough.

Core Takeaway: True revolutionists understand that transformation often involves collaboration.

5. The Widow Who Turned a Crisis Into a Business Model:

After the oil multiplied, she was instructed to sell the oil, pay her debts, and live off the remainder. The widow didn't just receive a miracle; she became an entrepreneur, turning her pain into profit and securing her family's future.

Core Takeaway: Thought revolutionists don't just seek temporary fixes but create lasting impact.

6. The Widow Who Shifted From Survival to Generational Wealth and Sustainability

Many in her position might have asked for ongoing charity, but she learned how to sustain herself and her children.

Core Takeaway: Her actions broke the cycle of poverty and dependency, a hallmark of revolutionary thinking.

In the end, what made the widow a thought revolutionist was her willingness to embrace a new way of thinking, act in faith despite uncertainty, and transform her circumstances through divine strategy. Though she was an unwilling victim of her situation, she chose to become a vessel of transformation. She proved that even the smallest resources, when surrendered to God, can lead to supernatural overflow.

As you embark on your own entrepreneurial journey, let the widow's example inspire you to embrace the mental shifts that come your way, while holding fast to your faith and integrity. A mindset reset is important in the 21st century as life keeps evolving at a faster pace every day. You alone have the power to rewrite your life's story by harnessing the power of a renewed perspective.

As I close out this chapter, I want to offer a gentle caveat to those starting a business and experiencing challenges in their marriage. The strain is not just from long working hours but also from the shift in business mindset. It is crucial to bring your spouse along on this journey so they can understand the sacrifices and changes you are going through as a new business owner and fully support you. While you may be taking all the risks, they are also in it with you.

CHAPTER 34

SETTING THE BAR

The Missed Vessel

I once heard a story about a man stranded at sea, praying desperately for rescue. A boat came by, and the captain offered to help, but the man refused, saying, "God will save me." Later, a helicopter hovered above, and again, he declined, still waiting for divine intervention. Eventually, the man drowned. When he stood before God, he asked, "Lord, why didn't You save me?" God replied, "I sent a boat and a helicopter—you just didn't take them."

How many times in life have we missed opportunities simply because we didn't recognize them for what they were? Perhaps someone told us a door was closed, or maybe we failed to grasp the urgency of the moment. In this chapter, The Missed Vessel, we explore how often people walk away from their breakthrough and it's not because it wasn't available, but because they didn't seek out all the facts, underestimated the importance of an opportunity, or relied on someone else's limited perspective.

The widow in 2 Kings 4 was given clear instructions—gather as many vessels as possible. But what if she had stopped too soon? What if her sons had overlooked a neighbor who had more jars to give? The size of her blessing was directly tied to the number of vessels she collected, and the oil only stopped flowing when there were no more vessels left. Now, imagine if they had gathered and doubled the amount—how much greater would the overflow have been? This story reminds us that the extent of our success is often determined by how well we follow through on divine instructions and how relentless we are in pursuing every available opportunity.

This reminds me of how often we unknowingly limit ourselves by relying on others to determine what is possible for us. Have you ever missed out on a job opportunity, a business deal, or a major investment simply because someone who didn't have all the information convinced you that the door was already closed? So many of us make critical decisions based on second-hand information from people who don't have the full picture. That's where we get in trouble: when we allow someone else's perspective to limit our destiny.

I see striking similarities between the widow and her sons and the story of Adam and Eve. Both the widow and Adam received clear instructions; one from Elisha, the other from God Himself. But the challenge wasn't just in receiving the message, it was in how they communicated it and acted upon it. Adam and Eve's failure to fully grasp and obey God's instructions led to their eviction from the Garden of Eden. Similarly, the widow's sons may not have understood the full weight of their mother's task. Had they gathered more vessels, the oil would have kept flowing. Their partial effort resulted in a partial blessing.

This is why I titled this chapter The Missed Vessel. Too often, the size of our blessing is not just dependent on God's provision but also on how well we execute His instructions. The widow's financial future was directly tied to how well her sons carried out the command to gather vessels. Their limited efforts resulted in limited success.

This chapter will challenge you to reflect on moments when you may have unknowingly left opportunities on the table. Too often, those who were not present when we received divine direction do not fully grasp the weight of what was entrusted to us. And even when we attempt to convey the message, we may not always communicate it in a way that leads to the best possible outcome. In business, career growth, and life, these are lessons we cannot afford to ignore: never leave potential on the table.

We will explore how we unintentionally limit our own expansion by allowing others to define the boundaries of our pursuit. We will learn how to ensure that no vessel or opportunity is missed. Because when God releases an overflow, it is up to us to make sure we are fully prepared to receive it.

We find a critical moment in the widow's entrepreneurial journey when, after following Elisha's instruction to gather vessels and pour oil, she reaches a turning point. Her son tells her there are no more vessels left to fill. "Bring me another vessel," she says, but he replies, "There is not another vessel." At that moment, the oil stopped flowing. The truth is that the widow could have continued to expand, but her business was limited by the perception that no more vessels were available.

This singular moment offers a powerful lesson for Christian business owners today: the limitation of growth is not always determined by external factors but often by *internal beliefs and personal decisions.* The widow had **potential** for further expansion, but by relying on her sons' limited perception of when to stop, she unknowingly limited the extent of her business success!

Even writing this chapter is incredibly frustrating for me! We must learn to push past "beyond enough" moments in our businesses. Too often, we impose limitations on ourselves that hinder our growth, performance, and even more importantly our greatness. There were no limits to Elisha's instructions on vessel gathering. Yet, when the widow stopped collecting empty vessels, she inadvertently capped her own potential. In the same way, modern-day entrepreneurs must break free from the **"enough"** mindset to unlock greater opportunities. One reason we fall into this "enough" mentality is the danger of outsourcing our vision, entrusting it to a company or person who does not understand the price we paid for it.

The widow's decision to rely on her sons for gathering vessels serves as a cautionary tale that true leadership often means taking full responsibility for your vision. It is crucial to not delegate life-changing decisions to children or others who lack experience. The truth is, whenever a leader chooses to be hands-off in their business, they risk becoming ineffective and disempowered. There must be a balance between empowering your team and maintaining proper oversight. There is a distinct difference between laissez-faire management (a hands-off approach) and micromanagement; though they may seem similar, they are fundamentally different.

While both approaches aim to promote innovation, independence, and trust, the key difference is that micromanagement still includes leadership guidance and support, whereas hands-off leaders intervene only when necessary. This can be detrimental, as by the time a hands-off leader or business owner steps in, it may already be too late, and the damage has been done. By allowing her sons to decide when to stop borrowing vessels, the widow unintentionally created a barrier to further growth. A wise business owner learns to empower others while maintaining the oversight necessary to sustain and expand their enterprise.

By examining the widow's decision to stop collecting vessels and how it ultimately restricted her growth potential, Christian entrepreneurs today can learn how to avoid similar limitations. We'll also ask critical questions about the nature of her choice and how we can apply her experience to foster greater business growth while maintaining biblical principles.

The first question we must ask is: Did the widow's sons truly gather all the vessels? Elisha's instructions were clear: gather as many vessels as possible and pour the oil into them. Yet, we must consider whether the widow's sons fully followed this command. Did they truly collect every available vessel? It's possible they gathered only from a limited group of neighbors or underestimated how many vessels they could have found if they had expanded their search. Perhaps some people offered them extra vessels, and they declined. Or, as children, they may have simply grown tired of collecting and preferred to play outside!

The sons, though essential in assisting their mother, were not the ones who received the instructions from the prophet. This would have affected their perception of what "*enough*" vessels meant. As business owners, we must ensure that our team understands the vision and magnitude of our mission. When they don't, it's easy for their limitations to become ours.

Another important question we must consider is whether the widow closed the door prematurely, or both literally and figuratively. The oil stopped flowing when the vessels ran out, but what if she had continued searching for more vessels? Could the blessing have continued? Closing the door too early can symbolize shutting down opportunities before they fully develop. For Christian business owners, this could mean retreating when success is within reach or halting expansion due to perceived limitations.

Another pressing question is: Did the widow's sons have enough time to gather all the empty vessels? We must also consider whether time constraints affected their ability to collect more. Business growth requires patience, yet external pressures such as time, financial limitations, or emotional exhaustion can cause us to stop before gathering all the necessary resources for expansion.

In today's fast-paced world, Christian entrepreneurs may feel pressured to rush through processes, believing they lack the time to explore every opportunity. However, God's timing is perfect, and delays or slowdowns can be necessary for greater long-term success. If the widow's sons had more time to gather vessels, her business might have expanded even further. Additionally, the widow's own perception played a crucial role in her decision-making. Did she truly believe her sons had gathered enough, or was she simply weary from the process and willing to settle for what they had collected?

When starting and running a business, the way we perceive our opportunities directly influences our success. If we see limitations, we tend to act within those limitations. But if we see abundance and potential, we push the boundaries of what's possible. As Christian business owners, we must ask ourselves whether our perception is aligned with the expansive, abundant nature of God's provision, or if it is hindered by fear, doubt, or impatience.

In today's world, gathering vessels can be seen as gathering resources, opportunities, and relationships that fuel our business success. So, how can we gather the right amount of vessels as 21st-century Christian entrepreneurs? We can do so by the following methods:

1. ***Seek Divine Guidance:*** Like the widow, Christian business owners must seek divine guidance in all their endeavors. We should regularly ask God for wisdom on when to expand, when to gather more resources and when to press forward.
2. ***Expand Your Network:*** Gathering vessels can also mean expanding your network of contacts, investors, and collaborators. Limiting yourself to a small circle may restrict your growth.
3. ***Don't Settle for the Minimum:*** It's easy to settle for "good enough" when things are going well. But remember, just as the oil only stopped when there were no more vessels, your business can only grow as far as the resources you gather.

This means you must take charge of your own capacity for growth—even the prophet was not in control of the widow's expansion. However, her business stalled when she accepted her sons' report that no more vessels were available. This serves as a warning to us all: true growth comes from actively expanding our capacity rather than relying on others' limited perceptions—even when those perceptions come from our own family and friends!

As entrepreneurs, understanding when to close the door is crucial, as timing can make or break success. Closing too soon might mean missing out on greater opportunities, while keeping the door open too long could lead to wasted resources or burnout. In business, this highlights the importance of strategically deciding when to scale and when to pause. There are moments when you must focus on filling the vessels you have, but there are also times when keeping the door open allows for the gathering of more resources and opportunities.

Another essential lesson from the widow's story is finding the balance between seeking counsel from others—whether children, employees, or peers—and staying true to God's original instructions. The widow listened to her sons when they said there were no more vessels, but we must ask: was it truly time to stop, or could more have been done?

The moment her sons declared that the vessels were finished, she should have reassessed the situation herself to ensure that was the case. Visionary leadership is intentional—it is the difference between deliberate success and mere happenstance. By relinquishing control of the vessel count, the widow allowed others to define her level of success. If you find yourself in this position as a leader, it's time to reclaim control over your enterprise and move beyond accidental or constrained business progress.

As business owners, we will often receive advice from well-meaning individuals who may not see the entire picture. While it is important to take counsel, we must always align it with God's original instructions and vision for our lives and businesses. At times, the pressures of the present, like debt, exhaustion and imposter syndrome, may cloud our judgment and make us more susceptible to stopping too soon.

While the term "imposter syndrome" may be relatively new, one possible reason the widow didn't push for more vessels could be a sense of inadequacy. After years of struggling, she might have believed she didn't deserve such success, or perhaps she feared the blessings would run out. This kind of imposter syndrome occurs when a person feels unworthy of the success or opportunities they receive. For many business owners, it becomes a significant obstacle. However, as Christians, we must remember that our blessings are not based on our worthiness but on God's grace. When God opens a door for expansion, it is not our place to question whether we deserve it—but to step forward in faith and obedience.

There are many modern-day and biblical examples of businesses and individuals who fell short of their full potential because they listened to outside voices or internal doubts instead of staying committed to their original vision. The Israelites, for example, wandered in the wilderness for 40 years—what should have been just an 11-day journey—all because they doubted God's promise to lead them into the Promised Land. Fear and hesitation kept them from receiving a blessing that was already available to them. If only they had acted in faith, they would have reached their destination much sooner.

Kodak is a modern-day example of a business that limited its growth by not adapting to new opportunities. Despite inventing the digital camera, the company hesitated to pursue it fully, fearing it would cannibalize its film business. This hesitation eventually led to their downfall as other companies took the lead in digital photography. Both examples demonstrate the importance of being open to expansion and not allowing fear, doubt, or limited perception to stifle growth.

As Christian entrepreneurs, the key to overcoming all these challenges is to stay rooted in God's guidance; understand the current business and market trends and, most importantly, be willing to expand when opportunities arise. Here are a few nuggets to ask yourself when that time comes:

Questions to Reflect On:

1. Am I gathering all the vessels that God has made available to me, or am I stopping short because of fear or doubt?
2. Am I closing doors prematurely, or am I keeping them open to allow for further expansion?
3. When do I take counsel from others, and when do I stick to the original instructions God has given me?

By continuously reflecting on these questions, we can ensure that we don't limit the growth and blessings God has in store for us. It is important that we set the bar for ourselves around what type of success we want to achieve, thus avoiding the ceilings that others place on our success. It's important to set your own standards and refuse limits imposed by others or by past circumstances.

Finally, the danger of full vessels represents complacency, revealing the limits of our current approach. There are times when we become content with what we have, lacking the ambition to move forward simply because we never expected to achieve the level of success we now enjoy. The danger of this mindset is that it often signifies untapped potential within us. In the widow's case, there was still more to receive, more to offer—but the flow stopped because she reached her perceived limit. Modern entrepreneurs must continually seek out additional "vessels" to capture every opportunity available, no matter how small or insignificant it may seem. True growth comes not from settling but from recognizing that there is always room for more.

In conclusion, if the widow had continued gathering vessels, her business could have expanded even further. For today's Christian business owners: the potential for growth is often far greater than we realize. The key is to remain open to God's leading, avoid limiting beliefs, and trust that the resources and opportunities we need are out there waiting for us to gather them. The lesson is clear: don't let someone else's perception of when to stop define your success. Seek God's wisdom, gather as many vessels as possible, and trust that He will provide the oil to fill them. Learn from the widow's restrictive choices and be challenged to proactively gather as many resources as you possibly can without fear of overreaching.

Know that the moment the widow's oil ceased, it was not an end but God's invitation to expand her vision and authority. And when we fully embrace this mindset, we position ourselves not only for business success but for long-lasting impact in God's kingdom.

CHAPTER 35

CEASING OF THE OIL

Seize The Moment

Has anything you worked on just simply ceased and how do you handle that moment? Was it a partnership or a job? How do you handle situations when they end? Do you embrace the end of a season, or do you stretch it out to make it last as much as you possibly can? How we handle the end of a season, relationship or situation speaks a lot to how we see and handle things altogether. Many of us struggle on the part of *'embracing the end of a season'* especially when there are no warning signs.

I recall a season of unexpected endings, a time when there were no warning signs. I was working for a particular company, consistently overperforming. I had exceeded expectations so much that one of the partners even sent me a handwritten card, expressing how grateful he was to have me on the team and how amazing I was. Well, well, well, my friends, fast forward three months. The day before Good Friday and just one day before receiving my $20,000 bonus, that same partner told me over a Zoom call that I was a low performer. What?! I had just completed leadership training, preparing to lead my own team! And now, suddenly, I was being dismissed?

I was **SHOCKED**! I reminded him of his handwritten card he had personally mailed to me, to which he dismissively hung up the Zoom call and handed me over to Human Resources, who seemed visibly uncomfortably and could only offer a vague apology. When they informed me that I could always return to the company, I simply laughed. No, I did not get my bonus, and I found out later from a number of other company alumni that they too had the same experience just before they were to get their bonuses.

While I might not have originally embraced the moment, many opportunities were afforded to me afterward, and I look back and realize that the oil ceased there because I was greater than what I was doing. I will not tell you that when your oil ceases you will be rejoicing, but I will tell you to look beyond the oil and seize your moment.

As we read, the widow's oil ceased flowing after the last vessel was filled. This moment holds profound significance for Christian business owners today, symbolizing the natural end of a season of provision or opportunity. The widow's oil was a miraculous blessing, but it was never meant to flow indefinitely. Likewise, in business, every opportunity has its season. Success is not just about recognizing when the oil is flowing; it's about preparing for when it stops as well. How we respond when a season ends can determine whether we stagnate or step into the next level of growth.

In this chapter, we will explore the significance of the oil ceasing and the critical lessons Christian business owners can learn from it. Recognizing when a business model, venture, or opportunity has reached its natural end is essential for sustained growth. We will also examine how to prepare for these transitions without fear, drawing from both biblical and secular examples of once-profitable businesses that eventually became obsolete. Finally, we'll identify key signs that indicate when it's time to shift from one business model to another and discuss how to navigate these transitions with wisdom and faith.

One of the most crucial lessons from the widow's story is that her oil had a finite flow—it ceased when there were no more vessels to fill. As business owners, we must recognize that opportunities are not always indefinite. The business that generates revenue today may not be profitable tomorrow. However, this reality should not create fear, but awareness. Just like the oil, every season in business has its limits. The key is to discern the right time to transition—to prepare for the end of one venture and the beginning of another.

While the widow's oil was a divine miracle, the ceasing of the oil points to practical lessons we can apply to business. Could the widow have prepared better for the ceasing of the oil? Here are some ways she might have:

1. ***Diversification of Resources:*** The widow relied solely on the oil for her business. Diversifying her income streams by exploring other ways to generate income alongside the oil could have ensured stability even after the oil ceased.
2. ***Long-Term Planning:*** Understanding that the oil would eventually cease, the widow could have planned for what to do when that moment came. Creating a long-term strategy could have helped her sustain herself after the miracle ended.
3. ***Investing the Profits Wisely:*** Instead of solely using the oil to pay off her debts, the widow could have reinvested part of her profits into other ventures or assets that would generate continuous income.

For modern Christian business owners, these lessons are critical. Just as the widow's oil eventually ceased, every business venture has a lifespan. The key is preparation—diversifying resources, planning ahead, and investing wisely. This is not a new phenomenon. Throughout history, once-thriving businesses and ventures have faded because they failed to adapt or anticipate change. Even in Scripture, we see examples of God-ordained provision that eventually came to an end.

One notable biblical example is the manna in the wilderness. In Exodus, God miraculously provided manna for the Israelites. Yet, when they entered the Promised Land, the manna ceased—signaling a new season of provision.

And they ate of the produce of the land on the day after the Passover, unleavened bread and parched grain, on the very same day. Then the manna ceased on the day after they had eaten the produce of the land; and the children of Israel no longer had manna, but they ate the food of the land of Canaan that year.
Joshua 5:11-12

This transition signified the end of a miraculous provision and the beginning of a new season in which the Israelites had to work the land and gather their own food. Just like the manna, the oil in the widow's story was never meant to last forever. Recognizing when God is shifting us to a new season is crucial to our overall success.

Businesses that became extinct all had one thing in common—they refused to pivot when their season changed. Whether it was failing to adopt new technology or ignoring market trends, their reluctance to evolve led to their downfall. As a business owner, recognizing the right time to transition from one business model or venture to another is crucial for sustainable success. Here are some telltale signs that it might be time to make a shift:

1. ***Declining Revenue:*** A consistent decline in revenue is a clear sign that the market is changing, and your business model may no longer be sustainable.

2. ***New Competition:*** If new competitors are entering the market and outperforming your business, it may be time to innovate or pivot to stay competitive.

3. ***Changing Consumer Preferences:*** As consumer preferences change, your business must adapt. Failing to meet new demands can lead to a loss of relevance.

4. ***Technological Advances:*** Advances in technology can render certain business models obsolete. Staying updated on industry trends and innovations is vital for staying ahead.

Just as the widow's oil ceased, businesses must know when to recognize the signs of an ending season and transition into new opportunities.

It's crucial to understand that the opportunity of today is often vastly different from the one of tomorrow. Markets evolve, technology advances, and consumer needs shift. What worked for the widow—pouring oil into vessels—was sufficient for that moment, but once the vessels were full and the oil stopped flowing, her next step would have been entirely different. Likewise, in business, the strategy that brings success today may not be the one that sustains you in the future. Recognizing when to evolve, pivot, or even exit a market is essential for long-term success.

Whether you want to believe it or not, there were some benefits as there were some limitations as well by the widow's oil ending. The widow's decision to stop pouring oil when there were no more vessels may seem like a limitation, but it also came with benefits. Let's explore both:

Limitations:

1. ***Missed Opportunity for Expansion:*** Had the widow gathered more vessels or sought additional ways to expand, she may have continued to grow her business.
2. ***Reliance on a Single Resource:*** By relying solely on the oil, the widow limited her options once the oil stopped flowing. Diversifying her income streams could have provided more security.

Benefits:

1. ***Financial Security:*** The widow was able to pay off her debts and live off the remaining oil, demonstrating that there are benefits to recognizing when an opportunity has served its purpose.
2. ***Completion of a Season:*** Sometimes, recognizing the end of a season allows us to transition into a new one without fear. The widow didn't need the oil to flow forever because it had served its purpose.

As Christian business owners, we must discern when an opportunity has reached its natural conclusion and be prepared to transition into the next phase—whether in business or life. The widow may not have realized that her oil came with a limited-time opportunity, but its abundant yet temporary flow teaches us a critical lesson: every opportunity has an expiration date. The key takeaway? Seize and maximize short-term blessings before they fade. Procrastination can rob you of opportunities that were meant to elevate you. The ceasing of the widow's oil is a powerful reminder that no matter how blessed we feel today, wise planning is essential for tomorrow's uncertainties.

When the oil ceased, the widow experienced a sudden shift from abundance to scarcity—a reality that many business owners face at some point. For Christian entrepreneurs, this highlights the need for strategic preparation: building contingency plans, diversifying income streams, and cultivating adaptability. The widow's miracle was never meant to last forever, serving as a warning against assuming infinite provision. Instead, it teaches us the wisdom of anticipating change and preparing for the next season before the current one ends.

If we do not bank on infinite provision, then we must learn how to thrive even after our oil ceases. The widow's cessation of the oil should serve as a warning that no blessing lasts forever if we don't prepare for its end. It is therefore important that you adopt a long-term perspective, manage expectations, and develop sustainable practices that enable you to thrive beyond your current season of success.

When the oil ceased, the widow faced a sudden shift from abundance to scarcity, a reality that many businesses owners encounter at some point. For Christian entrepreneurs, this underscores the importance of strategic preparation: building contingency plans, diversifying income streams, and embracing adaptability. The widow's miracle was never meant to last forever, serving as a cautionary lesson against assuming endless provision. Instead, it teaches us the wisdom of anticipating change and preparing for the next season before the current one ends.

Preparing for the end of a business venture or opportunity should not be viewed as a fearful event but rather, it should be seen as an opportunity to embrace a new season. Here are some practical steps Christian business owners can take to prepare for the ceasing of their "oil":

1. ***Diversify Income Streams:*** Relying on a single product, service, or client can be risky. Diversifying income streams provides security and flexibility when one revenue source ceases.
2. ***Plan for the Future:*** Develop a long-term strategy for your business that includes contingency plans for when current opportunities end.
3. ***Stay Informed:*** Keep up with industry trends, technological advancements, and market shifts. Staying informed allows you to anticipate changes and adapt before it's too late.
4. ***Trust God's Provision:*** Just as God provided the oil for the widow, He will provide for you in each season of your business. Trust that God's provision does not end when one opportunity ceases; He will guide you into the next.

Just as the widow experienced a natural cessation of oil once every vessel was filled, recognizing and navigating the end of your business season is important. You must enter your transition period with adequate strategic planning and faith in future provision. There are some business opportunities that when I get into them, if I do not like how they are panning out, I begin to develop an exit strategy.

I liken exit strategies to fire drills, with the difference being that I have no intention to re-enter the building once I exit. It is crucial to prepare for the closing of a golden window of opportunity. Being realistic is key; remember that, as the oil stopped flowing, it signified the natural close of one profitable season for the widow. Exit strategies, along with portfolio diversification, should be explored as profit margins shrink.

Once the widow's oil ceased, she faced the reality of limited resources, underscoring the need to diversify income streams. Learning how to expand your business portfolio ensures that a single product's end doesn't spell disaster for your overall enterprise. Developing strong exit strategies and pivoting effectively allows you to transition smoothly, ensuring that when one window closes, you're ready to open another with minimal disruption. There are clear benefits to having an exit strategy when your resources begin to dwindle, starting with the following:

1. ***Opportunities for Innovation:*** When one opportunity ends, it creates space for new ideas and innovations. Being prepared allows you to pivot quickly and take advantage of emerging opportunities.

2. ***Reduced Anxiety:*** Knowing that you have a plan in place for when the oil ceases reduces anxiety and fear of financial loss.

3. ***Continued Growth:*** By recognizing when to transition, you can continue growing your business instead of stalling when the current model no longer works.

The widow's story teaches us that the end of one provision is not the end of God's provision entirely. When the oil ceases, it signifies not a loss, but a transition—an indication that God has something new in store. As Christian business owners, we must learn to embrace these shifts with faith, trusting that God is guiding us into the next phase of both our business and our lives.

Faith is reflected in how we perceive our circumstances. The ceasing of the widow's oil was not a failure; rather, it marked the completion of a season. In business, there will be times when the oil stops flowing—when a particular opportunity or venture comes to an end. How we prepare for and respond to these moments will shape our future success. By recognizing the natural conclusion of one provision, we can proactively navigate seasonal downturns and chart new paths with confidence and purpose.

The widow's timely actions ensured her financial freedom before the oil stopped flowing. This is more than just a lesson in market shifts; it also underscores the importance of securing your business foundation before external conditions force a change. Business opportunities can become obsolete overnight, making it essential to embrace constant innovation and flexibility. By doing so, you ensure that your enterprise remains relevant and competitive in a rapidly evolving marketplace.

There are also valuable insights for entrepreneurs who engage in seasonal startups and high-impact ventures. Not every opportunity is meant to last forever, and some are designed to meet an urgent need before giving way to a new season. The widow's oil was a temporary miracle that addressed her immediate crisis, yet it also set her on the path to long-term transformation. Likewise, believers who launch seasonal startups can leverage these temporary ventures to create meaningful impact, positioning themselves for sustained success beyond the season.

Modern entrepreneurs can benefit from understanding that not every venture is meant to be a lifelong commitment. By seizing temporary opportunities with passion and precision, you can build capital and gain valuable experience that will fuel future business endeavors. Embrace the cycle of starting, harvesting, and transitioning—much like a farmer who understands that each season serves a different purpose and must be leveraged wisely. A farmer manages resources according to the season, adapting to shifts even as growing cycles become more unpredictable.

Similarly, we can navigate dwindling resources and the end of prosperous seasons by aligning our focus early, seizing opportunities before they vanish and adapting to economic changes. For wise business owners, reinvesting before the well runs dry is essential. Even the miracle of the oil had an endpoint. By learning from the widow's experience, Christian business owners can embrace transitions without fear, trusting that God's provision is always sufficient for each season.

Understand that not every phase of business is permanent. The widow's oil eventually ceased, indicating the natural end of that season. Know when to scale up, when to sustain your current operations, and when to pivot or exit a venture altogether. Those are critical decision points in entrepreneurship. Diversifying resources, planning for the future, and trusting in God's guidance will help us navigate the end of one opportunity and the beginning of the next with confidence and faith.

CHAPTER 36

CRITICAL CHECKPOINTS

Don't Ghost Your Advisor

I love the lessons of the widow's oil and how often people overlook Scriptural wisdom on the power of successful mentorship. One experience from years ago left a lasting impression on me, teaching me the true value of mentorship and the importance of staying connected to those who pour wisdom into our lives.

I once gave a young entrepreneur key advice that helped transform his struggling business. At the time, I was balancing ministry and my career, yet I made time to pray with him and offer guidance. Within a week, doors flung open, he was blessed with an extra car for his business, received final approval for his green card, and secured a multimillion-dollar cleaning contract with a major airline. It was a breakthrough moment!

Then there was complete silence. No calls. No updates. Not even thank you. Months passed, and when I finally reached out to check on him, my calls went unanswered. I moved on, assuming he was doing well—until one day, I received an urgent message. He was in crisis, on the verge of losing everything, and desperately needed my help.

This chapter is about critical checkpoints in life and business, the mentors and advisors God places in our paths, and why we must never ghost those who invest in us. Success isn't just about reaching the top; it's about sustaining what you've built—and that often requires staying connected to the people who have guided you along the way. Let's explore why mentorship is essential, how to recognize the right advisors, and the dangers of neglecting those relationships when everything seems to be going well.

How entitled have we become as people, treating preachers like prayer contractors, calling them up whenever we need something, making demands as if their time and guidance are owed to us? When he finally reached out, I asked him where he and his sisters had been over the past few years. He sheepishly listed his many problems, but as I listened, I realized that his situation was beyond my expertise. More so, I was unwilling to jeopardize my relationship for someone who had proven himself ungrateful.

I informed him that I could not help, and he was shocked by my response. Let's be clear that this was not about revenge; it was about protecting the relationships that mattered to me. The young man and his sisters had failed to future-proof their vision, and I was not going to risk my own relationships for his benefit.

Future-proofing your vision is essential for anyone seeking true success. The widow received additional guidance only after she returned to Elisha a second time. The truth is, sometimes a mentor provides just part of the puzzle, waiting to see what results you will produce. This is not a tactic to make you return to them, but a way to determine the kind of support you truly need to succeed. Even after filling all her vessels with oil, the widow instinctively knew her journey was incomplete—she needed further direction on what to do next.

This is a powerful lesson for Christian business owners: the need for continual guidance, mentorship, and instruction, especially after experiencing initial success. Many entrepreneurs fail because they assume that a small victory means they no longer need counsel. Ego, arrogance, and overconfidence can blind us to the reality that the journey is far from over and oftentimes, we do not yet have the full picture.

This chapter explores how the widow's humility in returning to the prophet serves as a model for business owners today, highlighting the importance of avoiding the pitfalls of arrogance and nurturing relationships with mentors and advisors who can guide us toward sustained success.

You might ask, why did the widow return for additional guidance? One major reason is that she had never been a businesswoman before. Lacking experience, she needed the prophet's further instruction. Her story demonstrates the wisdom of seeking additional direction and humility in trusting the word of the prophet.

In business, it's tempting to believe that once we've reached a certain level of success, we have all the answers. However, true wisdom lies in recognizing that guidance often comes in stages. The initial advice may just be the first step, and continued mentorship is essential to navigating the next phases of the journey to greatness.

The danger of a little success is the assumption that we know it all. After experiencing an initial breakthrough, it's easy to believe that we no longer need advice. The widow could have fallen into this trap; after all, she had filled all the vessels with oil, just as Elisha had instructed. By all appearances, her journey was complete. But she didn't make that mistake. Instead, she recognized the need for further instruction and sought additional guidance. Whenever business owners assume they have all the answers, they risk falling into the trap of arrogance, which can lead to the following:

1. ***Poor Decision-Making:*** The truth is that without proper ongoing guidance as a business owner, it is very easy to make decisions based on incomplete information or faulty assumptions.
2. ***Isolation:*** When we stop seeking advice from those who are experienced, we isolate ourselves from their wisdom and life lessons, leaving us more vulnerable to failure and disappointment.
3. ***Missed Opportunities:*** Opportunities for growth and expansion are often overlooked if we do not continue seeking input from those with greater insight, knowledge and experience.

Just as the widow understood that her work wasn't done, Christian business owners must recognize that ongoing mentorship is crucial for long-term success. Too often, people fail because they stop following the very path that once led them to success. The widow's initial achievement—gathering and filling the vessels—laid the foundation for a lasting legacy, but it did not guarantee it.

However, when she chose to continue learning under Elisha's mentorship, following all his instructions, she secured a better future. Modern entrepreneurs must plan beyond immediate wins, continually refining their strategies with the guidance of great mentors. Having a surplus does not automatically translate into stability, as some business owners mistakenly believe. Wise counsel not only provides the necessary steps for business growth but also helps prevent burnout, ensuring sustainable success.

Even when experiencing success—like the widow's overflow of oil—she wisely managed her resources by remaining open to ongoing advice. Wise counsel not only helps business owners make sound decisions but also protects them from burnout as they continue to grow their ventures.

If arrogance leads to poor decision-making, then ego can be considered a **"silent business killer."** Ego and arrogance often go hand in hand, especially when money starts flowing in. Many failed business owners once basked in the pride of their "we've made it" moment—only to stop listening to the very people who helped them succeed. This is where so many entrepreneurs come crashing down, much like Humpty Dumpty, who sat on the wall but couldn't withstand the fall.

The widow was devoid of any ego, a rarity for someone who had just collected enough oil to pay off her debt and take care of her sons. Although she had filled the vessels, she still needed guidance on how to use the oil to pay off her debts and live well. She didn't cut the prophet off after her initial success, but instead, she humbly returned to him for extra guidance.

The widow demonstrated true humility even after experiencing early success. In contrast, those who are arrogant often cut off their mentors or advisors, believing they have "arrived," only to make short-sighted decisions that jeopardize the long-term health of their businesses. This arrogance often leads to financial trouble, whether by spending profits unwisely, failing to reinvest in their business, or missing out on key growth opportunities. The widow's story serves as a powerful reminder that success should not breed arrogance. Instead, it should deepen our reliance on the wisdom of those who have guided us and contributed to our success.

There are numerous examples in the bible of individuals who cut off people in the early stages of their success. No greater example is that of King Saul, who was ordained by the prophet Samuel and once he was crowned king he began to act independently, so much so that as he grew more powerful, he disregarded the advice of Samuel and disobeyed God's commandments. This led to him eventually losing the kingdom along with dying next to his three sons.

> *The soldiers took sheep and cattle from the plunder, the best of what was devoted to God, in order to sacrifice them to the Lord your God at Gilgal." But Samuel replied: "Does the Lord delight in burnt offerings and sacrifices as much as in obeying the Lord? To obey is better than sacrifice, and to heed is better than the fat of rams. For rebellion is like the sin of divination, and arrogance like the evil of idolatry. Because you have rejected the word of the Lord, he has rejected you as king."*
>
> *1 Samuel 15:21-23*

Just as we see in the Bible, the same holds true in the secular world—many entrepreneurs rise quickly, only to fall just as fast. Some successful startups, after receiving mentorship and capital investment, choose to stop listening to continued advice, believing they can navigate the complexities of business on their own.

Too often, these companies collapse due to arrogance, poor leadership, and bad decision-making, proving the necessity of continuous guidance. For business owners who have a habit of ghosting their advisors, it is essential to maintain the very relationships that contribute to their success. It is your responsibility to nurture the connections that once served as a beacon of hope and direction. Success isn't just about seeking provision when needed; it's about ensuring that your mentors remain valuable resources long after your first major breakthrough.

The widow's second appointment with Elisha played a crucial role in preventing complacency from setting in. The power of a second appointment lies in the deeper level of access and accountability it provides—something the initial encounter often lacks, as it is usually driven by urgency or panic. Returning for guidance reveals a great deal about one's character and belief system. It reflects a posture of gratitude and humility. In the widow's case, despite her miraculous gain, she never assumed her journey was complete. Instead, she sought Elisha's counsel once again, and through him, she likely received fresh insights that helped her sustain progress and guard against complacency.

The question today is what areas in your business have you seen early success, and have you cut off those who guided you to that success? What steps can you take to reconnect with those mentors, and how can you begin seeking their advice again without it looking like you are taking advantage? And are you truly sorry for how you handled that relationship? If as a business owner or even as a minister, you have offended your mentor, there are certain steps you can follow in order to reconnect.

1. ***Admit Your Mistakes*** by humbly acknowledging that you may have distanced yourself from those who helped you out of arrogance and foolishness. This act of humility and accountability will go a long way in restoring relationships.

2. ***Seek Apology and Reconciliation,*** especially if your ego or arrogance caused a rift in the first place. You must be willing to apologize and seek reconciliation, but you have to make an effort. Mentors are often forgiving, especially when they see genuine humility.

3. ***Show Gratitude:*** Express sincere gratitude for the guidance and support you have received in the past. A thankful heart opens the door for future mentorship and access to their resources.

4. ***Commit to Continued Learning*** by demonstrating a willingness to continue learning from your mentor, recognizing that their advice is invaluable to your growth.

There are certain qualities that successful mentees exhibit when following their mentor's advice. The widow exhibited many of these traits and if we are to thrive as business owners and entrepreneurs, we should be open to following them, starting with the following:

1. ***Humility:*** The ability to recognize that we do not know it all and need guidance.

2. ***Patience:*** Understanding that success takes time, and that advice often comes in stages and sometimes after failures as well. I will talk about Failures and Successes in my 5-book series titled *"Igniting Your Vision."*

3. *Teachability:* A willingness to listen, learn, and implement advice from others, even if you do not fully understand what they are requesting.
4. *Gratitude:* Recognizing the value of the mentorship and expressing appreciation for the wisdom received.
5. *Perseverance:* Sticking with the process, even when it gets difficult, and continuing to seek counsel as you grow.

The widow displayed humility, patience, and teachability by returning to the prophet for further instruction. These traits are essential for any business owner who seeks to succeed long-term. One biblical example of a mentee following the advice of their mentor is that of Joshua and Moses. Joshua succeeded Moses as the leader of Israel, by following Moses' example and guidance.

Joshua was mentored by Moses, and by faithfully following God's instructions as conveyed through his mentor, he successfully led Israel into the Promised Land (Joshua 1:1-9). His humility and obedience to Moses' guidance became the foundation of his great success.

Secular Example: Steve Jobs and Tim Cook

A great example from the business world is Steve Jobs, the visionary founder of Apple, who mentored Tim Cook, the company's current CEO. After Jobs' untimely passing, Cook stepped into leadership, carrying forward his mentor's vision while also adapting it to meet evolving market demands and consumer needs.

Cook's ability to uphold Jobs' foundational principles while innovating for the future has been instrumental in Apple's continued success and market dominance. These examples highlight the power of mentorship and the ongoing need for guidance from those with greater experience.

Failing to get the whole picture or prematurely cutting off advice from a seasoned mentor can have long-term negative consequences. The widow could have assumed that once the vessels were filled, her work was done. However, by returning to Elisha, she learned how to use the oil wisely in paying off her debts and living off the remainder.

Business owners who fail to seek the full picture risk experiencing **Incomplete Success**, achieving some level of progress but never realizing the full potential of their business. Another major consequence is **Financial Instability**; without proper guidance, mismanaging profits or failing to reinvest wisely can lead to financial hardship or even the collapse of the business. **Burnout** is a common struggle for entrepreneurs who try to handle every aspect of their business alone. Without seeking help or advice, exhaustion can set in, leading some to give up entirely. God places people in our lives not only to offer financial guidance, but also to provide wisdom and directional support. Recognizing and embracing these resources is the key to long-term success.

As business owners grow and mature, there comes a time when they transition from being students to becoming mentors themselves. Those who have followed their mentors' guidance and achieved success can, in turn, help guide others on their entrepreneurial journey. To successfully transition from student to mentor, there are a few key qualities and skills that must be acquired along the way:

1. ***Wisdom:*** The ability to discern when you have enough experience to help others.
2. ***Generosity:*** A willingness to give back and share the knowledge you've gained.
3. ***Patience:*** Understanding that mentoring others takes time and commitment.
4. ***Humility:*** Remembering that you were once in the same position and that success is a continuous journey.

The widow's return to the prophet teaches us that mentorship is not a one-time event but a continuous process of seeking guidance and implementing the advice one has been given. The widow's reliance on Elisha for his continual direction in a new business venture underscores the importance of seeking wisdom before complacency sets in. This also helps mitigate the risks of going solo after a start-up's initial success.

By examining the widow's frequent consultations with Elisha the prophet, we recognize that her need for ongoing oversight could have been leveraged into helping her lean on him and fortify their relationships for future endeavors, if she had been interested in remaining in business for herself!

Contemporary Christians must understand that mentorship is essential beyond their first major payday. Early success is merely the beginning, not the endpoint. Continuous guidance is crucial for navigating new challenges and refining a business vision. The widow's story serves as a powerful reminder that success is not built on a single piece of advice, but through ongoing counsel, patience, and mentorship.

Christian business owners must embrace humility, seek continued guidance, and guard against arrogance and overconfidence. True success is not just about personal achievement but also about passing wisdom to others and becoming mentors in turn. The widow's story teaches us the power of lifelong learning, mentorship, and humility in business. Sustainable growth is only possible when we welcome ongoing counsel into our lives. Just as the widow's prosperity was built by following Elisha's guidance, so too must we remain open to wise instruction.

For modern-day Christian business owners, ongoing advice is essential for adapting to change and sustaining growth in an ever-evolving business landscape. It is crucial to resist the 'Solo Syndrome'—a mindset where individuals prefer to work alone, often at the expense of teamwork, collaboration, and meaningful relationships. This tendency is especially common among high-achievers, entrepreneurs, leaders, and creative geniuses who struggle with delegation, trust, or relying on others.

Business owners who suffer from **'Solo Syndrome'** are oftentimes in peril of flying blind once money begins to flow into their bank accounts. The widow's reliance on Elisha prevented her from making uninformed decisions when success first appeared as such; she did not allow early profits to breed isolation. Mentors are not just for difficult times but for good times as well. Have those critical checkpoints regularly while walking in humility by visiting those who helped set you up for success.

The widow continued to seek guidance from Elisha, even after her newfound success, ensuring her long-term stability. This reminds us that maintaining humility and regularly reassessing our path with expert advice is crucial for sustained achievement. Ultimately, preserving financial gain requires staying connected to mentors for long-term impact. By keeping in touch with her mentor, the widow safeguarded both her profits and future prosperity. In the end, it is the strength of ongoing mentor-mentee relationships that helps protect and multiply success over time.

CHAPTER 37

INNOVATION, SIMPLIFICATION AND MARKET DISRUPTION

From 'Empty' to 'Exponential'

I remember when I was first learning to ride a bicycle. I had watched others do it effortlessly, yet every time I tried, I wobbled, overcorrected, or fell flat. I thought I needed something extra—a better bike, training wheels, or even someone holding me up the entire way. But the truth was, I just needed to master balance. Once I did, everything changed. Business and entrepreneurship work the same way. We often believe we need something big, complex, or entirely new to succeed. But in reality, success is often about mastering the fundamentals—finding balance, refining what works, and scaling it with confidence.

The widow in 2 Kings 4 didn't need a new product—she just needed to recognize the potential in what she already had. Her oil wasn't extraordinary until she applied a fresh strategy to it, just like my bicycle didn't take me anywhere until I learned how to ride it properly. In this chapter, we'll explore how starting simple, thinking creatively, and leveraging what's already in our hands can lead to innovation—and even market disruption. Sometimes, all it takes is a shift in perspective to turn something seemingly insignificant into something exponential.

In the story of the widow and her oil (2 Kings 4:1-7), there are profound lessons for anyone looking to start a business venture. One of the first principles we see in this story is the power of simplicity combined with innovation. The widow's oil was an everyday commodity, something common, affordable, and accessible, but it became the key to her financial breakthrough because of the way she applied a fresh approach to an old idea. Here is where we will draw parallels between the widow's experience and modern-day business practices, showing how Christian entrepreneurs can take simple ideas and revolutionize them into market-disrupting concepts.

We will also explore how to develop a plan for generating innovative ideas that can be life changing. This includes challenging traditional business norms through creativity, leveraging tools like Generative AI, and forming strategic partnerships. Believe it or not, everyday resources have the potential to become major market disruptors—just like the widow's oil, which started as an ordinary household commodity.

When she used and packaged it creatively, it not only resolved her financial crisis but also became a profitable venture. Her story should inspire modern entrepreneurs to rethink the value of common assets and recognize their potential for innovation.

To succeed, we must learn to think beyond the obvious and maximize the tools already within our reach. The widow's decision to repurpose her small jar of oil through a simple yet creative approach shows that true innovation doesn't always require something new—it requires a fresh perspective. This should encourage us to challenge conventional uses of everyday resources to unlock new opportunities, products, or services.

One thing for sure is that to start, you must keep it simple. In my *"Igniting Your Vision"* series, the first book is titled *"Start Simple."* People always have these great grand ideas, but the truth is that starting simple is where most companies have experienced great success before growing into a conglomerate. Starting simple was also the widow's strategy, as it is one of the most effective lessons we can learn from how she started her business.

The widow started with a simple idea—a product that was both familiar and essential. She didn't attempt to invent something entirely new; instead, she took oil, a commodity everyone needed, and transformed it into a profitable venture by bottling it. As business owners, we often overcomplicate things, constantly searching for the next big innovation when, in reality, the solution might be right in front of us. **Simplicity does not equate to a lack of innovation.** In fact, some of the most groundbreaking business ideas have come from revolutionizing simple, everyday products or services. Facebook is a prime example—before it existed, we already had ways to communicate, but Facebook streamlined and redefined how we connect and interact, turning it into a global phenomenon. The widow's story demonstrates that simplicity, when paired with the right strategy, can serve as the foundation for remarkable business success.

Innovation often doesn't come from inventing something entirely new. Instead, it comes from taking an old idea and applying a fresh perspective to it. God has placed creativity within each of us, and by tapping into that, we can bring about life-changing financial breakthroughs. The widow's oil may have been a basic commodity, but her application of the prophet's instructions turned it into a business that rescued her from debt.

The first innovator in the Bible was Jacob, whose groundbreaking livestock strategy transformed his destiny. His story in Genesis 30:25-43 mirrors the journey of many modern innovators. They work tirelessly, often struggling, until they discover an ingenious idea that changes their lives forever. For many business owners today, this is their reality. Jacob is a powerful biblical example of how an old concept can be revolutionized. He worked for his uncle Laban, tending his flocks as part of their agreement. However, when the time came for Jacob to build wealth for his own household, God provided him with an innovative strategy. He selectively bred Laban's livestock using a method that increased the number of speckled and spotted animals, which were his wages. This simple yet divinely inspired idea turned Jacob into a wealthy man.

Now Jacob took for himself rods of green poplar and of the almond and chestnut trees, peeled white strips in them, and exposed the white which was in the rods. And the rods which he had peeled, he set before the flocks in the gutters, in the watering troughs where the flocks came to drink, so that they should conceive when they came to drink. So, the flocks conceived before the rods, and the flocks brought forth streaked, speckled, and spotted. Then Jacob separated the lambs, and made the flocks face toward the streaked and all the brown in the flock of Laban, but he put his own flocks by themselves and did not put them with Laban's flock.

Genesis 30:37-40

A modern-day example of a similar innovative idea is Facebook, whose inventor was Mark Zuckerberg. While he didn't invent communication, he changed the way the world communicated. Facebook simplified the process of staying connected, which previously required more effort through letters, phone calls, or face-to-face meetings. By revolutionizing an old idea, Zuckerberg created a platform that billions of people use today.

The widow's oil demonstrates how a simple, yet familiar resource can disrupt the market when leveraged creatively—much like how Facebook revolutionized communication by scaling up the common concept of social interaction. The journey of the widow with the jar of oil illustrates the transformative power of everyday tools and the spirit of innovation, much like Facebook's impact on social connection. These examples highlight that **God can provide us with creative, life-changing ideas,** even though something as simple as oil or livestock. The key is to remain open to His direction and seek opportunities for innovation.

In today's marketplace, applying innovation is essential. As modern-day Christians, how can we take an old idea and transform it into something revolutionary? It begins with asking the right questions and remaining open to God's guidance. Here are some steps to help you turn a simple idea into a game-changer:

YOUR MARKETPLACE

Step 1: Identify a Need:

Every successful business solves a problem or meets a need. Start by asking yourself: What need or problem do people face every day? The widow's challenge was financial, and she leveraged oil—a common, affordable resource—to address that need.

Step 2: Look for Gaps in the Market:

Often, the most successful businesses identify market gaps that others overlook. Facebook achieved this by simplifying and expanding global communication, making it more accessible. In your industry or community, what unmet needs or opportunities can you address?

Step 3: Keep It Affordable

Affordability is a key driver of market disruption. The widow had little to start with, yet the oil she possessed was enough. Likewise, your business idea should be cost-effective in its early stages. Start small and leverage the resources already available to you.

Step 4: Innovate Within Simplicity

Don't underestimate the power of simplicity. Some of the greatest innovations come from making existing ideas more accessible or efficient. Think of Uber and how it revolutionized transportation by simplifying ride-hailing.

Step 5: Seek God's Guidance

Above all, seek God's guidance. Just as the widow followed the prophet's instructions, listen for God's direction in your business decisions. He has placed within you the creativity to take an old idea and make it new again.

Step 6: Leverage Your Network

Leveraging your network—much like Facebook's use of social interaction—can drive significant growth. This aligns with the widow's strategic approach of borrowing jars to maximize her resource's impact. She didn't work alone; instead, she sought help from her community, demonstrating that relationships can amplify your reach and success. Networking and community support are invaluable in scaling your venture beyond what you could achieve on your own.

Now, the real work begins. Once you've identified a need, a market gap, and a viable idea, it's time to develop a business plan for your innovation. Here's how to create a cost-effective idea that can be launched from home. You can also take advantage of AI-powered assistant tools like ChatGPT, Claude, and Perplexity, which provide insights, generate content, and enhance productivity for individuals and businesses alike.

NEXT STEPS

A. Research Your Market

Look at similar businesses or services and find out what they're doing right, as well as what they're missing. Research will help you understand the landscape and how you can innovate.

B. Start Small

Your idea doesn't need to be grand at the start. The widow started with a small amount of oil and multiplied it. Begin with what you have and allow God to multiply it.

C. Leverage Technology

In today's world, technology allows us to start businesses from home with little to no overhead. Whether it's using social media for marketing, creating an online store, or utilizing tools like **Gen AI** for automation, technology can be a great asset in keeping costs low while expanding your reach.

D. Create a Scalable Plan

As you grow, make sure your business can scale. The widow multiplied her oil until all the vessels were filled. Have a plan in place for growth so that when the opportunity arises, you can expand without being overwhelmed.

E. Build Partnerships

Don't be afraid to join with other successful businesses. However, ensure that you have solid contracts and agreements in place to protect your interests. Partnerships can help you reach new markets and scale your business more quickly.

THE ROLE OF GEN AI IN BUSINESS INNOVATION

Gen AI (Generative AI) has become a powerful tool for business owners today. It can help you automate tasks, create content, and even develop new products and services. Here are a few ways you can leverage AI to innovate:

1. ***Market Research:*** AI can analyze data and trends to help you find gaps in the market.
2. ***Automation:*** AI tools can automate repetitive tasks, allowing you to focus on innovation and growth.
3. ***Product Development:*** AI can help you create prototypes, test ideas, and optimize products more quickly than traditional methods.

By embracing technology—including AI—you can challenge your thinking and approach business in new and innovative ways, much like the widow did when she transformed a simple product like oil into a profitable venture. If there is one key takeaway from this chapter, it is this: What simple product can I revolutionize to create market disruption in today's world?

Consider how David defeated Goliath with nothing more than a sling and a stone—common tools that no one perceived as a formidable weapon. His victory demonstrates that innovation isn't always about creating something new; sometimes, it's about using existing resources in a groundbreaking way. Likewise, innovation can come from the combination of two simple products into one powerful solution, much like David's sling and stone working together. His approach was not about the tools themselves but how he used them differently—an example of reimagining an old concept in a new way (1 Samuel 17:40-50).

While David's sling and stone belong to biblical times, Airbnb is more of a modern twist based on the same concept. Airbnb didn't invent short-term rentals, but it took up the idea of renting out a space and simplified it through an easy-to-use online platform. This concept disrupted the hospitality industry, turning Airbnb into a global business.

This is a call to action for business owners, whether you are Christian or not, to challenge yourselves to think on a broader level. Color outside the box that you have been operating under. Innovation requires you to challenge yourself, step out of your comfort zone, and think differently. Don't be afraid to explore new ideas, even if they seem too simple at first glance. **Ask yourself:**

1. What everyday problem can I solve in a new way?

2. How can I take an old idea and make it better, faster, or more accessible?
3. Where are the gaps in my industry, and how can I fill them?
4. How can I leverage new technologies, such as Gen AI, to innovate and grow my business?

The widow's story teaches us that innovation doesn't have to be complicated or expensive. It begins with a simple idea, followed by obedience and creativity.

In conclusion, innovation should be forward-thinking—designed not just for the present but for the future. The story of the widow and her oil is more than a tale of financial breakthrough; it is a powerful lesson in innovation, simplicity, and market disruption. As Christian business owners, we must remain open to God's guidance, embrace innovation, and be prepared to disrupt the market with creative yet simple ideas that address everyday needs.

In today's world, success comes from leveraging technology, embracing partnerships, and challenging ourselves to think differently. Don't be afraid to collaborate with others but always protect yourself with clear contracts and Non-Disclosure Agreements. Most importantly, seek God's wisdom in every step—just as the widow did when she transformed her simple jar of oil into a life-changing business venture. By applying these principles, you can not only build a successful business but also become a game-changer in your industry.

CHAPTER 38
A COMMODITY REIMAGINED

Monetize What You Have

Many years ago, I lost my job and had a burst of creativity. At that moment, I designed a unique set of items that could be used as party or wedding favors (of course, I'm not going to share the idea—duh!). That simple idea ended up sustaining me, helping me pay my rent for the next three months until I found employment again. It was something people genuinely needed for their weddings. In fact, I had created several items for one particular wedding, and when the bride returned from taking pictures, she discovered that her guests had even stolen her own favors!

She cried, and of course, I created some complimentary ones for her and her husband. The moral of the story? I took an everyday household product and turned it into something I could monetize. Now, ask yourself: What is in your home, or what skill do you have, that could be monetized and completely transform your financial situation? What could you start with little to no investment? And most importantly, how do you think you will fare if you take that first step forward?

In the story of the widow and her oil, we see one of the most powerful examples of producing something that was not only valuable but also in demand. After following the prophet Elisha's instructions, the widow filled her vessels with oil, something that people needed, wanted, and were willing to pay for. The result? She paid off her debts and had enough left to live on. The lesson here is that what she produced was **sellable**.

As a business owner today, the question you need to ask yourself is this: **Is what I'm producing something that the market wants? Is it sellable?** The widow's oil was a product that fulfilled a need in her community, and its simplicity made it desirable. Likewise, your business product or service must not only meet a need but must also be something people are eager to buy. This chapter will guide you through understanding market demands about creating a sellable product and developing the confidence to talk about and promote what you've made.

The first question you must ask yourself is: Are you producing what the market wants? The lesson from the widow's oil is that it wasn't just valuable, it was essential! In those days, oil was a common household necessity, used for cooking, lighting lamps, and religious practices. The widow's success came from producing something that everyone needed.

The next question is: Have you identified the market demand for your product? As a business owner, one of the most critical steps in product development is identifying what people truly need or want. A high-quality product with low demand will still result in failure, no matter how great it may be. The widow's oil sold well because it fulfilled a daily necessity for her community. Here are three essential questions you must ask yourself:

1. What is the need in the market?
2. Is my product something people will use often or regularly?
3. What pain points does my product solve for my customers?

The answers to these questions will help you identify whether your product has a strong market demand. Consider how certain industries like food, clothing, and technology thrive because they meet ongoing, universal needs. Your business must do the same, especially if you can turn your creativity into a cash-making product. Just like the widow's product found a market, so can yours, if you have the right product.

The widow transformed her modest jar of oil into a commodity that met an essential need, proving that even a simple resource can become a profitable product when viewed through an innovative lens. This serves as an invitation for modern-day Christian entrepreneurs to reimagine their everyday assets as opportunities for market disruption and financial breakthroughs. By recognizing and harnessing the inherent value of everyday essentials—just like the widow's oil—we too can turn ordinary products into profitable assets. This highlights a crucial step in the entrepreneurial journey: identifying potential revenue streams.

The next step in monetizing your product is ensuring that it is both affordable and marketable. For any business to thrive, affordability is key—something the widow understood well. Her oil was not only a necessity but also accessible to her customers. In today's competitive marketplace, pricing your product right can be a game-changer. If you want to profit from your passion, you must master the principles of market demand and value.

Though the widow's business was driven by necessity rather than traditional passion, the widow's recognition of the intrinsic value of her oil shows that every resource holds worth when aligned with market demand. You must be able to identify and capitalize on the true value of your offerings, ensuring they fulfill a critical need while generating profit. What do you have in your home that is just lying around idle that you can turn into making money? The truth is that the widow took an idle jar of oil and turned it into an income stream, creating her own formula for revenue!

She transformed a neglected jar of oil into a thriving business, proving that proactive effort can turn dormant resources into continuous revenue streams. Her story serves as a powerful lesson for entrepreneurs: idle assets can become active sources of income through strategic action and faithful stewardship. The widow monetized what she had, building a sellable product from scratch. Her ingenious use of limited oil highlights the power of leveraging existing resources, no matter how modest they may seem. By starting with what you already have and applying creative thinking, you can develop a marketable product that drives financial success.

In many cases, companies that thrive today understand the importance of balancing quality and pricing. Many fashion designers, for example, cater to two distinct markets: celebrities seeking exclusivity and everyday consumers wanting to feel special in what they wear. To meet these demands, they produce two types of products—luxury lines for those who can afford them and more affordable collections for the masses. This strategy ensures they effectively serve both ends of the market, maximizing their reach and profitability.

While affordability is important, it is equally essential to elevate your product and make it marketable. Ask yourself:

1. How can I make my product stand out from the rest?

2. What added value can I provide?
3. How can I create a brand story that resonates with my customers?

For instance, Apple has been able to sell its products at premium prices by emphasizing not just the technology but the user experience. Their focus on design, simplicity, and innovation has made Apple products desirable across the globe.

The next thing for many business owners is how to sell their products. For new entrepreneurs, and even seasoned ones, the biggest challenge isn't their product itself but how to talk about and sell their product. The widow's story demonstrates her courage to go back and sell her oil to the same people she had once borrowed from. This requires a level of boldness and confidence that every entrepreneur must develop.

You must learn how to talk about your product—selling begins with storytelling. It's not enough to have a great product; you must communicate its value in a way that resonates with others. From my years in consulting, one of the first lessons I learned was the art of storytelling. It not only clarifies what you're selling but also transforms data and complex ideas into compelling narratives. I come from a family of storytellers, and my father was the one who taught me this skill. Consulting, however, showed me how to monetize storytelling by leveraging data and the power of persuasion. If you can make your story relatable, you can sell your product.

Here are some tips for talking about your product effectively:

1. ***Know Your Product Inside and Out:*** Be able to explain not just what your product does, but how it benefits your customer.

2. ***Practice Your Pitch:*** Rehearse how you will talk about your product so that you can do it confidently and concisely.
3. ***Highlight the Value:*** Focus on the unique benefits that your product offers, and how it solves a problem for your customers.
4. ***Leverage Social Proof:*** Share testimonials or stories from satisfied customers to build credibility.

Selling your product to complete strangers can feel intimidating, especially for new entrepreneurs. Many struggle with fear and self-doubt when it comes to selling, feeling nervous about approaching potential customers or unsure of how to ask for the sale. The widow's innovative approach to handling her limited oil shows how necessity can spark groundbreaking ideas that meet urgent needs. However, even the best innovation means nothing if you cannot sell your product effectively. While I encourage modern entrepreneurs to harness crisis-driven creativity to develop practical and profitable products, it's just as important to remember that you have to sell what you create. Even the widow had to step out of her comfort zone to sell her oil.

From my experience working in an IT environment, I've seen that when a cloud-based product is developed, it's often bundled with a service or maintenance package. You can apply the same principle to your business. One practical way to overcome the fear of selling is to focus on service rather than sales. Instead of worrying about how to make money, shift your mindset to how you can help your customers with your product. When you frame your business as a way to serve others, selling becomes more natural and far less intimidating.

Let us explore some biblical examples of people who had products or ideas that were both sellable and profitable at the same time, starting with the story of Joseph, the second in command to the Pharoah of Egypt!

A. Joseph's Administration of Grain (Genesis 41):

Joseph took Egypt's grain—a necessity—and leveraged it to sustain people across the land during a time of famine. His ability to manage the supply strategically not only saved Egypt but also made it prosperous. Because grain was an essential resource in a time of great need, Joseph was able to sell it effectively and create a lasting impact.

B. Lydia the Seller of Purple (Acts 16:14)

Lydia was a thriving businesswoman who sold purple cloth—a luxury item in her time. She discovered her niche by catering to those who could afford and desired high-end fabrics, establishing herself in an exclusive market where she excelled.

Both Lydia and Joseph found success by combining the right idea with the right product, proving that identifying a need, producing a valuable offering, and selling it effectively can change the course of history. Today, modern-day widow-like entrepreneurs are applying the same principles, transforming everyday essentials into revenue streams. Just like the widow who turned a common household commodity into a profitable asset, these entrepreneurs recognize the market potential in the simplest of resources and leverage them for financial success.

Learning how to identify and transform everyday essentials into revenue streams is what Sara Blakely of Spanx did with her invention of Spanx, as mentioned in a previous chapter, in which she took a woman's undergarment issue and through innovation solved a problem. Another individual who leveraged a simple concept is Blake Mycoskie, founder of TOMS Shoes—for every pair of shoes purchased, another pair would be donated to a child in need. This idea, coupled with a quality product, created a movement that resonated with consumers globally.

Mycoskie's ability to align a product with a greater purpose made it not only profitable but also impactful and charitable. He demonstrated that financial success and social good can go hand in hand by turning common resources into pillars of stability and generosity. These examples prove that sellability doesn't always require a groundbreaking idea—it requires identifying a need, providing a solution, and effectively communicating your story.

Imagine the courage it took for the widow to go back and sell oil to the very people she had borrowed from. It's not easy to approach those who have helped you in the past and now try to sell them something. Yet the widow's story reminds us that sometimes our past struggles are part of the journey to success.

One of the biggest challenges in starting a business after facing personal setbacks or failures is confronting those who know your past. Some of your future customers may be people who are familiar with your struggles, which can lead to feelings of shame or discomfort, making you hesitant to move forward. However, remember that they are also witnessing your growth. Instead of allowing your past to hold you back, embrace it as a testament to your resilience. The widow did not shy away from those who knew her debt—she returned to them with confidence because she had something valuable to offer: a product they needed.

Remember what I talked about earlier regarding the art of storytelling? Well, here is where you get to turn your story into your strength. As a business owner, your story can become one of your greatest assets (it should not be long-winded). Be open about your challenges and how you overcame them, since people are more likely to buy from someone they can relate to, and your transparency can build trust and loyalty with your customers.

There are so many essential lessons from the widow's journey as it pertains to business, monetizing your product and its sellability. Here are a few of them.

1. ***Produce Something That is Needed:*** The widow's oil was a necessity for her community. Likewise, your product must meet a need.
2. ***Make it Affordable:*** Her oil was accessible to everyone. Your product should offer value at a price point your target audience can afford.
3. ***Be Courageous:*** The widow had the courage to sell her oil to those who knew her debt. Don't be afraid to approach customers, even those who know your history.
4. ***Leverage Your Story:*** The widow's journey from debt to success became part of her story. Don't be ashamed of your past; use it to inspire others and build connections with your customers.

In conclusion, never be ashamed of your past—no matter how colorful or complicated it may be—as long as you have learned from it and taken ownership of your mistakes. As Christian business owners, we must recognize that our experiences, challenges, and even failures are all part of the journey that shapes our success. They add to our story, our resilience, and our unique perspective. This is why the widow's story is not just about oil—it is about redemption, courage, forgiveness, and perseverance.

Never be ashamed of the difficulties or poverty you may have endured to get where you are today. Oftentimes I meet people who want to erase that part of their lives, pretending like that never happened! But you do yourself a great disservice as that is the reason why you are so successful today. This is also the widow's story as well. Her keen decisions, rooted in necessity, transformed scarcity into wealth, which highlighted her crucial role in strategic market entry and timely innovation.

Just like the widow, your experiences are part of your testimony—and they will resonate with others facing similar struggles. By sharing your story and standing confidently behind your product, you can inspire others and build lasting success for your business. Your journey may be the very thing that encourages an aspiring business owner to move forward instead of giving up. Never underestimate the power of your story—it could be the catalyst that changes someone's path forever.

By having a sellable solution, you allow one decision to turn your scarcity into prosperity. Understand that a well-timed, strategic decision can transform a desperate situation into a thriving enterprise, offering life lessons in seizing opportunities amid adversity. By re-envisioning a simple jar of oil as a valuable product, the widow unlocked a market opportunity that many overlooked. There lies in you the transformative power of innovative thinking that needs to be unlocked, so that even the most ordinary resource can yield extraordinary profit for you when you reimagine an old product creatively.

Let the widow's journey inspire you to move forward with boldness. Whether it's the people who once supported you or the challenges you've overcome, every experience can be transformed into an opportunity for growth and success. The widow's courageous decision to turn a humble jar of oil into a thriving business embodies the essence of entrepreneurship. As modern Christian business owners, embrace her lesson—take bold steps, lean on divine guidance, and create ventures that not only generate income but also provide lasting stability and impact.

Believe in the value of your product, the power of your story, and the certainty of your success. When you trust God and take courageous steps forward, your breakthrough becomes inevitable.

CHAPTER 39

SALES, STRATEGY AND STEWARDSHIP

Running with Your Oil

What if I told you that now that you've identified your oil, the next step is simply learning how to package and sell it? And that if your product is marketable, you are already on your way to financial freedom? How would you view the God-given gifts you've been blessed with? How would you approach your life moving forward? The story of the widow's oil offers a clear and powerful lesson about the impact of following divine instruction. When the prophet Elisha spoke to the widow, his guidance was simple but transformative. He told her: **Go, sell the oil, and pay your debts.** It wasn't just about producing the oil; but what was she going to do with it, meaning she needed to take action.

Elisha's commandment to ***"go"*** is a message that still resonates today, especially for Christian business owners. It's not enough to have a good product or a great idea; you must be willing to **run with it**. You must be proactive, courageous, and diligent in turning that idea into a thriving business. Too often, many of us create something valuable, whether it's a product, a book, or a service, but all we do is sit on it. We hesitate, second-guess ourselves, and even allow friends and family to talk us out of it, and then fail to take action.

But Elisha's advice to the widow wasn't just to make the oil—he told her to sell it. He made her see its value so she could pay off her debt and secure her family's future.

This chapter guides Christian business owners in doing the same: recognizing their product's worth, selling it effectively, and managing finances wisely, especially in paying off debt.

In life, success requires action. Like the widow, we must understand the assignment. Elisha didn't just tell her to pour oil—he told her to sell it. The lesson is clear: even the best product won't succeed without action. Many have great ideas but never act. As a business owner, it's your responsibility to market your product so people buy it.

Fear of failure and rejection often hold people back from marketing their products. Many hesitate, trapped by fear and procrastination. Yet, Elisha's faith and instructions pushed the widow to act. Today's Christian entrepreneurs should adopt the same mindset—"Go and sell." Here are practical steps to help you take action:

A. Develop a Marketing Plan:

In today's world, having a great product isn't enough. You must know how to market it. That starts with a basic marketing plan that outlines:

1. Target audience: Who is most likely to buy your product?
2. Value proposition: What makes your product unique or valuable?
3. Marketing channels: Where will you promote it—social media, email marketing, word of mouth, etc.?

B. Leverage All Tools, Including Online Ones:

In the 21st century, the internet is a powerful tool for selling and marketing your product. Key platforms include:

1. ***Social Media:*** Instagram, Facebook, and LinkedIn help you reach a broader audience.
2. ***E-commerce Websites:*** Shopify and Etsy make it easy to set up an online store.

3. ***Email Marketing:*** Building an email list and sending regular updates or promotions keeps customers engaged.
4. ***Leverage Your Network:*** As a business owner, your first customers will often be people in your network, which includes family, friends, and community members.
5. ***Word of Mouth:*** Customer testimonials and referrals are powerful. Encourage satisfied customers to share their experiences.
6. ***Promotions & Discounts:*** Attract initial customers by offering special deals. This can encourage people to try your product and spread the word.

Having the right marketing strategy and leveraging online tools can take your business to the next level. Just like the widow needed her neighbors' vessels, you will need partnerships to grow your business. Don't hesitate to collaborate with other businesses, influencers, or mentors to expand your reach.

Recognizing the value of your product is a crucial part of selling. Elisha's instruction to the widow wasn't just about moving inventory, it was about helping her see that she had something valuable to offer. As a business owner, you must recognize the worth of your product and have confidence in what you're offering. I have a little saying on my desk: "Know your worth and then add tax to it." That same mindset applies to your product. It's up to you to determine its value. Here are three key factors to help you decide:

1. ***What Problem Does it Solve?*** People buy products that address a need or solve a problem. Be clear on how your product improves your customers' lives.
2. ***How Does it Compare to Other Products?*** Research your competitors and identify what makes your product unique. What benefits set it apart?
3. ***What are People Willing to Pay?*** Pricing is key. Study the market, see what similar products cost, and set a price that reflects your product's true value.

These are key questions to answer before setting the right price for your product. Pricing can be challenging but getting it right from the start is crucial. Here are some effective strategies:

1. ***Cost-plus Pricing:*** Calculate the cost of producing your product and add a markup to ensure you make a profit.
2. ***Market-based Pricing:*** Research into what customers are willing to pay for similar products and price your product competitively.
3. ***Value-based Pricing:*** Price your product based on the value it offers to your customers, especially if it offers something unique that competitors don't have.

These are key questions to answer before setting the right price for your product. Pricing can be challenging, but getting it right from the start is crucial. By recognizing the value of your product, you can set a price that reflects its worth, while ensuring profitability. As a business owner, staying focused on the mission—especially financial responsibility—is crucial. Elisha's instruction to the widow wasn't just about selling the oil; it was about using the profits wisely to pay off her debts. In the same way, business owners must remain disciplined with their earnings, prioritizing financial obligations rather than getting sidetracked once money starts flowing in.

The Bible strongly emphasizes the importance of living debt-free. Proverbs 22:7 states, "The rich rule over the poor, and the borrower is servant to the lender." Debt can be a heavy burden, restricting both freedom and opportunity. For the widow, selling the oil wasn't about luxury—it was about settling her debt and securing her family's future. Similarly, as a business owner, eliminating debt should be a top financial priority. As discussed in earlier chapters, it's tempting to spend your first profits on luxuries like a fancy car or a designer handbag. However, this mindset can lead to financial disaster. The widow remained focused on her mission—paying off her debts—not indulging in unnecessary expenses.

There are other biblical examples of individuals who paid off their debts besides the widow with the oil. One notable figure is Nehemiah (5:10-12), who rebuked the nobles and officials for lending money at high interest rates to their fellow Jews. He urged them to stop this practice and return the lands, vineyards, and houses they had taken from debtors. Nehemiah's example highlights the importance of fairness and integrity in debt management.

Just as the Bible provides examples of individuals who displayed financial indiscipline, history also offers numerous worldly figures who struggled with money management. One major celebrity was Johnny Depp, the actor who earned over $650 million from movies like the Pirates of the Caribbean franchise, but reportedly lost most of it due to lavish spending and poor investments. At one point, it was rumored that he was spending $2 million monthly, including $30,000 on wine! Similarly, the late Michael Jackson's estate suffered severe mismanagement despite generating billions of dollars. At the time of his death, he was reportedly $400 million in debt.

There are many lessons to be learned from the mistakes of these celebrities. Unlike the widow, who managed her resources wisely, they were prone to overspending. Each of them lived beyond their means, often making poor investment choices. While the widow strategically multiplied her oil, these celebrities failed to manage their wealth effectively—and ultimately paid the price for it.

Both celebrities and everyday people are often guilty of ignoring their debts. Once the widow earned money, she paid off her debt immediately instead of allowing her debts to pile up without a clear repayment plan or a path forward. Successful business owners and celebrities often lack the humility to seek help when facing financial challenges. This wasn't the case with the widow, who sought guidance from Elisha. Unfortunately, many celebrities either refuse to listen to financial advisors or make reckless decisions. These examples emphasize the importance of using your earnings wisely, particularly when it comes to paying off debts.

As mentioned in an earlier chapter, not all debt is inherently bad. Understanding the difference between good and bad debt can help you make wiser financial decisions. Remember, good debt is debt used to invest in your business and generate more income. This includes business loans for expansion, which can, in turn, increase your revenue. Real estate investments, such as purchasing a property for your business, can also be a smart financial move if the property appreciates in value or provides a steady rental income.

Bad debt is any debt that neither generates income nor improves your financial position. This includes credit card debt—while it can help build your credit, high interest rates can quickly spiral out of control, especially when used for non-essential purchases. Taking out loans for luxury items that do not appreciate in value or generate income is also a poor financial decision.

Poor financial decisions can lead to unpaid debts, which can have serious consequences both financially and reputationally. As Christians, failing to honor our obligations can be even more damaging, as it erodes trust. When you fail to repay your debts, people become less likely to trust you in the future, harming your reputation and straining relationships—both personally and in business.

The truth is that carrying large amounts of debt can lead to financial instability and hinder business growth. Some banks may view you as a financial risk, especially when interest payments start eating into your profits. Missed payments not only damage your credit but can also lead to legal issues—or even bankruptcy. The best way to avoid these tough situations is to steer clear of bad debt altogether. However, if borrowing is necessary, only take on as much debt as is truly needed.

This means borrowing only what you can reasonably expect to repay. The next step is to create a budget—know exactly how much you owe and develop a clear plan to pay it off quickly. Avoid letting debt linger, as the longer it remains, the harder it becomes to fulfill your obligations. Stay disciplined by sticking to your financial goals and paying off debts before indulging in other expenses. This requires resisting temptation and staying focused on building your business. Make debt repayment a top priority to prevent accruing unnecessary interest. Finally, establish an emergency fund; a financial cushion is essential to help you avoid taking on unnecessary debt during a crisis.

Once you've paid off your debts, staying disciplined is essential to avoid falling back into financial trouble. Here are a few key strategies:

1. ***Create a Savings Plan Immediately***—Set aside a portion of your profits to build financial security and prevent future debt.
2. ***Stick to a Budget***—Be intentional about how you spend your money, prioritizing necessities and cutting out unnecessary expenses.
3. ***Invest in Growth***—Instead of spending profits on luxuries, reinvest them into your business to ensure long-term success.

The widow's willingness to address her debt immediately laid the foundation for fast-tracking her financial recovery. By prioritizing debt repayment, she established a cornerstone for building lasting financial freedom. Turning her oil into profit underscores the importance of aligning spiritual trust with practical action to achieve financial liberation. It's not just about praying—it's about taking the necessary steps to back up that faith with action.

Now that we've emphasized the importance of debt repayment, it's time to focus on sales and strategy. The first step is to take action—run with your product. Do not sit idle or allow self-doubt and fear to hold you back. The widow didn't have the luxury of hesitation; with her family's survival at stake, she leaped into action immediately!

Selling the oil right away helped reduce her urgent debts. By bringing her oil to market, she transformed her crisis into a solution, using what she had to create financial stability.

This concept challenges you to monetize your assets strategically, ensuring that every resource in your home contributes to a debt-free future. The widow recognized her opportunity and took decisive action, immediately bringing her product to market. If you're a business owner reading this, understand the importance of moving with urgency—your product needs to hit the market now. Timing is critical in entrepreneurship. This chapter serves as your call to action: move with urgency and confidence. Ensure your product reaches the market before the opportunity fades.

I want to leave you with several practical steps to take action today.

1. ***Launch Immediately***—Drop the spirit of perfection before it steals your opportunity. Don't wait for everything to be perfect before you start. Many successful businesses begin small and scale up over time. Start with what you have.

2. ***Set Small, Achievable Goals***—Break down your business goals into smaller, actionable steps. Whether it's setting up a website, making a few sales, or promoting your product on social media, every step brings you closer to success.

3. ***Stay Consistent***—I write down five things I want to accomplish each day and work toward them. If I don't finish everything today, I make sure to get it done tomorrow.

And the dreaded "get feedback"—yet the widow sought additional guidance from Elisha, a man of God. I love feedback! It once helped me keep my job during layoffs because I had always expressed a desire for it. Feedback is the key to growth, evolution, and long-term success in business. Just like the widow sought wisdom from Elisha, you should seek guidance from mentors, business coaches, or trusted advisors who can help refine your product and strategy. Most importantly, keep moving forward. The key to success in business is momentum. Even if progress feels slow, do not stop. Consistent action over time is what builds a thriving business. Stay the course—do not slow down!

In conclusion, the most powerful lesson from the widow's story is that we all have something of value to offer the world. However, success requires action. We must recognize the worth of our product and practice financial discipline to achieve greatness. As Christian business owners, we are called to be faithful stewards of the resources God has given us. By embracing the lessons from the widow's story—selling wisely, eliminating debt, and managing finances with wisdom—we can build successful businesses that honor God and bless others.

The widow ran with her oil—she exemplified a relentless spirit, taking her product to the market, fueled by divine guidance, and selling it. Be inspired to harness that same determination by transforming immediate action into resource monetization.

True success comes when we apply a faith-driven strategy, just as the widow did when selling her oil. Only then can we achieve powerful, lasting results.

CHAPTER 40

THE POWER OF YOUR LEGACY

Beyond the Last Jar

Have you taken the time to consider what your legacy will look like long after you're gone? What will the world say about your contributions to society? Are you someone who mentors the next generation, or do you prefer to live life on your own terms, giving nothing in return? Do you believe in the idea of "pulling oneself up by their bootstraps," or do you recognize that not everyone has the same opportunities in life? In my five-book series, *"Igniting Your Vision—Ending Triumphantly,"* I emphasize the importance of leaving behind a worthy legacy—not just for your children, but for the world you live in.

While this chapter explores the widow's miraculous journey from poverty to wealth—where she ultimately lives off the remaining oil—we know that life is about more than just the money we gain. The widow's story reaches its conclusion when she seeks Prophet Elisha's final instructions on paying off her debts. He assures her that she has gathered enough to sustain herself and her sons for the rest of their lives. This remarkable moment illustrates God's abundant provision when we faithfully follow His guidance.

This story also teaches us that God's plan is not for us to live burdened by debt or scarcity but to experience the fullness of life He has prepared for us. It's important to note that when the widow first met the prophet, she came to him in desperation, begging for help. Elisha, in response, guided her on how to solve her financial crisis. However, the next time she approached him, she was no longer a desperate widow but a businesswoman seeking further mentorship. This transformation highlights not only her financial growth but also her personal and spiritual development.

The widow didn't just nurture and fill up her vessels; she also nurtured her relationship with the man of God! Her discipline in setting aside full vessels taught her the importance of preserving what she had earned. Modern Christian entrepreneurs can learn from her example by not only managing their resources wisely but also cultivating meaningful relationships. Both are essential for ensuring lasting growth and long-term stability.

She learned that there was life beyond mere survival—something many Christians today struggle to realize. The widow's journey wasn't just about getting by; she and her husband had likely lived paycheck to paycheck, simply making ends meet. But through faith and action, her story transformed from one of survival to a life of abundance and purpose. This chapter contrasts basic subsistence with a thriving, faith-driven approach to business—one that not only sustains but also enriches lives and communities.

As Christians, it's crucial to understand that God desires us to live free from the weight of debt and to fully enjoy the fruit of His blessings. The widow's story is not just about survival—it's about thriving. Her obedience to Elisha's instructions opened the door to a life of relative comfort and freedom. Tragically, this was a life her husband never got to experience. In this chapter, we will reflect on the widow's journey, examine the concept of "living off the rest of your oil," and explore what it truly means to walk in the fullness of God's provision.

God's provision for the widow wasn't just enough to get by—it was more than enough. The oil that filled her borrowed jars provided sufficient income not only to pay off her debts but also to sustain her and her sons for the rest of their lives. This is what we call "abundant living"—a powerful reminder that God's resources are never limited by our circumstances. Yet, many of us struggle to fully trust that God has already prepared an abundant life for us.

In fact, many of us live with a scarcity mindset, convinced that there isn't enough for us to live debt-free or achieve financial freedom. Yet, the widow's story serves as a powerful reminder that God's blessings are abundant and overflowing. When we place our trust in Him and act in obedience, He provides far more than we can imagine.

"And my God will supply every need of yours according to his riches in glory in Christ Jesus."
Philippians 4:19

The widow's life after the miracle was one of freedom from financial bondage. No longer did she live in fear of creditors coming to take her sons. Across the world, debt remains a constant source of anxiety, preventing many from experiencing the peace and abundance that God promises. The key to living beyond debt is twofold: first, trusting in God's provision, and second, taking practical steps toward financial freedom. We must believe that God not only desires to bless us spiritually but also to provide for us financially.

"Now to him who is able to do far more abundantly than all that we ask or think, according to the power at work within us."
Ephesians 3:20

One of the most striking aspects of this story is the total contrast between the widow's newfound financial freedom and the life her husband lived. He was a man of God, devoted to the ministry, yet he died in debt, unable to provide for his family. We should all take a moment to reflect on his life and ask ourselves a very important question: Was her husband living up to the full capacity of what God intended for him?

Now, ask yourself the same question: What if, after all the years you've spent on this earth, you come to realize that God had a greater package for you—but you were too afraid to access it? What a revelation! It's possible that the widow's husband, despite his faithfulness and dedication to ministry, had a limited understanding of God's ability to provide. While writing this book, I had an opportunity arise—a ministry-related event with a group of women. However, I was uneasy about the financial direction the event was taking. After hanging up the phone with the organizer, God spoke to me clearly: "Sandra, she does not know ME as the God Who Provides because she has never tried or trusted ME financially."

The very next day, I decided to pull out of the event. Her response was telling—she admitted that she couldn't trust God to provide for the ministry. I smiled, not out of superiority, but out of deep pity because, at that moment, she had confirmed the very word God had spoken to me the night before. Without any judgment, I recognize that many Christians today face similar challenges. We have faith in God to serve in ministry and strive to live righteous lives, yet so often, we place limitations on ourselves by failing to fully trust in His supernatural provision.

According to Scripture, the widow's husband—a disciple or associate of Prophet Elisha—dedicated his life to serving in the kingdom, yet he still died in debt! Could this have been avoided if he had fully understood and embraced God's principles of provision? What steps could he have taken to free himself from a limited mindset? How could he have crafted his future differently? And most importantly, did he have what it took—like his wife—to develop a transformative faith that changes everything?

It's critical for every believer to examine their own life and ask whether they are living according to the fullness of God's promises or are operating from a place of limited faith. Are we, like the widow's husband, caught in cycles of debt, or are we trusting God to lead us to financial freedom?

Throughout the Bible and history, we see countless examples of individuals who found themselves burdened by debt, only to be delivered by God's grace and wisdom. The truth is that debt and deliverance often go hand-in-hand. One powerful example is found in Nehemiah 5, where the people of Israel cried out because they were drowning in debt, having mortgaged their fields just to pay taxes and afford food. Nehemiah intervened, confronting the wealthy and urging them to cancel the debts of the poor. This act of mercy not only restored the people's dignity but also gave them the opportunity to rebuild their lives.

In another part of the Bible, the prodigal son's parable, while it is not directly about financial debt (Luke 15:11-32), illustrates how reckless living can lead to poverty and despair. However, the father's forgiveness and restoration of the son symbolize God's willingness to restore those who have lost everything. Debt and deliverance are not just biblical stories but true ones as well, such as the story of Dave Ramsey.

This well-known financial advisor was once deeply in debt; yet through discipline, biblical principles, and hard work, he became debt-free and now teaches others how to achieve financial freedom. The famous queen of television, Oprah Winfrey overcame extreme poverty and debt early in her career. And like Ramsey, through sheer determination and wise financial decisions, she has become one of the wealthiest women in the world, using her platform to help and coach others.

Both Dave Ramsey and Oprah Winfrey exercised their faith, just like the widow. Her single act of faith—filling vessels with oil—catalyzed a lifetime of transformative change, freedom, and opportunity. The widow moved from surplus to security because she tapped into her oil's full potential. Her surplus wasn't just a temporary fix; it became the foundation for lasting security. When we maximize our God-given resources, we can transform short-term blessings into long-term financial stability.

One of the great lessons of the oil is that as it flowed beyond the widow's immediate needs, she experienced abundant provision that reshaped her future. When we choose to live in the overflow of what God has in store for us, it leads to a life of continuous blessings that extend far beyond mere survival. The widow's obedience not only cleared her debts but also set the stage for a debt-free legacy. This teaches us the importance of using surplus resources wisely to secure a future unburdened by financial strain.

Oftentimes, we hear about legendary basketball and football players whose careers have ended with nothing left to show for all their success. This wasn't the case for the widow. When her oil finally ceased, it didn't mark the end—it signified the beginning of a new legacy for her family. We must challenge ourselves to think beyond immediate gains and build a lasting impact that ensures freedom for generations.

Elisha's instructions gave the widow a clear roadmap for transforming her scarcity into abundance, turning her time of dire need from crisis to comfort and serving as a launchpad for a secure and debt-free future through disciplined stewardship.

What does it mean to "live off the rest of your oil"? For the widow, it meant living in comfort and freedom, sustained by the miracle God provided. For us, it can mean the same, but it's essential to reflect on what "enough" looks like for each of us.

Each person's definition of "enough" will differ. For some, it may mean a modest lifestyle, free from debt and financial stress. For others, it may involve building wealth to create opportunities for future generations. The key is to define what contentment looks like for you.

"But godliness with contentment is great gain. For we brought nothing into the world, and we can take nothing out of it. But if we have food and clothing, we will be content with that."
1 Timothy 6:6-8

Another question we must ask ourselves when God has blessed us is whether we maintain or reduce our lifestyle. How do we plan to manage our resources? Do we continue at the same level, or adopt a simpler, more frugal approach to ensure long-term financial security? Part of wise management is understanding that having more doesn't mean we should spend more. The widow had enough to live on for the rest of her life, but it required careful stewardship of her resources.

The widow's miraculous provision was a direct result of her obedience to God's instructions through Elisha. By following his commands precisely, she reaped the full benefits of God's provision. Throughout Scripture, obedience to God's guidance consistently leads to blessings. When we align our finances, relationships, and spiritual lives with His principles, we open ourselves to the fullness of His provision.

"If you fully obey the Lord your God and carefully follow all his commands I give you today, the Lord your God will set you high above all the nations on earth. All these blessings will come on you and accompany you if you obey the Lord your God."
Deuteronomy 28:1-2

One of the most important lessons from the widow's story is the need to stay on the path to financial freedom. This requires discipline, obedience, and wisdom in managing resources. Even when the oil stopped flowing, the widow's obedience ensured that she had enough for the rest of her life.

Once the widow paid off her debts, she was free. However, staying free from debt requires a commitment to wise financial practices and avoiding the temptation to fall back into debt.

Steps to Avoid Debt

1. ***Create a Budget:*** A clear budget helps you manage your money and ensures that you live within your means.

2. ***Build an Emergency Fund:*** Having savings set aside for unexpected expenses can prevent you from taking on debt in times of crisis.
3. ***Live Below Your Means:*** Even when your income increases, maintain a frugal lifestyle to build wealth and security.
4. ***Seek Wise Counsel:*** Surround yourself with mentors or financial advisors who can guide you in making sound financial decisions.

Avoiding debt after achieving financial freedom is crucial, as falling back can be devastating. The consequences—stress, strained relationships, and loss of trust—can be overwhelming. God desires us to live in freedom, but it is our responsibility to maintain it through wise stewardship of the resources He provides. Manage your blessings wisely by strategically reinvesting part of your overflow while saving as well, ensuring that each blessing contributes to a lasting legacy for you and your family.

In the end, God promises each of us a full life, and the widow's story is a testament to His desire for His people to live in freedom and abundance. While everyone's journey may look different, the promise remains the same: if we follow God's instructions, we will experience His provision in ways beyond our imagination. Whether you are overcoming debt or managing your finances wisely, the widow's story offers lessons for us all. Trust in God's provision, follow His guidance, and live with the confidence that He has more than enough for you to live off the rest of your oil.

CONCLUSION

UNLEASHING THE POWER OF YOUR OIL

Faith, Family, and Fulfillment

Writing this book was an immense joy. To be frank, I pushed myself in ways I never thought possible to create a finished product that anyone could relate to, regardless of social or economic status—or whether they are Christian or not. This book was written with the everyday worker and business owner in mind, with the hope that its words would be easy to follow, relatable, and practical while nurturing faith and inspiring you to pursue that business or dream you may have buried away.

As we reach the end of this journey of the **40 Invaluable Life Lessons of The Widow's Oil**, it's clear that this timeless story carries with it profound wisdom for the everyday Christian business owner and individual seeking a life of purpose and abundance. The widow's experience reminds us that our oil—those unique gifts, talents, and resources that God has placed within us—holds the key to unlocking a life free from debt and filled with endless possibilities.

My prayer for you is that you take the first step toward transformation by locating your oil. Just as the widow discovered her source of provision in the midst of despair, may you also seek out the unique gifts and resources God has placed within you that may have remained dormant. What skills, experiences, or passions do you possess, and how are you harnessing them to their fullest potential? By identifying and nurturing your oil, you can begin to build a life that not only sustains you but also impacts those around you.

If you live in America, you're in one of the most debt-ridden countries in the world—yet we still claim to be a global power! If you're reading this book, I want you to commit to paying off your debt. Confronting your debt is a sign of taking full responsibility for your choices—good, bad, or indifferent. The widow took ownership of her financial obligations, and once she did, God provided a way out. He can do the same for you, but you must be willing to face the truth and take action.

Paying off your debts isn't just a financial goal—it's a pathway to freedom and peace. God desires for you to live without the weight of financial stress. By applying the principles in this book—setting a budget, seeking wise counsel, and living within your means—you can take meaningful steps toward financial freedom. True wealth isn't just measured in money but in the peace of mind that comes from wise stewardship.

Finally, as you step into this new chapter of your life, embrace the promise of a life filled with abundance. The widow gained not only financial stability but also purpose and joy. God's provision isn't reserved for a select few—it's available to all who seek Him wholeheartedly. As you navigate life and business, remember that your journey isn't just about personal success but also about serving others and glorifying God through your work.

As you reflect on the widow's transformation from survival to a thriving entrepreneur, I invite you to see your own life as an evolving journey. Her story is more than a tale of financial rescue—it's a testament to the power of faith, personal accountability, and familial responsibility. This is a call to modern-day Christians to integrate their spiritual beliefs, family values, and business wisdom to build a life that honors God and nurtures those they love. It's about looking beyond limitations and embracing divine provision and creativity in every area of life, just as God did for the widow and her sons. By doing so, you can expand your impact and create opportunities that influence your community.

I want to urge all believers to use their **"oil"** wisely, protecting and investing it in order to build a brighter future marked by hope, stability, and purpose. Learn from the transformative power of managing and reinvesting your surplus in a way that sets you up for ongoing prosperity. The widow's disciplined approach to using her oil as a resource teaches us that laying a foundation of abundance today ensures a legacy of provision for tomorrow.

Today, I urge you to stand on the shoulders of the widow as your final act of obedience—so you may live abundantly beyond your last drop. Pay off your debts to secure your family's future. Be faithful, be diligent, and be disciplined, so your loved ones can enjoy the prosperity God has set aside as their legacy.

Let this be your call to action: it's time to rise up, recognize your oil, and cultivate it with diligence and faithfulness. Each chapter of this book has equipped you with invaluable insights to navigate life and business. Now, it's your turn to act.

1. ***Identify Your Oil:*** Reflect on your gifts and how they can serve others.
2. ***Commit to Financial Health:*** Take the necessary steps to pay off your debts and embrace a lifestyle of stewardship.
3. ***Embrace Abundance:*** Live boldly, trusting in God's provision and sharing your blessings with those around you.

In closing, remember—the widow's oil did not stop flowing until the last vessel was filled. Your journey doesn't end here; it is only the beginning of a lifelong pursuit of abundance and purpose. As you step into the fullness of God's plans for you, carry with you the lessons from the widow and her oil. Trust in His provision, walk in obedience, and watch as He transforms your life, allowing you to move beyond survival into the richness of a life well-lived.

Draw inspiration from the widow's strategic steps—from borrowing vessels to selling her oil—and let this book serve as a roadmap for modern-day entrepreneurs, whether you are Christian or not. I encourage you to embrace her wisdom in planning, executing, and scaling your business ventures for long-term, sustainable success. Remember, your success is not just for you; it can become a blessing for future generations and your community. May you discover the power of your oil, break free from the chains of debt, and live a life overflowing with purpose and provision. The best is yet to come!

In Him

Sandra Ekpenyong

SALVATION PRAYER

Perhaps you have read this book today and have realized that you are not where you are supposed to be in your relationship with Jesus Christ, or you may have even backslidden. Here is an opportunity to say the sinner's prayer.

Heavenly Father,

Today, I invite You into my life, surrendering my will, my spirit, and my soul to You. I acknowledge that I am a sinner and sincerely repent for the sins I have committed. I humbly ask for Your forgiveness and grace.

I confess Jesus Christ as my personal Lord and Savior. I believe in Your only begotten Son, Jesus Christ, and that through the shedding of His blood on the Cross of Calvary, my sins have been washed away. I stand as a new creation in Christ because I have fully believed. I affirm my faith in His baptism, death, and resurrection, knowing that my life is now hidden in Him, and I am saved.

I now thank Jesus for His undying love and grace on the Cross, and for granting me access to the throne of grace in times of trouble and tribulation. I accept the Holy Spirit as my guide and teacher on this new and wonderful journey of abundant life. Lord, transform my life and mold me into who You desire me to be, now that I am saved. Amen.

PRAYER FOR ENDING DEBT

If you are finding yourself in debt, I pray that this prayer will start to help you find your way out and clarify your next steps as God did for the widow with the jar of oil.

Heavenly Father,

I come before You today on behalf of every reader **of 40 Invaluable Lessons of the Widow's Oil** who is burdened by financial debt. Just as You miraculously provided for the widow, I ask that You release divine wisdom, provision, and breakthrough into their lives.

Lord, open their eyes to the resources already in their hands and grant them the wisdom to multiply what You have given them. Help them to be faithful stewards of their finances, to make wise decisions, and to trust in Your supernatural provision.

Break the stronghold of debt over their lives and replace lack with abundance. Grant them favor, unexpected opportunities, and the discipline to walk in financial freedom. May they stand on the promise of Deuteronomy 28:12—that they will lend and not borrow. In Jesus' name, I declare that debt is broken, financial wisdom is released, and a season of overflow begins. Amen.

ABOUT THE AUTHOR

The End… or Just The Beginning?

I hope you've enjoyed reading this book as much as I've enjoyed writing it! Being able to share my words and be a part of your journey is an incredible privilege. If this book has brought you clarity, encouragement, love, peace, or direction in any way, I am truly grateful. Thank you—not just for purchasing this book, but for inviting me into your space and allowing me to walk alongside you through these pages.

I'd love to stay connected! If you'd like to receive the first chapter of any of my upcoming book series including *Biblical Dysfunctional Families: Mini-Series Part, I* and *12 Questions Every Christian Should Ask Before Getting Married*—visit www.thesandrae.com or scan the QR code below. These chapters will be available starting **October 10, 2025.**

www.thesandrae.com

https://bit.ly/Inspire2Live

While you're there, explore my website for **exclusive specials, freebies, and our Reader's Corner**, where you can:

- Sign up for my free monthly blog
- Download weekly inspirational quotes
- Tune into my podcast, Inspire2Live, on Spotify

I would like to specially request that if this book has been a blessing to you, please take the time to drop a review whether on my website, Amazon or whatever platform you use to purchase this copy. I am also dropping my latest book trailer for the father or daughter in your life titled "*The 13 Different Father and Daughter Relationships Of The Bible and Their Modern-Day Lessons.*" You can purchase a copy in print, audiobook, or PDF format on my website and other major platforms as it drops on Father's Day, June 15, 2025.

The 13 Different Father-
Daughter Relationships

And there's more! Starting **January 2026**, you'll be able to download **free devotionals** to accompany my books and workbooks helping you deepen your journey of faith, healing, and personal growth. Consider it as my special gift to you!

Once again, thank you for being a part of this journey. May these words continue to bring **healing, hope, and love** into your life.

Forever Grateful

Sandra Ekpenyong

Made in the USA
Monee, IL
05 November 2026

67810736R00298